Musicology

Professor Joseph Kerman was born in 19_ _ _ London, the son of an American journalist, and was educated at University College School, also for a time at the Trinity College of Music. After brief wartime service in the US Navy, he studied musicology under Strunk and organ under Weinrich at Princeton University. Since 1952 he has been on the faculty of the University of California at Berkeley; in 1972–4 he was Heather Professor of Music at Oxford. He is a Fellow of the American Academy of Arts and Sciences, a Corresponding Fellow of the British Academy, and an Honorary Member of the Royal Academy of Music. Among his publications are *The Elizabethan Madrigal*; *Opera as Drama*; *The Beethoven Quartets*; *Listen* (with Vivian Kerman); *The Masses and Motets of William Byrd*; *The New Grove Beethoven* (with Alan Tyson); and an edition of Beethoven's so-called 'Kafka' Sketchbook. He is a founding co-editor (since 1977) of the journal *19th-Century Music* and a regular contributor to the *New York Review of Books*.

Joseph Kerman

Musicology

Fontana Press/Collins

First published in 1985 by Fontana Paperbacks
and William Collins,
8 Grafton Street, London W1X 3LA

Copyright © Joseph Kerman 1985

Set in 10 on 12pt Linotron Sabon
Reproduced, printed and bound in Great Britain by
Hazell Watson & Viney Limited,
Member of the BPCC Group,
Aylesbury, Bucks

Hardback ISBN: 0 00 197170 0
Paperback ISBN: 0 00 686002 8

To Vivian
ancora

Contents

Acknowledgments

This book is, ultimately, one musician's analysis of modern ideas and ideologies of music. It deals with musicology and other fields of music study mainly as he has apprehended them in the United States and Britain in the years since the Second World War. I should first acknowledge, admit, or simply advise the reader that in looking back at this period, I have drawn a good deal on writings of my own germane to this broad topic. References to these writings will be found in the Notes and the list of Main Works Cited.

Looking at the present, as I have tried to do by reading widely in the current literature, what I find most impressive are various signs of novelty, evidence of new approaches that are being tried not by all, of course, but by many writers. Perhaps this impression is simply the result of paying closer attention than usual, but I do not think so. Thinking about music seems to be undergoing a rather rapid change just now. The latest issues of journals and the newest publishers' catalogues offer constant surprises, and in my mind this book has even assumed what advertisers call 'time value'. I am therefore especially grateful to those who have sent me prepublication copies of material that could be considered here before it was generally available. Also, if it does not seem too fatuous to do so, I should like to acknowledge the work of young musicians and scholars who seem to be moving music study in new directions. Some of them will be mentioned in the following chapters.

This was a hard book to write. Many friends and associates read parts or all of it in draft form, and I have profited very greatly from their comments. The most usual and, at first sight, the most gracious formula on these occasions is for an author to list and thank such readers, stressing also that any errors or *bêtises* that remain are due to him alone. There is another formula, though, which seems more appropriate in the present case. This book is by design a personal one, to the point of idiosyncrasy, and often I have neither accepted advice ('Give it up') nor responded to suggestions in ways that my friends surely hoped. Better that they not be named specifically, so they cannot be subject to any imputation of complicity with my viewpoint or my analysis – it would be a particular shame, certainly, if they were to feel any constraint about commenting on these. But the fact that they are not named does not mean that I am any less grateful to them all. I might indeed have given up save for the encouragement I managed to construe out of their always kind, always astute, sometimes touchingly concerned assistance. And often their direction and correction was indeed accepted.

I will therefore thank by name only those whose complicity with me is hopeless anyway, Vivian Kerman and Gary Tomlinson.

This project was supported by a fellowship from the National Endowment for the Humanities and by a Humanities Research Fellowship from the University of California at Berkeley. To write a book of this kind, it is essential to have access to a first-rate library and – almost as important – one that is really easy to use; and the Berkeley Music Library, under Michael A. Keller, has once again been a lifeline as well as a joy. Lawrence Archbold and Thomas S. Grey lent expert assistance in assembling bibliography, preparing notes and the index, and checking some details.

J.K.
Berkeley, December 1983

1. Introduction

'Musicology' is a coinage that is recent enough – the *OED* dates it to 1919, even though the *Musical Quarterly* commenced publication with a famous leader 'On Behalf of Musicology' in 1915 – so that there still exist pockets of somewhat surly purists who take exception to its use. It early suffered a modification or contraction of meaning. Adapted from the older French term *musicologie*, itself an analogue to the nineteenth-century German *Musikwissenschaft*, the word was originally understood (as *Musikwissenschaft* still is) to cover thinking about, research into, and knowledge of all possible aspects of music. Musicology ranged from the history of Western music to the taxonomy of 'primitive' music, as it was then called, from acoustics to aesthetics, and from harmony and counterpoint to piano pedagogy. Subtle and elaborate categorizations of knowledge were proposed, starting with the classic formulations of Hugo Riemann and Guido Adler in the nineteenth century and continued by not a few German scholars down to the present day. The last person to work seriously with 'systematic musicology' in English – it was the fixation of a long and great career – was Charles Seeger, the guiding spirit of modern American ethnomusicology. After reprinting several avowedly preliminary formulations of a comprehensive classification of music and music study in his collected essays, published at the age of ninety, Seeger completed two more extensive redactions of it before his death a few years later.

But in academic practice, and in broad general usage, musicology has come to have a much more constricted meaning. It has come to mean the study of the history of Western music in the high-art tradition. The academic musicologist teaches courses in the music of the Renaissance, in the symphony, in Bach, Beethoven, and Bartók. The popular musicologist writes programme notes for chamber-music concerts and intermission features for opera videocasts. Furthermore, in the popular mind – and in the minds of many academics – musicology is restricted not only in the subject matter it covers but also in its approach to that subject matter. (I say 'restricted' rather than 'constricted' here, for this approach is not the result of any paring down of an earlier concept.) Musicology is perceived as dealing essentially with the factual, the documentary, the verifiable, the analysable, the positivistic. Musicologists are respected for the facts they know about music. They are not admired for their insight into music as aesthetic experience.

Which is the subject of this book – musicology in the ideal, comprehensive, original definition, or musicology in the restricted, more mundane, current one? The broad or the narrow? The answer lies somewhere in between. Few people today could claim to write with much authority about the broad range of musical knowledge as mapped out by Adler or Seeger. Even those who could would need an outsized book to deal with so large a subject – and in any case, I am distinctly not one of those few. Still, a glance at the table of contents of this book may suggest to the reader that my view of the history of Western art music is less narrow than it might be. In what ways, I shall try to explain in a moment. It will be necessary first to say a word about other directly relevant disciplines of music study: music theory, analysis, and ethnomusicology.

Everybody understands what musicology is, at least in a general way. Music theory is much less widely understood, even by musicians, and to non-musicians it is usually a closed book. The latter can hardly be blamed, for music theory is invariably technical in nature, sometimes forbiddingly so. The former entertain a number of different estimates as to the relation of theory on the one hand and its ambivalent adjunct, analysis, on the other.

Theory, says *The New Grove Dictionary of Music and Musicians*, 'is now understood as principally the study of the structure of music'. Another way of putting it – hardly more informative – is that music theory is the investigation of what makes music 'work'. Thus the range of its subject matter extends from the formation of scales and chords to procedures for the distribution of pitches in time – such as counterpoint and twelve-tone or serial operations – to principles of musical form and even semiology. Choosing our words with great care, we might say theory deals with those aspects of music that might be thought analogous to vocabulary, grammar, syntax, and rhetoric in the field of language. And musical analysis as a technical procedure might be thought analogous to parsing, linguistic reduction, and *explication du texte*. While theory clearly is an indispensable part of the study of any one of the world's music systems, musicians who call themselves theorists nearly always confine themselves to Western art music, past and present. It is characteristic, too, that even when they deal with past music, they decline to deal with it in historical terms.

Ethnomusicology is popularly understood to mean the study of non-Western music – or 'musics', as the ethnomusicologists themselves prefer to put it. Indeed, they have their own all-inclusive definition of ethnomusicology, Alan P. Merriam's famous phrase 'the study of music in culture'. They see the whole world of music – Western art music, Western folk and popular music, non-Western musics both simple and complex – as their dominion; it is no accident that Seeger the systematic musicologist was also a father of modern ethnomusicology. Still, what has in fact occupied ethnomusicologists most intensely are the highly developed art musics of Indonesia, Japan, and India and the less developed musics of the American Indians and subsaharan Africans. These are studied to yield accurate technical descriptions on the one hand, and information about the musics' roles in societies on the other. There are no generally accepted names for students of Western popular musics such as jazz, rock, or reggae, or for students of European folk music (a field that now flourishes particularly in Eastern Europe). One has the impression that the ethnomusicologists would be glad to swallow them up.

The musicologist likes to think of himself as a historian, like the art historian or the literary scholar, and aligns himself with the goals, values, and style of traditional humanistic scholarship. That is why although he is a relative latecomer to the academy he (and even she) has had a relatively easy time there. Typically musicologists write or aspire to write essays and books in ordinary academic English, with the result that their work can be read outside the profession more easily than can that of theorists or ethnomusicologists. The ethnomusicologists' alignment is with anthropology; they are likely also to have special sympathies with some nation, 'world', or class other than that of their own origins. Seldom are their articles and reports free of social-scientific apparatus, if not jargon. Music theorists are the hardest to generalize about. Some of them lean in the direction of philosophy, and some write papers in a self-generated language as highly specialized as that of symbolic logic. But the more fundamental alignment of music theory is with musical composition: for if theorists have an intellectual interest in the structure of music, composers have this same interest from their own strictly practical viewpoint.

And indeed, while people have presumably been intrigued by theory for as long as music has existed on any level of sophistication – in all literate cultures, treatises on music theory predate by many centuries essays in music history or criticism – theory has acquired a special urgency in this century on account of the movement in the arts known as modernism. There will be a good deal to say about modernism in this book; one way or another, it remains a determining issue in the ideology of many musicians – and in particular, of many whose views we shall have to consider. In music, modernism falls into two broad phases. The first phase was accomplished just before the First World War, with works such as Debussy's *Jeux*, Stravinsky's *Le Sacre du printemps*, and Schoenberg's *Pierrot lunaire*. The second was launched directly after the Second World War, with the compositions of Boulez, Stockhausen, and Cage.

Unlike great changes in art of the past, modernism has not resulted in a new consensus; that negative fact is practically a part of its programme. We no longer agree on how new music is to 'work'. Hence composers continue actively to seek new ways of making it do so. Modern theory is sometimes not (or not only) descriptive, then, but rather (or also) prescriptive. Much of the power and prestige of theory derives from its alignment, at least until very recently, with the actual sources of creativity on the contemporary musical scene.

So it might appear as though the three disciplines I have sketched above divide up the subject matter of music fairly equably among them. Musicologists deal with Western art music before around 1900, theorists with the same after 1900, and ethnomusicologists with non-Western musics and Western music outside the elite tradition – folk and popular music. Generalization on this level, even in the conventionally safe preserve of a book's Introduction, makes the head spin, yet this is probably a fair enough description of what happens as far as day-to-day work and year-to-year publication are concerned.

Musicology, theory, and ethnomusicology should not be defined in terms of their subject matter, however, but rather in terms of their philosophies and ideologies. Even without going into detail at this point, we can probably see that when they are defined in this way, the disciplines overlap appreciably in the musical territory they cover. It may be suspected, furthermore, that it is often where two or even all three systems can be said to compete for the intellectual control of territory that we will find the most promising fields of study.

And in the areas of overlap all is not equable. Ethnomusicologists, as has already been remarked, are disposed to see as their province the entire universe of music, encompassing the more limited domains of musicologists and theorists. While they have not plunged into work on Western art music to show exactly what they mean, some of them have repeatedly called for an 'ethnomusicological approach' to this music. It is a message that musicologists repeatedly claim they are taking to heart, and one that they do indeed, in some cases, take substance from for basic orientations of their work. Theorists, so far from concentrating exclusively on the composers' immediate concern, the music of modernism, have also developed powerful doctrine about the so-called standard repertory of music. By proposing analytical models for the canonic masterpieces of Bach, Mozart, Beethoven, Brahms, and the other familiar masters, they come up with quite a different view of musical repertories than do the musicologists, who treat the same works within a much wider empirical context. Particularly with music of the nineteenth century, as we shall see, a confrontation and accommodation between the two viewpoints is offering an avenue of fresh under-standing.

History, anthropology, the analysis of structure . . . it will be noticed that nothing has been said so far about another thoroughly traditional method of considering the arts. Criticism – the study of the meaning and value of art works – does not figure in the explicit programmes of musicology or theory. (For the moment the reader is asked to take this on faith; the point will be substantiated – and qualified – later.) Ethnomusicology encompasses the meaning and value of music along with every-thing else about it, but what is usually considered is the meaning of a musical genre to its culture and the value of a musical activity to its society. This is rather different from the sort of thing we mean by Shakespeare criticism or the body of criticism that has grown up around *Paradise Lost* or *Notes Toward a Supreme Fiction*. In music-academic circles, the term 'criticism' is little used. It is, in fact, positively distrusted.

Part of the problem is the vexing common usage of the term 'criticism' in musical parlance to mean the reviewing of concerts for daily or weekly papers – that and nothing more. Journalistic criticism has a very bad odour among the profession. The folklore of journalism is rich in rascally tales of music critics who switched over one fine day from the sports pages to revel in a life of ignorance and spite. People tend to forget that within living memory composers and musicologists as reputable as Virgil Thomson and Jack A. Westrup practised daily journalism for a time, and that someone as profoundly knowledgeable and civil (or, rather, humane) as Andrew Porter has devoted himself to it for decades.[1] But whether practised badly or well, and it is usually practised badly, criticism conceived of in journalistic terms always places the writer under severe limits of space and level of technical discourse. To mention only one simple index of this: music reviews are never illustrated by examples in music notation, in the way that poetry reviews cite lines of verse, and art reviews regularly employ admittedly rough-and-ready reproductions of some of the works exhibited. This makes it almost impossible for the critic to do one very simple and necessary thing. He cannot refer to a detail.

What I would call serious music criticism – academic music criticism, if you prefer – does not exist as a discipline on a par with musicology and music theory on the one hand, or literary and art criticism on the other. We do not have musical Arnolds or Eliots, Blackmurs or Kermodes, Ruskins or Schapiros. In the circumstances it is idle to complain or lament that critical thought in music lags conceptually far behind that in the other arts. In fact, nearly all musical thinkers travel at a respectful distance behind the latest chariots (or bandwagons) of intellectual life in general, as we shall see many times in the following pages. Semiotics, hermeneutics, and phenomenology are being drawn upon only by some of the boldest of musical studies today. Post-structuralism, deconstruction, and serious feminism have yet to make their debuts in musicology or music theory.

There is, of course, musical analysis – though most people prefer not to call that criticism. As applied to music, the term 'analysis' has come to mean the detailed 'internalist' explication of the structure of particular compositions. (And a highly technical process this explication turns out to be, with its fine print and its doctored musical examples, its tables, reductive graphs, and occasional mathematical excursuses.) Analysis, as I have already said, is closely associated with music theory and often subsumed under it, as if analysis were merely theory's demonstrative adjunct. And if so – if the primary activity is theory – one cannot complain that what the analysts are doing is too narrow. A theoretical demonstration may legitimately be as abstract as the demonstrator needs in order to make his point.

M.—2

But questions arise when one tries to look at things the other way around, and subsume theory under analysis as its enabling support structure. (There are ample historical grounds for this way of looking at things, as will be explained below, in Chapter 3.) In this view, the primary activity becomes analysis; and when analysis becomes a primary way of approaching the work of art, it has to be seen as a type of formalistic criticism. At this point it can also be legitimately complained about in terms that go beyond its own self-imposed frame of reference. Why should analysts concentrate solely on the internal structure of the individual work of art as an autonomous entity, and take no account of such considerable matters as history, communication, affect, texts and programmes, the existence of other works of art, and so much else?

Qua criticism, musical analysis is limited and limiting; yet it is also capable of more rigorous and powerful determinations in its own sphere than are available to formalistic criticism in any of the other arts. That is why the serious critic cannot help being both fascinated and exasperated by analysis. The potential of analysis is formidable, if it can only be taken out of the hothouse of theory and brought out into the real world.

In my own work I have sometimes attempted to do this, but more often I am to be found on the junction between criticism and musicology, between musicology conceived more broadly than in purely positivistic terms, and criticism conceived more broadly than in purely formalistic ones. Among the primary 'facts' about pieces and repertories of music (past and present) are their aesthetic qualities (past and present). There is a widely held conviction that musicologists are, if not actually failed musicians, then at any rate persons of sharply limited musical sensibility – persons who know a lot of facts about music and very little about 'the music itself'. That could be true of certain musicologists. But with the majority of them, in my experience, it is not so much a matter of inherent unmusicality as of a deliberate policy of separating off their musical insights and passions from their scholarly work. I believe this is a great mistake; musicologists should exert themselves towards fusion, not separation. When the study of music history loses touch with the aesthetic core of music, which is the subject matter of criticism, it can only too easily degenerate into a shallow exercise. At the same time, I also believe that the most solid basis for criticism is history, rather than music theory or ethnomusicology.

Earlier it was suggested that the view of musicology in this book is somewhat broader than it might have been had its author accepted the conventional current view of his subject. Such breadth follows from the set of beliefs about history and criticism just mentioned, rather than from the actual range of music that occupies me, and that will be dealt with in the following chapters. For better or for worse, I am not very much interested in non-Western music or in the popular music of the West (for worse, in that this must betray a real limitation of mind and sensibility; for better, perhaps, in that it may lend a certain intensity to what I do within these limitations). But I *am* interested in the art music of the Western tradition, interested and engaged, and to this music I would bring as many critical tools as possible. In practice, this entails a good deal of experimentation with analysis, and a good deal of impatience with the viewpoint conventionally regarded as 'historical' in the dry sense. Another way of putting it might be to say that my conception of history is more comprehensive than that of more conventional musicologists.

We began with two familiar or at least standard definitions of musicology, one broad, one narrow. They correspond, of course, to two views of the subject which determine the work of actual scholars; and for me the broad view is too broad and the narrow view too narrow. The one is suspect on account of its schematic quality and a certain chilliness of academic ambition that goes with it, the other on account of its undeniable tendency to shy away from 'the music itself'. What I uphold and try to practise is a kind of musicology oriented towards criticism, a kind of criticism oriented towards history. More of this in Chapter 4.

2

The way we think about music – as professionals or as amateurs; as critics, historians, theorists, whatever – is important at least partly because of the way it impinges on music that is composed, performed, and listened to. Ideas can influence music: though it is just as glaringly obvious that the flow also runs in the other direction. Ideas about music come into being as a response to music that is already there. Since this book is an account of ideas and ideologies of music as I have apprehended them since the Second World War, in the United States and Britain, it will be well to begin by recalling the main outline of musical developments in that period.

As in many areas of thought and artistic expression – perhaps in all – the end of the war marked the beginning of a period of major change, in which virtually every aspect of music was transformed. Almost all the transformation took place in the first fifteen or so postwar years, furthermore; thereafter things have been relatively static, perhaps even disappointingly so. But it would be hard to think of another period lasting less than a generation in which so much happened to so many branches of the art of music as in 1945–60.

What I have called the second phase of modernism in music erupted with remarkable speed after 1945. In terms of historical process, incidentally, this presents a sharp contrast with the situation after the First World War, where it was the immediate prewar generation that witnessed just such another major development, the development of modernism in its first phase. By 1950, young Europe's discovery of Schoenberg and Webern, Debussy and Messiaen was already an old story; Darmstadt and Donaueschingen were established forces and the Paris Conservatoire the unlikely site of Messiaen's revolutionary analysis classes. The earliest studios for electronically generated music were in the advanced stages of construction. And the theorizing was well under way. Messiaen and Eimert had published full-scale treatises, and smaller but more fervid writings by Boulez and Stockhausen were beginning to appear. *Die Reihe* started

publication in 1955, by which time the first important compositions of Boulez and Stockhausen, Barraqué, Xenakis, Pousseur,
Ligeti, Berio, Maderna, and Nono had all been heard and were
beginning to make their impact.

Die Reihe is one of those periodical titles (like that flower of
Victorian Wagnerism called *The Meister*) that tells it all.
European avant-garde music was a celebration of Schoenberg
and especially Webern's idea of the twelve-tone row. The
principle of serialism was extended from pitch to other musical
'parameters' such as duration and dynamics. *Die Reihe* must be
one of very few German journals on any subject that have ever
been translated issue by issue within a few years of publication
for dissemination in English-speaking countries. Still, not many
composers from those countries joined in directly with the continental avant garde in the earliest days. From Britain, where
modernist composition had never established itself in the 1930s,
there was no one to join. The Americans were content to continue working at home. A number of native composers had been
writing twelve-tone music for some time – and of course
Schoenberg himself was right here, teaching, along with many
more musicians associated with the Schoenberg school than
were living at that time in any other country. Milton Babbitt
conceived of and composed the first piece of music with
durations serialized as well as pitches in 1947, actually a little
ahead of Messiaen's independent effort along similar lines.

Babbitt's rigorous mathematical style of music theory left no
room for the variously metaphysical, confessional, and Marxist
strains that were coming out of Darmstadt. His treatise of 1946
was not and never has been published, but this in no way
impeded his influence as a teacher. With Roger Sessions, he was
the inspiration for a group of young composers and theorists at
Princeton which would later be associated with *Perspectives of
New Music*, an American answer to *Die Reihe*.

Another strain of prewar American music was gaining definition and force in this period. The rediscovery of Ives, usually
dated approximately from the time of his death in 1954,
coincided with a surge of interest in Cage, in indeterminacy,

happenings, minimalism, and (again) writings in the form of lectures, non-lectures, squibs, interviews, and 'silences'. This too was 'theory' of a sort – and a much more accessible sort than the other, it must be admitted. Also much more media-wise. The meteoric rise of interest in serial and chance music was accompanied by an eclipse, at least in prestige, of more conservative music. It seemed symbolic that the main Eastern establishment figures in their fifties, Roger Sessions and Aaron Copland, both turned to serialism at this time. This was as nothing, however, compared to the sensation produced by the similar turn by Stravinsky, in his seventies, on the West Coast.

Partly as a result of the eclipse of conservative contemporary music, the polarization of musical life between the old and the new seemed to grow even more intense under the second phase of modernism than under the first. As the decades passed, music-lovers found themselves listening at concerts and on the newly marketed long-playing records to the same old music, over and over again. The best-loved Puccini operas and Mahler symphonies were now more than fifty years old. Advanced twentieth-century music seemed no nearer to acceptance. The left accused symphony orchestras, opera companies, and other standard concert institutions of turning themselves into museums, museums without modern wings which people could walk through (for when contemporary pieces were played, people walked out). Critics of this persuasion were further disquieted by the vigorous revival of even older music, such as that of Vivaldi and Telemann, to say nothing of the twelfth-century *Play of Daniel* which was so stylishly presented by the New York Pro Musica Antiqua in 1958. The right persisted with attacks on the avant garde. The polemic of Henry Pleasants's *The Agony of Modern Music* of 1955 was to echo down through the decades to Leonard Bernstein's *The Infinite Variety of Music* of 1966, Samuel Lipman's *Music after Modernism* of 1979, and (presumably) beyond.

In Britain conservative music was not eclipsed, chance music never had much of a chance, and serialism did not make a serious impact until somewhat later. A younger generation of composers needed to grow up, such as the group who were students at the Royal Manchester College in the mid-1950s, strongest among them Peter Maxwell Davies. Well before this, however, something else was happening under the aegis of a composer who had once wanted to study with Alban Berg but who now turned sharply away from the avant garde. Benjamin Britten's work is best understood as an emphatic continuation of the revival of British music that began in late Victorian times – the 'English musical Renaissance', if this term may be extended to generations past those of Parry and Vaughan Williams. Britten's triumphant establishment of English opera starting with *Peter Grimes* in 1945, his 'realizations' of Purcell and English folksongs, his celebration of an East Anglian rural-cum-marine idyll at Aldeburgh, even his provision for generational continuity through music written for children – all this can be seen as a single impetus. Not everyone liked Britten's music, but by 1960 he was already becoming that highly improbable phenomenon for the second half of the twentieth century – a 'classical' composer with whom a substantial part of a nation could identify.

It is true that this all looks a lot clearer today in retrospect, and that more conservative and less perceptive critics were quite capable of missing important things that were taking place in musical composition of the 1950s. (I was among them.) This was hardly the case as regards popular music. The precipitous decline of the big bands was widely observed, while much attention was paid to survivors such as Stan Kenton and the indestructible Ellington. The resurgence of jazz for small ensembles was predicated on radical new styles, the 'bop revolution' of the 1940s soon refracting into the dazzling kaleidoscope of modern jazz. The fusion of jazz with 'classical' music, an ideal since the time of Gershwin and the early Copland, never took place. Or, at least, it took place on the terms of jazz musicians such as Ellington and Ornette Coleman, not on the terms of classically trained musicians such as Mátyás Seiber and Gunther Schuller.

Shaken by its own modernist movement, jazz even produced its own antimodernist reaction in a faceless new Dixieland tradition. As modern jazz grew more esoteric and less popular, other kinds of popular music developed from sources humbler than those of jazz to meet the needs of the mass audience and those who purveyed to it. First rhythm and blues, then rock and roll, and finally rock were swept forcefully into everyone's consciousness. The rather astounding rock explosion in Britain (to some observers, though not to all, the final decisive confirmation of that English musical Renaissance) came a little later, once again. But the Beatles and many other groups in Britain were already playing in the 1950s, though the gold records had not yet begun to be issued. A fertile ground for all kinds of jazz, blues, and country music had been prepared by the American presence in Europe during and after the war. As Charles Hamm has pointed out, it was only in the wake of America's decisive political entry into the world scene that American popular music finally became an undisputed world language.[2]

Obligatory, in discussions of postwar music, is mention of the impact of electronic technology for recording and generating music. Though the electronic studio equipment of the 1950s seems almost unbelievably clumsy by today's standards, it produced the first and still seminal monuments of electronic music. The Beatles were soon to try their hand at a little electronic composition – and as for performance, the whole rock phenomenon is certainly unthinkable without electric guitars, Moogs, and those terrifying amplification systems which made Woodstocks possible. In a quite different area, new vistas were opened up for ethnomusicology. Field work, which had relied on sound recording since the days of Edison, was revolutionized by the battery-powered tape recorder, while all the musics of the world were disseminated in the West by long-playing records. A little later the Beatles were playing sitars, too, and Benjamin Britten was writing *Curlew River* on a Japanese model.

In all this welter of audio-technological advance, nothing was more important than the simple fact of the long-playing – and low-priced – record. People have been fascinated, even horrified, by the power of recording technology and marketry to establish whole genres of popular music, let alone the careers of individual performers and groups. The postwar concert repertory has also been decisively guided by records: consider the new popularity of Haydn and Mahler, of opera of all kinds, and of Baroque and other early music. Consider also not exactly the popularity but at least the availability of the corpus of modernist and other important music from the first half of the twentieth century, and even from the second.

But the crucial thing, I believe, was that now listeners could and did obtain great masses of music of all kinds and were able to *browse* through it on recordings, in something like the way they were used to browsing through literature of all kinds in books. Previously only professional musicians had been able to move around in music with such (actually less) flexibility by reading scores. The range and sheer amount of music known to non-musicians and musicians alike went up exponentially; musical composition, musical performance, and musical consumption were all affected by the electronic revolution of the 1950s, but consumption was affected most. No wonder the audience for music increased (and with the record audience, also the audience for live music at concerts). No wonder the young Colin Davis at postwar Oxford could remark that the *cachet* formerly reserved for poetry now seemed to be accorded to opera.

The new radical music created a demand for and received its new radical theory. 'Demand' is too strong a word, perhaps, but the great mass of music newly made available on records might be said to have called up its new criticism, too. A need was felt for modes of understanding, approach, or at least accommodation to increasingly sophisticated types of modern jazz and popular music, Indian ragas and Japanese koto performances, the bewildering array of medieval, Renaissance, and Baroque music of the West and – last but not least (and not the least bewildering) – music of the twentieth-century avant garde. Criticism in the broadest sense, taken to include everything from scholarship to journalism, proliferated in dissertations, monographs, journals, newspapers, and in that newest locale for the musical feuilleton, the LP record sleeve.

That the most coherent body of thought to develop should centre around Western music of the past was not a requirement, only the unavoidable consequence of academic history. Musicology – the history of Western art music – had thrived in the universities of German-speaking countries for more than fifty years before the war, and habits of mind formed at those times and in those places have been with us ever since. There have been legitimate grumblings about the slow acceptance into the academy of ethnomusicology, music theory, and criticism, but in fact by 1960 some important first steps had been taken, at least in ethnomusicology and theory. Before the war ethnomusicology had only a marginal place in universities here and abroad, and music theory only a marginal place in conservatories. Serious criticism existed at best – and it was not a very good best – in fugitive issues of little magazines.

Musicology before the war was not restricted to Germany, of course. It was practised everywhere, though everywhere less intensely and in a less organized way. The tradition in Britain was small, largely amateur, and distinguished. In the United States things were similar but rather less impressive – until the Hitler years, when the influx of refugees from Europe transformed music along with so many other aspects of American artistic and intellectual life. Musicology became institutionalized at major universities, and most of the powerful professors of the postwar period, with the exceptions of Oliver Strunk at Princeton and Gustave Reese at New York University, were members of the European diaspora. To mention only the most influential, Willi Apel was at Harvard and later Indiana, Manfred F. Bukofzer at Berkeley, Hans T. David at Illinois, Otto Gombosi at Chicago and later Harvard, Paul Henry Lang at Columbia, Curt Sachs at NYU, and Leo Schrade at Yale. From this time on, musicology has been expanding in the American academic setting at an expanding rate.

It was a fortunate time to enter the field. What was unfortunate was that the work of some of the most effective and best-placed of these teachers was cut off so soon. Bukofzer and

Gombosi died as young men in 1955, and in 1958 Schrade returned to Europe. This left Princeton, in particular, where Strunk had been joined by Arthur Mendel, in a favourable position; under Mendel, who was equally effective as an administrator and as a teacher (and indeed as a performer of early music), Princeton became the main music-intellectual centre in America. This was also because of the serious work fostered there in music theory, allied to composition, in which the commanding figures were Sessions and Babbitt, as has already been mentioned. The other strong theory programme established at the time, under the influence of Schrade at Yale, was associated less with composition than with music history.

And it was perhaps predictable that ethnomusicology should have received no comparable impetus at those particular institutions. Indiana University and Wesleyan University in Connecticut were outposts of ethnomusicology in those days, but it seems fitting that the most emphatic programme should have been developed in the West, at the University of California at Los Angeles. The force behind this development, which coalesced in 1961 with the establishment of a highly effective Institute of Ethnomusicology, was a young composer who had studied with the great Dutch ethnomusicologist Jaap Kunst, Mantle Hood. Its *éminence grise* was Charles Seeger, who had also started out life as a composer, who had sparked a music department at the university as long ago as 1912 (at Berkeley), and who had given the first courses on ethnomusicology ever offered in America, at the New School for Social Research in New York in the 1930s.

Similar developments took place in Britain but, once again, rather later. A recent survey of musical scholarship in Britain remarks on how slowly institutional support seems to be taking hold, and on how stubbornly ingrained patterns of amateurism continued in this area.[3] Yet the immediate postwar years did see some decisive advances. Although the serious study of theory and analysis was possible only in private, with refugee scholars in the Schoenberg orbit such as Erwin Stein and Hans Keller, heady stuff was published in new or newly invigorated journals such as *Music Survey, The Score, Tempo,* and the *Music Review.* The scholarly publication series *Musica Britannica,* by getting launched on the same wave as the 1950 Festival of Britain, did receive institutional support, from the Arts Council; this series, devoted to the publication of musical monuments from Britain's past, serves or served as a major focus for musicological work. A different sort of focus, also important, was provided by the indirect support of the BBC. On the Third Programme musicologists and historically minded performers joined forces to broadcast an unbelievable amount of early music. If English musicology is characterized by high-level popularization and a concern for the actual sound of early music, and American musicology by seminars, dissertations, and other insignia of academia, we can see the difference also in certain primary institutions supporting them.

But there was also, in Britain, growth of academic support. The clutch of new universities founded in the 1950s contributed to the institutionalization not only of musicology but also of theory; York specialized in avant-garde music, Southampton and Sussex in theory. At the older foundations there was the astonishing fluke of three senior musicologists appointed to chairs in the single year 1947 – this in a country which up to that time had had only one real musicologist-professor, Edward J. Dent at prewar Cambridge. (All university appointments in Britain are flukes, or so it sometimes seems to outsiders.) Jack A. Westrup went to Oxford, Anthony Lewis to Birmingham, and Gerald Abraham to Liverpool. Also in that same year a younger man was appointed lecturer at Cambridge who was to have as great or even a greater impact. Thurston Dart immediately proved to be an almost explosively dynamic teacher, and in the 1960s he was to establish a music department at King's College in the University of London on radical terms – radical not only as regards musicology. Ethnomusicology and avant-garde music were on the syllabus, as well as the historical performance of music, which was always the focus of Dart's musicology. In 1982 King's actually established a professorship, for Arnold Whittall, in Musical Theory and Analysis.

3

The rapid development of musical scholarship in the postwar period has to be charted principally in terms of influential scholars and enabling institutions, as I have tried to do very briefly above. Institutions of various other kinds also deserve to be mentioned: the learned societies with their journals, committees, and annual meetings; fellowship programmes – especially, perhaps, that of the Fulbright Commission; and publishers such as W. W. Norton in New York who specialized *inter alia* in music textbooks and 'official' scholarly books on music. And perhaps I might also put in a word for the students of the postwar generation, since I was one of them: a generation which in both England and America appears to have produced as many bright – well, anyway, interesting – young musicians who were attracted to musical scholarship as to musical composition. This may well be considered to be a rather surprising turn of events; and doubtless in strictly logistical terms it would also have to be counted as a decisive one. It probably had a good deal to do with the new availability of music of all kinds on long-playing records. People desire or decide to become musicologists, composers, or ethnomusicologists because they have heard music that excited them – old music, contemporary music, or music of non-Western cultures. And whether students go into scholarship or composition is sometimes determined less by their supposed intellectual or creative proclivities, I think, than by their attitudes towards modernism.

When they go into scholarship, they publish too much. This is a state of affairs music shares with all other branches of academic life today; it has been analysed and deplored on many occasions, and I would have nothing really new to add to what others have incisively said about it.[4] But I do think it necessary, before concluding this sketch of postwar developments in music, and before embarking on a more detailed analysis of the course of postwar musicology, to underline this condition. The situation may not, in fact, be at its worst in music, but there is no blinking at the fact that a great deal of so-called intellectual work is done on a low level. No editor of a journal, and no reader of manuscripts for university presses, has been spared the shock of seeing a piece of work he has firmly rejected pop up like a cork in someone else's magazine or monograph series. We are all a part of the problem. Half of the academic community writes when it has nothing to say, it seems, while the other half conspires to get that writing published.[5]

Perhaps, then, the above account of the rapid development of postwar scholarship in music is altogether too rosy. One would like to think that the great expansion of activity entailed a corresponding expansion of good work; but it would be impossible to say confidently that this second expansion has been proportional to the first. It would in any case be a dispiriting task, as well as a very dull one, to try to survey the field comprehensively and impartially. No, the coverage in the following chapters will be nothing if not selective. The reader has already been alerted to the criteria governing the selection. We shall examine certain lines of thought in musicology and in related disciplines, lines that illuminate the coming together of those disciplines and the growing orientation of musicology towards criticism.

2. Musicology and Positivism: the Postwar Years

What is the impetus behind musicology? Why do we study the history of music? This was a question posed by Arthur Mendel at the beginning of his well-known paper 'Evidence and Explanation', which became a sort of musicological credo for many in the 1960s.* His answer was really an evasion:

> Our primary reason for studying history . . . is, I hope, the same as the primary reason why the best minds study anything: because we have a passion for understanding things, for being puzzled and solving our puzzles; because we are curious and will not be satisfied until our curiosity rests. 'Man, who desires to know everything, desires to know himself' (p. 4).

This dictum of R. G. Collingwood's, or something like it, is often invoked in order to supply an ideal impetus for musicology as a kind of abstract investigation, a pure working of the mind among the multiple mysteries of music's past and present. It is invoked especially by those who without understanding science very well would like to attach the term 'scientific' to thought about music.

Mendel knew better. The puzzles to which he had turned his presumably free-floating curiosity during the essential span of his career as a musicologist were puzzles about Bach, the com-

---

* For notes marked with an asterisk (rather than an arabic number), the reader should refer directly to the list of Main Works Cited, page 243. When the titles of articles or books are already present in the text, as here, the list will provide full bibliographical information. When, as sometimes happens in the course of a discussion of an author's works, articles and books are referred to in the text (and asterisked) without being actually named, the full titles can be found in the list under the name of the author.

poser with whom more than any other he had identified in his other career, as a conductor from the 1930s to the 1950s. Even more specifically, they were puzzles about the Passion According to St John, a work which he had performed in a particularly memorable fashion. As he went on to say in the same paper, music historians have another type of interest in their subject matter over and above that of political and social historians. 'Apart from the fascination of establishing facts, and relations between facts, we are interested in the musical works themselves – as individual structures and as objects of delight. Our interest in Mozart's Jupiter Symphony is different from the political historian's interest in Napoleon or the social historian's interest in the steam engine.'[1] It is this second, 'different' interest in music as an object of delight, I believe, that provides the primary impetus for many, if not most musicologists, including (as I also believe) Mendel himself. It is an interest that can be called *critical*.

The interest, like the delight, may be direct or attenuated. While one musicologist studies Bach's passions, another may study the Lutheran passion as a genre and another the music of Bach's less great contemporaries. Another may work on the aesthetic theories of the age, or its social configuration for music, or on the many intricate systems of tuning or temperament that were put forward in Bach's lifetime for keyboard instruments. Even so narrow a study as this last one is predicated on the fact of the musicologist caring (or at least, once having cared) about the music of Bach and his time *as music*. Musicologists of another kind study music as a coherent element in the culture of its time in the broadest sense. Others investigate the contemporary performance conditions of Bach's choral music and put the facts to work in an actual performance, as Mendel had done in his days as director of the Cantata Singers in New York.

The naive reader may find it hard to believe, at first, that musicologists can love some of the music they study – Byzantine chant, fourteenth-century English descant, German lute music. But they can. Love is a many-clangoured thing.

Behind all this, of course, is the assumption that music of the past is of aesthetic interest – and this assumption, it should be stressed, is of relatively recent vintage. The historical sense in music is much newer than in literature, where canonic texts have been handed down for millennia, or in art, where temples and cathedrals stand for centuries and galleries have been cultivated since the Renaissance. But a musical tradition is not made up of texts and artifacts. Music is evanescent, and until recently the repertory of Western art music did not extend back more than a generation or two; in the deepest sense, music history extended back no further. (Exception must be made for Gregorian chant and some other kinds of liturgical music.) The Renaissance composer and music theorist Johannes Tinctoris announced that there was no music worth listening to that hadn't been composed in the last forty years or so. This was in 1477, when Tinctoris was himself about forty years old.

The late eighteenth-century musician no longer spoke about Handel in this way (nor Corelli, nor Palestrina). But the real change came with the first decades of the nineteenth century, when Haydn, Mozart, Beethoven, Weber, and Rossini were not supplanted by the next good composers to come along – as Machaut and Dunstable had been, for Tinctoris, by Ockeghem and Regis. Instead their music was accorded a place in what turned out to be a more or less permanent canon. It was an era of basic change in the nature of musical repertories, in the social conditions under which Western art music was composed and presented, and in musical aesthetics, music theory, and musicology.[2]

The historical sense of music, and with it the intellectual or academic reflection of this called musicology, was in the nineteenth century closely bound up with nationalistic and religious ideology. 'And this man, the greatest musical poet and the greatest musical orator that ever existed, and probably ever will exist, was a German. Let our country be proud of him; let us be proud, but, at the same time, worthy of him!'[3] With these famous and fateful words J. N. Forkel, the first real German musicologist, ended up his Bach biography of 1802 which initiated the revival of that composer's music. Bach represented to the nineteenth century the German spirit and also the Lutheran spirit, and it is no accident that outside Germany his music made the greatest impact in a country that was neither Catholic nor resistant to German thought – a country whose prince consort, indeed, was a cultivated German musical amateur. After Forkel, the music that musicologists cared about, and that in consequence they devoted their books and their editions and their performances to, was generally the music of their own national tradition or – if sacred music was in question – of their own faith.

In the nineteenth century this was so much taken for granted, and the exceptions were so few, that probably no one would have thought of pointing it out. Nor would it have been pointed out, before the twentieth century, that musicologists were lavishing their attention almost exclusively on music identified with the upper and middle classes.

Today, when they see European musicologists studying the less important music of their homelands, Americans are sometimes bemused and start wondering about chauvinism or even propaganda. But anyone who has lived in Europe knows how deeply such native music can touch people who feel it to be part of their own tradition. This is true even when the music in question looks quite indifferent from the other side of the border, let alone the Channel, let alone the Atlantic Ocean. In Britain, nearly every musicologist does some work on British music or at least on the music of British-domiciled composers (Winton Dean on Handel, Alan Tyson on Clementi); it is a common pattern for British scholars to start out with native music with which they have a sense of shared identity and then go on to other things. In this respect the situation has not changed basically since the nineteenth century, when the Musical Antiquarian Society published the first scores of music by Byrd, Wilbye, Dowland, Purcell, and other British worthies, as early as the 1840s. The Rev. John S. Bumpus wrote *A History of English Cathedral Music 1549–1899*, the publisher William

Chappell edited *A Collection of National Airs* and *Popular Music of the Olden Time*, and the composer Sir John Stainer issued facsimiles and transcriptions of *Early Bodleian Music*. A major international figure such as Edward J. Dent, who wrote his first book on Allesandro Scarlatti in 1905 and went on to Mozart, Handel, and Busoni, also wrote a classic study of *The Foundations of English Opera*.

(Availability of source materials, it must be admitted, can sometimes set musicologists off as well as national feeling. The music in Stainer's *Dufay and his Contemporaries*, a pioneer work on the secular song of fifteenth-century France, was taken from a continental codex that had found its way to Oxford, where Stainer was Heather Professor of Music. Tyson's work on Beethoven began with the contemporary English editions of his music, neglected by continental Beethoven scholars. American research in European music began as a major activity only in the age of microfilm, jet travel, and Fulbright fellowships.)

Earlier generations of American musicologists worked on American music, just as Britons worked on British, Germans on German, and so on. Oscar G. Sonneck, who as music librarian of the Library of Congress in 1901–17 built up the great music collection there, is credited with initiating serious American music studies and has given his name to a Sonneck Society which fosters them today. Theodore Baker, best known for his *Biographical Dictionary* of Western musicians, still in print, published the first study of American Indian music as early as 1882. An even earlier and greater scholar, Alexander Wheelock Thayer, is best known (to most people, indeed, exclusively known) for his formidable biography of Beethoven. But in the 1840s Thayer did extensive research into the origins of American hymnody, which was his first love, and in the 1850s he flooded *Dwight's Music Journal* with contributions on every aspect of American music from folksong and Indian children's songs to Benjamin Franklin's musical instruments and George Bristow's opera *Rip Van Winkle* of 1855.[4]

Musicology – the point has been sufficiently hashed over in the Introduction – is now almost always understood to mean the study of the history of Western art music. The cases just mentioned show that musicologists of the past sometimes studied not only art but also folk music and music of non-Western cultures — especially if this was close to home and therefore close to their hearts. To the names of Chappell, Baker, and Thayer others could of course be added from among twentieth-century musicologists. Nonetheless musicologists work predominantly, overwhelmingly with art music, and the reasons for this seem obvious enough. Like most scholars, they come from the middle class; they are indeed likely to be moving up within its spectrum. It is middle-class values that they project and seek to protect, and Western art music since the nineteenth century has been the province of the middle class. (We can call this if we wish 'elite' music, though the term seems more appropriate to the seventeenth century than to the nineteenth, let alone to the twentieth with its wide dissemination of music of all kinds by radio and records.) Behind scholarship, and behind what I have called the 'critical' interest which drives most musicologists, there is nearly always the impetus to nurture traditions with which the scholar can associate or identify, or which have at least contributed to such traditions historically. These traditions, as has already been suggested, are likely to be controlled by class as well as national and religious ideologies.

Hence it is to East European musicologists that we owe the richest studies of European folk music, to the Germans our knowledge of the chorale and the chorale prelude, to the English our appreciation of Taverner, Tye, and Tallis, and (at least initially) to the Benedictine monks of Solesmes our knowledge of the earliest ritual music of the Catholic Church. And it is to musicologists of the greater Western intellectual community — Germans like Nottebohm, Frimmel, and Brandenburg, Frenchmen like Prod'homme and Rolland, Britons like Tovey, Anderson, and Tyson, Russians like Lenz and Fishman, Americans like Thayer, Sonneck, and Solomon — that we owe our understanding of Beethoven, who more than any other figure seems to epitomize the music of that shared community.

Is it the case, then, that musicologists deal only with music of the past – with music, indeed, of the rather distant past? Certainly this does not follow from our working definition of musicology as the study of the history of Western art music. History runs up to the present. Only in cant usage does 'history' mean 'the past'. For someone driven by a passion for understanding things, or by a passion for musical objects of delight, there is no logical distinction between today's music and yesterday's, or between the day before yesterday's and that of a century or a millennium ago.

This point has been urged by, among others, Frank Ll. Harrison, in a widely read essay on 'American Musicology and the European Tradition'.* 'Traditionally the function of musicology has been in the first place to contribute to the fostering of composition and performance by adding to the sum of knowledge about music,' wrote Harrison, and he went on to interpret the history of European musicology in this light, laying special emphasis on the Bach revival and the Gregorian chant movement as sources for musical composition in the nineteenth century. (Theodore Baker's dissertation, incidentally, was the source of melodies used by Edward MacDowell in his 'Indian' Suite.) Musicology in the twentieth century should also ally itself closely to contemporary musical life, which for Harrison is manifested most intensely by popular music, music that has to be understood first and foremost in terms of social use and value. 'Looked at in this way, it is the function of all musicology to be in fact ethnomusicology, that is, to take its range of research to include material that is termed "sociological".'[5]

Harrison's polemic motive here is transparent, however, as is also his tactic of turning from a descriptive to a hortatory mode as he turns from the nineteenth to the twentieth century. Musicologists today are mostly musical conservatives, and everybody knows it. It was the crisis of modernism that made the difference: even though there was a magical moment in prewar Vienna when private composition students of Alexander von

Zemlinsky, Schoenberg's teacher, and of Schoenberg himself were simultaneously members of Guido Adler's musicological seminar at the university. Webern, Egon Wellesz, and less well-known figures such as Karl Weigl and Paul Pisk were all Adler PhDs. Wellesz and Pisk went on to dual careers as musicologists and composers.

There were other exceptional figures, outside of Vienna: for example Dent, a founding member and first president of the International Society for Contemporary-Music in 1923, and the author of a book on Busoni. Charles Seeger was at the centre of the New York contemporary-music scene of the 1920s and early 1930s. But by and large the response of musicologists to the first phase of modernism was retrenchment. Like many composers and other musicians in the years before and after the First World War, they found themselves reacting strongly against the music of Romanticism; yet they were reluctant (or frankly unable) to follow the modernists on their path. In this reluctance they were joined by most music theorists, incidentally, who tended to assume even more dogmatically antimodernist stances.

By coincidence, an internal dynamic within the discipline of musicology was then leading scholars to the rich, largely un-studied field of medieval polyphonic music. So musicologists gravitated towards the esoteric remote past just as modernist composers hurtled into what seemed to many like an equally esoteric future. With the second phase of modernism, after the Second World War, lines were drawn even more sharply, though with this difference: by now the anti-Romantic reaction has passed and musicologists, as we shall see, have moved back with confidence to the study of nineteenth-century music.

In their attitudes towards nineteenth- and twentieth-century music there is a broad similarity, I believe, among modern musicologists in the United States, Britain, and other lands. (A large exception should be made for the extensive studies of twentieth-century music conducted since the 1960s by the group of musicologists around Carl Dahlhaus in Berlin.) Where the Americans today appear to differ is in their lack of involvement with their own music. Mendel was entirely typical in devoting his energies to such distant (but powerfully attractive) figures as Bach and Josquin Desprez. This, as we have just seen, was not the case in the nineteenth century, and the current state of affairs is one to which Harrison and others have reacted with surprise and even some indignation. At this point we will not need to look far for an explanation. The ideology of twentieth-century musicology is antimodernist and 'elite', and in America a substantial native tradition of art music did not come into being until the age of modernism. Bristow and MacDowell could hardly sustain a scholarly movement of this character in the way that Josquin and Sweelinck could, or Bach and Beethoven, or Glinka and Mussorgsky. It is to be doubted that British musicology could sustain itself for very long on Stainer and his contemporaries.

To the extent that Americans practise traditional musicology, then, they do so on a genuinely international basis, out of their sense of America's sharing in the Western tradition of art music. This is a perfectly tenable position, in spite of complaints about it sometimes heard from Americans; indeed, this international orientation has been extolled as one of American musicology's special strengths. It is sometimes also complained that the German musicologists who emigrated to the United States in the 1930s and 1940s influenced students to concentrate their attention on European (though often not German!) music. They did, of course – even those of them who also turned to the study of American music, such as Hans T. David and Hans Nathan – but their influence was a secondary consideration, as well as a passing one. Students were already committed to Western art music anyway. The main reason American musicologists do not work more with American music is because there is so brief a tradition of art music that can be taken seriously.

One should not, in any case, overstate the isolation of American musicology from American music. The line from Sonneck to today's Americanists was never broken. There were important figures in the 1950s, and new ones emerged in the 1960s – scholars who, in an ironic reversal of a common pattern we have mentioned in Britain, started out with Dufay, Març-

Antoine Charpentier, and Debussy before turning to popular music, Ives, and Stephen Foster. Harrison was right to this extent: work on the American 'vernacular' tradition in music, as H. Wiley Hitchcock has called it, is best understood not as traditional musicology but as a special outgrowth of ethnomusicology.

3

The rapid development of musicology in America and Britain after the war is something I have sketched out in the Introduction. On the world scene, it soon became clear that the postwar generation of musical scholars – scholars of all kinds – would no longer be dominated by Germans, as earlier generations had been. This may have been a reason or at least a pretext for the decision of the International Musicological Society to move out of continental Europe for the first time and hold their triennial congresses in Oxford and New York.

Some differences between the two occasions light up some differences between the two erstwhile *Länder ohne Musikwissenschaft*. The Oxford meeting in 1955 is now remembered largely for an idyllic summer evening when the delegates floated up and down the Thames to the sounds of ancient music in a grand old Victorian barge – one of a fleet which has, alas, to a large extent been mothballed or worse since those times. Not much of that congress remains save memories because the proceedings were never published. Professor Westrup simply stuck the papers in the room behind his office and made no discernible move to get them printed. In the summer of 1961, on the other hand, New York was so far from idyllic that certain delegates shut themselves up in their air-conditioned hotel rooms and reputedly never ventured down to the meetings. But the first fat volume of proceedings, containing more than forty round-table and symposium papers, was actually published before the congress – a bit of post-Sputnik efficiency which has never been repeated (and which no one in his right mind today would even contemplate repeating).

By 1961 the international colloquy included a cautious number of official participants drawn from the postwar generation; among them were about a dozen Americans and four or five Englishmen. It seems a convenient time to take stock. And indeed a formal inventory was drawn up at exactly that time.

In typical institutional fashion – typical for America, that is, if not for Britain – an entity named the Council of the Humanities at Princeton University determined to commission a series of over a dozen books on 'Humanistic Scholarship in America' and secured the requisite foundation support. The book on *Musicology*, which came out in 1963, was the work of three authors who had established their scholarly careers since the war. The central essay, on 'American Scholarship in Western Music', was written by Claude V. Palisca,* a Gombosi student who had come to Yale after the departure of Schrade. It is a revealing document. Equally revealing, though perhaps more surprising, the other two essays draw up preliminary battle lines in a shadow war between musicology and ethnomusicology which has been waged sporadically ever since. We have already quoted from the one by Frank Harrison, and will return to both of them later.

What would an interested reader of the time have learned from Palisca's inventory? Under 'Areas of Research', that American musicology was concerned mainly with music of the Renaissance, followed by the Middle Ages and then the Baroque era. On the other hand, the Classical and Romantic periods were 'comparatively neglected'. These are the periods encompassing nearly all the music in the concert repertory, from Haydn and Mozart to Richard Strauss and Debussy. 'Practically no attention' was being paid to music of the twentieth century. As for American music, 'this is a subject that has only a negligible role in graduate study and is treated as a serious research specialty by only a handful of American scholars, few of them in teaching positions'.[6]

Palisca had some explanations for this imbalance. Whether he was right to link the popularity of Renaissance studies to a general surge of interest in sixteenth-century choral music, which he attributed to Archibald T. Davison and the Harvard Glee Club, I cannot say. But he was certainly right to observe that the émigré scholars were carrying over the model 'problem areas' of prewar European musicology when they laid stress on the Renaissance and Middle Ages. Although Palisca did not say so, the neglect of twentieth-century music followed from the basic ideological orientation of musicology, and the neglect of nineteenth-century music could plausibly be attributed to the great 'distaste for romanticism during the last quarter-century'. Yet it should be said that while this distaste may indeed have been intense among the German refugees of the 1930s, by 1963, in the wake of triumphant Wagner and Verdi revivals and the new popularity of nineteenth-century composers such as Berlioz and Mahler, it had pretty well evaporated.

Under 'Notable Achievements' the reader of *Musicology* would have found one or two pages on biographies and general histories, a few more on dictionaries and monographs, and a great many more on 'Critical Texts'. He could hardly have been blamed for concluding that the main work of musicology consisted of bringing out editions – mostly of Renaissance music. To be sure, Palisca also listed 'Periodical Literature' as a major outlet for musicological work, without offering to survey this in the detail accorded to critical texts, problem by problem and field by field; and perhaps he was only running true to the form of his generation in not venturing an analysis of the periodical literature in terms of the *type* of work it represented, in terms of idea. The emphasis was heavily on fact. New manuscripts were discovered and described, archives were reported on, dates were established, *cantus firmi* traced from one work and one composer to another. Musicologists dealt mainly in the verifiable, the objective, the uncontroversial, and the positive.

The presentation of the texts of early music and of facts and figures about it, not their interpretation, was seen as musicology's most notable achievement. It is not only that a virtual blackout was imposed on critical interpretation – that is, the attempt to put the data that were collected to use for aesthetic appraisal or hermeneutics. Even historical interpretation was scanted. In this area, most of the activity consisted of arranging the events of music history, considered as an autonomous phenomenon, into simplistic evolutionary patterns – an activity which soon came under sharp criticism, as we shall see in Chapter 4. Much less attention was paid to the interaction of music history with political, social, and intellectual history. And less attention yet was devoted to the attempt to understand music as an aspect of and in relation to culture in the large.

'The musicologist is first and foremost a historian,' wrote Palisca, but he should really have added: a historian in his role as a chronicler or archaeologist, rather than as a philosopher or an interpreter of cultures of the past. In such a situation, needless to say, there was a dearth of interest in philosophizing or theorizing about what musicologists were doing. The most significant effort along these lines, Mendel's 'Evidence and Explanation' paper of 1961 which was cited at the beginning of this chapter, is not even mentioned in the *Musicology* volume.

To read about musicology in the 1950s is to experience an intellectual time-warp. It is remarkable how closely words written by R. G. Collingwood about German positivistic historiography in the nineteenth century fit the musical situation seventy-five years later, both as to the dominant strain of work and the dissatisfactions that were beginning to be voiced:

Historians set to work to ascertain all the facts they could. The result was a vast increase of detailed historical knowledge, based to an unprecedented degree on accurate and critical examination of evidence. This was the age which enriched history by the compilation of vast masses of carefully sifted material, like the calendars of close and patent rolls, the corpus of Latin inscriptions, new editions of historical texts. . . . But all through this period there was a certain uneasiness about the ultimate purpose of this detailed research. It had been undertaken in obedience to the spirit of positivism according to which the ascertaining of facts was only the first stage of a process whose second stage was the discovery of laws. The historians themselves were for the most part quite happy going on ascertaining new facts; the field for discovery was inexhaustible and they asked nothing better than to explore it. But philosophers who understood the positivist programme looked on at this enthusiasm with misgiving. When, they asked, were the historians going to embark on the second stage?[7]

The emphasis on critical editions, once again, was symptomatic. Palisca reported the symptom accurately but failed to mention the epidemic it reflected, a widespread phobia as regards historical interpretation. Not much real history was part of the daily work of the discipline Palisca was surveying.

Thus many – though not all – of the landmarks of musicology produced by the older generation were conspicuously long on 'hard' information and short on interpretation. Most impressive, perhaps, were the historical surveys of *Music in the Middle Ages* and *Music in the Renaissance* by Gustave Reese. A scholar who produced no more than a dozen specialized articles in a lifetime, half of them after the age of sixty, Reese had an enviable talent for digesting and directing the work of others. His books are vast compilations of historical information with an absolute minimum of interpretation or indeed selection. It was mainly from the Reese books, I believe, that we obtained our image of music history as an unbroken patchwork quilt extending back evenly into the dim reaches of the past. One worked on one's own patch. Each was as good – as important, as necessary for the continuity and integrity of the quilt – as any other.

Some, though, were certainly more difficult to work. Willi Apel and Leo Schrade devoted major efforts to the editing of fourteenth-century French polyphony, at that time a largely unworked patch and one of the most difficult. Oliver Strunk, who for the last forty years of his life turned to the study of the millennium-long history of Byzantine chant, is a particularly pure case. Editing his pathbreaking studies on this topic in 1977, his student (and my fellow-student) Kenneth J. Levy evidently felt some comment was necessary on such devotion to a seemingly recondite area at the expense of others to which Strunk had previously made contributions, areas ranging from medieval polyphony to Palestrina and Haydn. 'There are, at bottom, just two tests for the worthiness of a musicological undertaking,' wrote Levy, '(1) that it be concerned with first-class music; and (2) that it be concerned with a first-class problem.'[8] But in Strunk's own preface and the essays that follow, one gets very little sense that the first of these tests has been passed, or even set – only the second.

(The one book Strunk published in his lifetime was a landmark of another kind: *Source Readings in Music History*, an invaluable anthology of excerpts in translation from canonic works of music theory, philosophy, and criticism drawn approximately evenly from the ancient and medieval periods, the Renaissance, the Baroque, the Classical, and the Romantic. The quilt admitted of no foreshortening.)

There is certainly something of a puzzle here, for in fact most of these older scholars pursued interests considerably broader than the problem-oriented investigation represented most clearly by the work of Strunk. They were trying in some cases, possibly, to ascend to the second stage of the positivists' programme, referred to by Collingwood in the citation above. Otto Gombosi was obsessed by an overarching theory of rhythm, Manfred Bukofzer had a remarkably clear head for historical generalization, Curt Sachs, Paul Henry Lang, and Edward E. Lowinsky worked in their different ways at cultural history, and Schrade ranged from *Rezeptionsgeschichte* to biography and beyond. Lang was chief music critic of the *New York Herald Tribune* for nine years. Why did so little of this rub off on to the students of the 1950s?

No doubt part of the explanation can be expressed by some such formula as 'there were giants in those days'. I believe another part can be found in the adherence of those giants to European patterns of education which they failed to see would go only so far in a different setting. What they did not fail to see was the distressing lack of 'background' in students who did not have the advantages of *Gymnasium* training, and this seems to have made some of them obsessive about academic rigour. They insisted less on strictly musical credentials than on multiple language examinations, massive factual surveys, hierarchies of seminars leading to the Doctoral Seminar, and the completion of great crippling projects of a mechanical kind to convince the teacher that the student was ready to move on to the next stage. (As a parenthesis, it may be added that the lynchpin of the curriculum in those days was the seminar in the notation of medieval and Renaissance music. While such courses were supposed to provide an entrée to the music itself – were said, indeed, to provide the best possible entrée – they in fact focused not on music but on rather low-level problem-solving. Since young musicologists were so insistently taught to transcribe the archaic notation of early music into modern dress, it is hardly surprising they tended to become editors of critical editions and, in many cases, not much else. Dropping the notation course from the required list, some of us felt, was a first step in the liberation of musicology.) In any case, when in 1949 Sachs ended up a public plea for a wider view of musicology with this half-ironic salute to what he called 'the nothing-but-specialists' –

> However, let us be grateful to the nothing-but-specialists. They are indispensable as spadeworkers and stone-breakers. . . . We need detail work, patient, careful, faithful, done for the sake of knowledge and for nothing else; and students, above all, should keep to this kind of neat and devoted research[9]

– it may be suspected he voiced attitudes held by most of the émigré teachers. How will students who have been programmed to be 'nothing-but-specialists' turn into scholars with broad, original, humane horizons? Sachs does not say. In the event, the metamorphosis was not often witnessed. Perhaps American students never grasped what was supposed to happen to them. Perhaps, in class, they were never even told.

One important teacher was not a German and did not follow the hieratic, paternalistic system he had observed in Europe.

Strunk had a dislike for all the paraphernalia of academia – he himself held no college degrees at all, not even a BA. Anyone walked into any of his seminars, and in these he never offered or appeared to instruct; an immensely reserved and austere figure, he simply worked alongside the students. It would be invidious to say that he produced the best musicologists of the 1950s and 1960s, but it will probably be agreed that he produced the most diverse and independent-minded: perhaps also the most grateful and devoted.[10]

A crotchet of Strunk's that earned particular gratitude from me was his distaste for PhD dissertations. Dissertations had to be written, that was evident; but he left them strictly alone. Once he had helped a student formulate the relevant historical problem – and he had a genius for this – it was easy enough to get at the solution. In my case, as best I recall, it was impossible, once he had pointed out the right direction, not to run into thickets of evidence showing how smoothly the English madrigal of the late Elizabethan period had been taken over from one strand of the contemporary Italian madrigal tradition. (Like so many dissertations at the time, mine was on a Renaissance topic.*) The takeover, it developed, was encouraged by prominent men of letters who were themselves busy imitating Italian models at the time, and masterminded largely by one man, the politically and commercially astute composer Thomas Morley. It was facilitated by widespread copying and plagiarizing of translated Italian madrigals that were actually published in London.

Characteristically, Strunk advised me to limit the dissertation to a presentation of these and other such facts. Just as characteristically, he said nothing when I disregarded this advice and went on to a miniature critical study of the main madrigal repertory, the music of Morley and his younger followers Thomas Weelkes and John Wilbye. As Strunk viewed the situation, the factual findings were new and interesting, but that Weelkes and Wilbye were the best of the English madrigal composers was an old story which my critical exegesis was not likely to embroider to any appreciable extent. He was right; the criticism in that dissertation does not add up to much. It is just that I would have found it impossible to conduct the factual investigation without conceiving of it as an aid to richer engagement with the best music that came within its range.

One should not, however, minimize the potential for intellectual stimulation in factual investigations of the kind Strunk inspired. The joys of problem-solving are savoured by humanist scholars as much or almost as much as by scientists. 'We have a passion for understanding things, for being puzzled and solving our puzzles' – Mendel was not just making this up. It was fascinating to discover, for example, that the famous anthology of madrigals for Queen Elizabeth, *The Triumphes of Oriana*, probably was conceived of with specific preferment in view – Morley needed to get his music-printing monopoly from the Crown renewed; fascinating to discover that his own main contribution to the book, the six-voiced madrigal 'Hard by a Crystal Fountain', certainly was produced by rewriting a madrigal by the then-popular Venetian composer Giovanni Croce, phrase by phrase and practically bar by bar. Fascinating to me, that is: how far can such matters ever engage those who are not themselves caught up in the excitement of discovery? However this may be, in the 1940s and 1950s there was indeed a great deal of basic research that had not yet been undertaken. I have written slightingly above about the making of editions, because I think there is something wrong with a discipline that spends (or spent) so much more of its time establishing texts than thinking about the texts thus established. But the fact remains that absolutely central texts were still unavailable in those years. Readers who are acquainted with other fields of research – in literature or art, history or science – may find it difficult to appreciate the primitive state of musical documentation in the 1950s (and remember that one could not just go and look at the original manuscript or publication, as one could with a poem or a play, because pieces of music are generally transmitted in separate instrumental or vocal performance parts which have to be put together as a score before the whole can be comprehended). Dozens of Haydn symphonies were published in score for the first time in this period, as well as minor works by Beethoven, major works by Dufay and Josquin, and *practically the whole corpus of music* by important secondary figures of the Renaissance and Baroque eras such as Giaches Wert and Louis Couperin. To hazard a comparison from literature, it is as though the 1950s saw the first publication of Chaucer's *Troilus and Criseyde*, the second half of the *Orlando furioso*, seven volumes of Goethe including juvenilia, ephemera and the *Ur-Faust*, and the complete works of Lovelace and Herrick.

Those who like editing also like to discuss methods of editing. The most predictable sections of the learned journals are those devoted to the worrying of certain perennial bones of contention in the editing of old music: barlines, editorial accidentals, note-reduction, the format of critical apparatus, and the rest. Certain editions have become notorious whipping-boys in the process. Reading about them over the years, one can get the impression that much scholarly editing of music was and is done in a mindless fashion. Yet almost any edition is better than none, and no edition can meet every legitimate need of the specialist, who sooner or later has always to go back to the original documents themselves.

In any case, new standards of textual criticism and editorial rigour were established for music by the complete edition of Bach's works which was started in 1954 at Göttingen and Tübingen, to replace the famous old Bach-Gesellschaft Edition of 1850–1900. This was true in a literal sense, for *Richtlinien* derived from the New Bach Edition have repeatedly been drawn up in Germany for later projects – including some for which they are poorly suited.

Perhaps the most brilliant achievement of positivistic musicology after the war was attendant on this New Bach Edition. The fresh scrutiny of documents surrounding Bach's work resulted in an astonishing revision of their chronology, and with that a whole congeries of ideas about Bach's pattern of activity as a composer. This was a German product *par excellence*, with only a few American and British collaborators. It is nonetheless worth a brief discussion here as an outstanding example of what positivistic musicology could do – and what it has chosen not to do further.[11]

The new Bach research in fact dramatizes the relation between postwar neopositivism in musicology and the original nineteenth-century movement. For what was involved was a wholesale extension of the already impressive accomplishments of scholars who had been active some seventy-five years earlier, Wilhelm Rust and especially Philipp Spitta. The work of Spitta, a crusading positivist,[12] had long been regarded as a paragon of musicological method, and its authority had scarcely been challenged in the interim. The philological methods employed by the new Bach scholars, principally Alfred Dürr and Georg von Dadelsen, will be familiar enough in concept to those acquainted with similar work in art history and literary studies.* The details may have a certain interest, however, as unquestionably the outcome has.

As sophisticated editorial work got under way, some very unexpected things began to turn up about the accepted chronology of Bach's music. This was particularly true of his cantatas, a corpus of over two hundred large-scale works comprising the greater part of his surviving output. Since the Lutheran church cantata is typically linked by its words to a specific day in the church year, cantatas were typically used again and again in different years. They have come down to us in scores and/or sets of performance parts, which may or may not be complete and may or may not match the score, if any; some of these sources are autographs, others copies. Some can be traced to a performance in one year, some to a performance in another year – when the cantata might have been revised – and some can be seen to have been used on more than one occasion. Liturgical and local performing practices changed from town to town and from church to church. All of this could be investigated and the results brought to bear on the problem of dating the musical sources. A further complication arises from the circumstance that several different levels of pitch were in use for the organs which played in the cantatas, so that certain instrumental parts had sometimes to be recopied in different keys to make them fit with a newly pitched organ.

Spitta had successfully grouped the thousands of manuscript pages of cantata sources according to their watermarks. But watermarks in this period cannot be dated independently, only by inferences drawn from what is written on the papers. For writings by Bach himself, Spitta attempted to chart the state of the composer's handwriting as he grew older; unfortunately this remained pretty constant. So special attention was now devoted to other copyists, some of whom changed their orthography more than Bach did – and some of whom came to write so much like the master that it took refined methods to distinguish their writings at all. The idiosyncrasies of the compositors of Shakespeare's plays have not been studied more minutely than the handwritings of Bach's wife, his oldest sons, his main pupils, and various scribal *anonimi*. As an example of the intricacies of the problems encountered, twenty-one hands had to be unscrambled in the surviving materials for a single large work, the Passion According to St John, which Bach revived with modifications on several occasions.

When the results were in, it was discovered, first and foremost, that Spitta had committed one truly monumental error. A substantial and particularly famous group of cantatas, the 'chorale cantatas' based closely on traditional hymns, or chorales, is transmitted largely on a single type of paper which Spitta assigned to the 1730s and 1740s. But that paper and the handwritings on it now pointed inevitably to the single *Jahrgang* 1724–5. This was only Bach's second year as Cantor in Leipzig. He had, in short, written twice as much in the two-year period as Spitta thought (twice as much, probably, as anyone thought he could have written in so short a time, though now it is easy to see that plenty of other cantors wrote just as fast and just as copiously). What is more, already in 1725–6 Bach can be seen to have produced many fewer cantatas than in the previous years.

The traditional assumption had been that Bach devoted his major energies as Leipzig Cantor to church music from 1723 to around 1744, with something of a dropping off in the later period. Now it developed that the bulk of the church music – nearly all the cantatas – predated 1730. The sheer amount Bach produced makes it clear that borrowing from earlier music must have been much more widespread than was assumed before, though of course the procedure had been well documented by the time of Spitta. Secular cantatas such as birthday odes were provided with sacred words; concertos and other instrumental pieces were pressed into service, sometimes receiving words and even added contrapuntal voices to carry them. 'Chronology' in these circumstances began to take on a very ambivalent meaning.

But the new Bach scholars could say with some justice that their science was brushing away superstition, for when one looked more closely at Spitta's dating it became clear that more was behind it than a simple miscalculation. The idea of having the cycle of chorale cantatas come late in Bach's lifetime fitted only too well with the orthodox nineteenth-century view of the composer. According to this view, a career dedicated essentially to the music of the Lutheran liturgy reached its climax in that form of cantata which depended most deeply on the music of Luther, the chorale, itself.

Now, to put it brutally, it began to look as though Bach's attitude towards Lutheran church music had cooled appreciably quite early in his Leipzig years. It was an agonizing prospect for many West German musicians, if an eminently satisfactory one for their colleagues in the East. A Bach myth was shattered, and remains shattered, even though as the result of later research Bach's withdrawal from church music is now seen in a less decisive and less brutal light.

Indeed, it was perhaps only after this demythification that two of the most interesting newer lines of Bach research could have developed – lines which both start at the gap which seems to have opened up in Bach's activity in the 1730s, and which both lead outside of Lutheran Leipzig. One was due to a student of the older Bach scholar and theologian Friedrich Smend, Christoph Wolff, who emigrated first to Canada and then to the United States. Wolff in 1968 drew attention to a small but important group of late Bach compositions based on the *stile antico*, a conservative style still maintained in the Catholic Mass and motet in direct line from Palestrina.* Not only did Bach employ this style in part of his own B-minor Mass and other works, he orchestrated a Palestrina Mass first published in 1590 and transcribed or made additions to such staunchly Catholic contemporary works as a Mass by the Bolognese composer G. B. Bassani and the famous *Stabat Mater* of Pergolesi. Though strictly (perhaps too strictly) delimited in scope, Wolff's is one of the very few major Bach studies of recent decades to concentrate on the matter of musical style. And it is a pity he has not pursued this kind of work.

A student of Arthur Mendel, Robert L. Marshall did his first work with sketches and other evidence of the compositional process that can be discerned in Bach's autograph manuscripts. More recently Marshall has been emphasizing not the antique but the modern elements in Bach's later music.* In 1730, as is well known, Bach angled for a position at Dresden – Catholic Dresden, seat of the Saxon court, where he often travelled to give organ recitals. Under the Italianate composer J. A. Hasse ('Il Sassone') and his wife the *prima donna assoluta* Faustina Bordoni, Dresden was just then becoming the German centre for modern Italian opera. Marshall finds evidence of operatic style in the magnificent Gloria Bach sent to Dresden (perhaps for Faustina?), in his secular cantatas, which he now wrote in increasing numbers, and in the favourite sacred cantata for coloratura soprano and trumpet obbligato, *Jauchzet Gott in allen Länden* (No. 51). In his instrumental music he adopted features from such post-Baroque composers as Domenico Scarlatti and his own son Carl Philipp Emanuel. Some rather modest flute sonatas attributed to Johann Sebastian, which sound so rococo that people have tended to reject the attributions, Marshall sees as authentic further testimony to the composer's modernist inclinations. So along with the myth of Bach as a latter-day Luther, another myth is coming into question, that of Bach as a stubborn conservative out of sympathy with his times.

Wolff's work from the late 1960s and Marshall's from the 1970s represent promising new departures from the Bach research of the 1950s. Yet all Bach scholars – including those younger than Wolff and Marshall – seem obsessed, even oppressed by the enormous weight of paleographical and graphological apparatus left over from that great positivistic enterprise. What they have not begun to tackle is a critique of the broadly accepted scheme of the evolution of Bach's musical style from his periods in Weimar, Cöthen, and Leipzig. This legacy of Spitta's has not proved so easy to shake as has his flawed chronology. If the chorale cantatas of 1724–5 come *before*, not *after* the Passion According to St Matthew of 1727, what are the consequences of this chronological information for our understanding of these works? And now that we know that parts of the Passion are from ten to twenty years older than the rest, how are we to experience the work as a 'unity'? Perhaps our concept of unity in musical works needs revision; the Bach scholars should be in a position to speak to this. Clearly we can no longer accept (if we ever did) that Bach's style in, say, cantatas went through a process of linear development; but the alternative cannot be a tacit model of a style that never changed at all. That would indeed offer a *reductio ad absurdum* of chronological investigation. What use are correct dates, except to the gazetteers, if they do not help us understand the music in its historical context? Bach research has for some time been poised on the brink of the classic positivistic dilemma: more and more facts, and less and less confidence in interpreting them.

The positivists' interest in musical style seems to be mainly in its possible use as a guide to chronology – and this interest may indeed be merely *pro forma*, for they are always ready to counsel caution, if not outright scepticism, about such use. Here the argument is not whether 'external evidence' is preferable to 'internal evidence' when we have it; of course it is. The argument is whether to admit the sensitive interpretation of internal evidence when external evidence is lacking or inconclusive. But distrust of interpretation is programmatic among the traditional German Bach scholars. That this attitude was shared by American Bach scholars, at least of an older generation, will appear in a moment; it also came naturally to the leading British Bach specialist, Walter Emery, who incidentally also doubled as a text critic of Icelandic saga. 'What Bach scholarship needs today', wrote Emery in 1961, 'is not only more facts – both fresh facts, and corrections of traditional errors – but also greater caution in interpreting facts.'[13] He said nothing about any need to direct those facts to a new appreciation of Bach's music as music.

Some older scholars, it is interesting to note, were made a little uneasy by this situation. One was Friedrich Blume, a leading figure in both prewar and postwar German musicology, even though Blume himself assented to the demythicization of Bach almost too eagerly. 'A rather exaggerated dogmatism is prevalent at the moment,' he observed – this was in 1963 – 'the belief that only that is true which results from the close textual investigation of the original sources and that whatever does not result from it cannot be true. The climate of scholarship will change, however, and the textual scholars will not have the final word. The purely textual will be followed by a more interpretative phase.'[14] Brave words; but in the austere climate of Göttingen and Tübingen interpretation of a strictly musical nature remains to be undertaken. While sophisticated debates continue about the date of the St Matthew Passion, a comprehensive new critical account of it or of the whole massive corpus of the church cantatas forms no part of the positivists' programme. Only in 1982, with the appearance of an ambitious study of the Passion by a young Canadian musicologist, Eric Chafe – a study strongly influenced by Smend, incidentally, and still largely consumed by complex arguments about sources and dating – has a fresh start been made towards the aesthetic appreciation of that great work.*

5

It seems particularly apt that the most significant presentation in English of the neopositivistic theory of music history should have emerged directly from the background of Bach research, the great postwar success story of German musicology conceived from this position. Gracefully enough, the presentation was given by a leading American Bach specialist at a plenary session of that 1961 New York Congress of the International Musicological Society which was mentioned some pages earlier. Arthur Mendel's title was 'Evidence and Explanation', and he contrived to turn an exploration of those topics into a tract on the theory and practice of music history in general.*

How does the historian know what he knows, and on what basis does he say what he says? The true basis, said Mendel, is deduction, and he proceeded to expound a model for causal explanation in history due to the analytical philosopher Carl Hempel, then at Princeton. According to this model, which was much discussed at the time, an 'explanandum' is to be inferred from clearly defined 'antecedent conditions' according to a clearly formulated 'covering law'. If we see a ship on the sea and then look five minutes later and see it somewhere else, we infer from this evidence that it has occupied a series of different positions in between. We must formulate a general law according to which our observation of the ship in two positions at two moments – the antecendent conditions – allows us to deduce that it has travelled from one point to the other.

This perhaps slightly curious example was taken from Collingwood's influential *The Idea of History*, where it served a somewhat different argument. The ship can also serve, I think, to lead us to the heart of Mendel's inquiry. As has already been noted, this grew out of postwar Bach research – which started him thinking seriously about historical method in the first place, says Mendel at the beginning of his paper, and which supplied him with the one specific historical question raised, however briefly, at the end. Did Bach actually part with the famous autograph manuscript of his Brandenburg Concertos (as had been assumed) on the date of the dedication written in it, March 1721 – and hence necessarily derive all later copies of the concertos from some other source? Just how much does the evidence of that dated autograph allow us to explain?

What Mendel cared about was rigorous thinking about low-level facts, facts like Collingwood's ship. To the extent that he was echoing Hempel's well-known injunction to historians that they root out 'the assumptions buried under the gravestones "hence", "therefore", "because" and the like', his article can be read as part of a growing critique of musicological method from within the profession. And to that extent Mendel's own endemic personal scepticism had a healthy effect on more than a few Princeton students who have gone on to do serious work.

But Mendel's effort to extend Hempel's model from 'low-level' explanations in music history to 'high-level' ones – to explanations of the relation between two composers' styles, for example, or of particular musical events in particular pieces of music – was not healthy in the least. His paper argued against several familiar objections to the sweeping positivistic position. According to William Dray, history cannot be covered by laws such as those employed in science because it deals with one-of-a-kind events. But scientists have their laws without assuming the existence of 'invariable uniformities', Mendel argued, citing Bertrand Russell: 'As soon as the antecedents have been given sufficiently fully to enable the consequent to be calculated with some exactitude, the antecedents have become so complicated that it is very unlikely they will ever recur.' According to Isaiah Berlin, historical explanation needs to be 'thick' rather than 'thin', and thickness requires qualities of insight and imagination over and above the application of logical models. But *all* explanation, thick or thin, scientific or historical, is hypothetical (here Mendel cites Popper); and while Mendel cautiously grants the necessity of thick explanation in history, he argues that the processes of thick and thin explanation differ only in degree:

To establish the fact that Ockeghem died in 1495 [or to] establish the historical relations between Josquin's lament, *Nymphes des bois*, and Ockeghem's death, or between *Nymphes des bois* and the chant melody of the *Requiem aeternam*, or between polyphonic settings in general and *cantus prius facti*, or between all compositions that make some use of preexisting material and that material, or between Josquin's style and Ockeghem's, we have to use the same processes. But the higher we go in the scale of generality, the harder it is to make the empirical tests Hempel specifies and the more our explanation will assume the character of a hypothesis or an outline (p. 13).

A seamless continuum is posited between the process of explaining facts thick and thin, high- and low-level. Berlin's 'imagination and insight' are subsumed under a 'fictive' element said to be present even in the simplest hypothesis, and present in thick explanation merely to a greater degree.

Mendel seems to grant even more when, a little later, he agrees with Collingwood that the historian must re-enact or enter imaginatively into the material he is treating. Collingwood had developed this idea freely from Dilthey and Croce, and when Mendel transposes it freely to music history, asserting that for the musicologist aesthetic interest in his material is essential, that indeed 'in the music-historian the musician and the historian are inseparable and indispensable to each other', he comes within hailing distance of a concept of musicology oriented towards criticism. But after granting this much, Mendel makes an all but Jesuitical turn and grants nothing. The historian's aesthetic experience 'is not evidence'. Committed to an *a priori* method, the positivistic method of Hempel, Mendel was content to exclude values which he actually admitted adhere to his subject matter, music. 'The aesthetic relation to the musical work exists and is necessary to the music-historian' – but evidently Hempel's supposed rules of evidence are a higher necessity.[15]

The unhealthy influence of this doctrine, which puts quasi-scientific methodology first and assumes a methodological continuum in the treatment of all kinds of low- and high-level phenomena, can well be imagined. For while Mendel said that thick explanation is necessary in history, he did not say this in a very loud voice. Small wonder that musicologists impressed by his precepts tended to shy away from the relative uncertainty, difficulty ('it is harder to make the empirical tests'), and 'fictiveness' which he claimed adhered to all investigation above the lowest, Collingwood-ship levels. Mendel did the same in his own work. He established important facts and texts: facts about the history of musical pitch and the text of the St John Passion. He coedited a book of Bach documents. He also tried and cheerfully admitted failure to develop computerized methods of musical style analysis.

Positivism is still probably the dominant mode in musicology today. At a later point I shall speak briefly of its latter-day manifestation in Britain. In the United States musicologists who have never pondered 'Evidence and Explanation' have absorbed the ideology unconsciously from the unusually stodgy shelf of the textbooks that guided their graduate study. (As was remarked in passing in Chapter 1, the publisher with a corner on 'official' musicological texts is W. W. Norton, or was until recently.) The common observation that yesterday's intellectual orthodoxy is reflected most baldly in today's textbooks certainly holds for music. Musicology stays with the old ways because they seem so simple – because even their difficulties seem conceptually so simple: though it should be said that positivism has a way of deflecting attention from even such difficulties as are implicit in its materials. This seems, in fact, to have been what was worrying Mendel. His tract can be seen most sympathetically as a warning against the kind of simplistic thinking that positivism encourages but does not, at its best, necessarily entail.

Such intellectual interest as musicology can show today emerges out of several strains of reaction to positivism, and out of attempts, either associated with them or not, to develop a new musicology. To a large extent these attempts have themselves emerged from the confrontation of musicology with theory and ethnomusicology. The coming together of these disciplines has had, so far as I can see, a more invigorating effect on musicology than on the other two. In any case we should now look at theory, and its ambivalent adjunct analysis, before coming to see how it has affected the musicology of the present day.

3. Analysis, Theory, and New Music

Metaphysics is older than historiography, and the theory of music is a great deal older than musicology. Theory, according to the author of the article in *The New Grove Dictionary of Music and Musicians* – he is Claude Palisca, already known to us as the chronicler of American musicology – 'is now understood as principally the study of the structure of music'. In past centuries and millennia, however, as they are surveyed in the *Grove* article, almost any kind of disciplined thought about music seems to have been admitted under the blanket of theory. In an ingenious demonstration, Palisca bodies out a plan of universal musical knowledge set forth by the theorist Aristides Quintilianus in the second century AD into a taxonomy of the sort prepared by systematic musicologists such as Riemann, Adler, Seeger, and others today. 'Theory', in its root meaning of contemplation or speculation, like 'musicology', or the science of music, can be taken to cover the study of music in any or all of its dimensions.

The history of music theory, in this broad sense, is part of the subject matter of musicology; and the first thing to ask about theory in any historical period is what musical elements theorists felt it necessary to speculate about. (The next thing to ask is for whom the individual theorist was writing – for musicians, men of taste, students, or other theorists.) Theory, like aesthetics, has to be understood historically, for the theory of an era reflects its musical concerns, themselves bound up with the problems of contemporary music as they were then conceived.

Therefore it is no surprise that one central branch of late twentieth-century theory has been concerned with the 'problematic', as Adorno would say, of composing music in our time.

To see today's theory as 'a spin-off of avant-garde composition', as one theorist has put it, is to see a recurring strain in theory over the ages. If we may judge from the surviving writings of Aristoxenus, the first considerable body of writing on music that has come down to us, the main things that musicians at the time of Aristotle needed to get straight were the tuning of scales and their organization into modes and keys. In the Middle Ages, theorists wrote about the intricate notational systems developed to record what was then a newly developing element of musical composition, rhythm. Theorists of the Renaissance wrote about the simultaneous sounding of pitches to form consonances or dissonances, and the way successions of pitches, or musical lines, are to be combined to form counterpoint. Early eighteenth-century theorists wrote about chords and how to connect them.

All of this, clearly, is essential source material for historians dealing with the period in question. Indeed, in the late nineteenth century, before the cracking of all the codes that allowed for the transcription of early polyphony, one of the first major studies of late medieval music was made largely on the basis of a comprehensive survey of medieval theory; and ever since the time of W. H. Wooldridge and the *Oxford History of Music*, the most industrious and sophisticated interpreters of theory among musicologists have been the medievalists. More and more work has been done on the music theorists of later centuries, however. One area of special recent interest is the doctrine of musical rhetoric expounded by Renaissance and especially Baroque writers. This has provided, among other things, practical inspiration for the development of a new style of performing Baroque music.

Tuning, rhythmic configurations, consonance and dissonance, chord formations – no doubt all these fall under the capacious mantle of Palisca's term 'structure'. When musicians use this term today, however, they generally mean the structure of total works of art – what makes compositions 'work', what general principles and individual features assure the music's continuity, coherence, organization or teleology. They mean musical form, broadly construed to denote the shape or ordering of trains of sounds in time. Scales, counterpoint, and harmony are structures in another sense (structures on another structural level, one is tempted to say). And the notion of a musical composition having, in this large sense, structure or form that is a matter of signal importance is one that evolved at a particular moment in history. It is a historical fact about the present that theoretical speculation about music – old music as well as new music – is dominated by theories of form.

The Canadian composer and theorist William E. Benjamin has recently declared himself on the subject of music theory 'as currently practised in the United States and its intellectual satellites'. (By satellites he means not only Canada but also, one must assume, Britain, where theory and analysis on the American model has been gaining much ground recently.) Theory as currently practised, according to Benjamin,

> is an unnatural confluence of two streams of thought which ought to, and inevitably will, reject one another because they represent mutually contradictory values. The first stream is the Schenkerian tradition and all that is tributary to it; the second is a spin-off of avant-garde composition and consists in generating the system, mechanisms, formulas, lists, strategies and rule-structures which support this type of composition. These streams have entered into a curious marriage of convenience, perhaps because of a fear of going it alone in a hostile musical world, and cohabit to the point of sharing space in the minds of individual theorists.[1]

This is certainly a highly constricted (and highly emotional) reading of the situation. That Benjamin's dualistic scheme leaves no room for the study of medieval or Baroque theory was perhaps to be expected; such work is carried out by persons who call themselves musicologists, not theorists, and their interest is in interpreting theory, not generating it. More surprising is that his scheme consigns to limbo work such as that of the musical semiologists of Montreal, for example – to look no further than 2000 miles across Benjamin's own country – and that of

Leonard B. Meyer, which, like it or not, must be granted to be the most sustained effort (four books) at a comprehensive theory of music produced recently in English-speaking countries, and one that has made an impact even within the music-theory establishment which Meyer has tended to shun. Then the generous array of theoretical and analytical writing about music of the so-called tonal period, from Bach to Brahms, is all channelled into a 'Schenkerian' stream – as though Heinrich Schenker and his followers owned private fishing rights to the standard repertory, and as though Schenker's idiosyncratic flies and casts were accepted by the musical world at large. Let us simply call this 'tonal theory'. As for the paradox of 'mutually contradictory' strains of theory coexisting in individual theorists' heads, if Benjamin does not actually resolve this in his article, he makes its solution abundantly clear. We shall see that their confluence is not all that unnatural.

Yet for all its myopia, this vision of modern theory as reported by one of its most able younger practitioners cannot be discounted entirely. For it does represent reality of a sort. It represents the reality of an academic situation which was marked, until quite recently, by oppressive orthodoxies to an extent that made musicology and ethnomusicology seem eclectic and positively hospitable to new ideas by comparison. Theory has been a small field built around one or two intense, dogmatic personalities and their partisans. That is changing; it was a bit late in the day for Benjamin to be writing as he did in 1981, I think. But it was (and still is) a bit early to see what significant new directions theory is taking. Meyer recently observed sagely that music theory seems at present (1982) to be in a 'pre-paradigm period'.[2] An even more recent questionnaire sent to a group of thirty-odd American theorists – mostly younger theorists who are not composers – elicited responses over a bewilderingly wide range of largely independent pursuits.[3] About the most that can be said is that the old orthodoxies have clearly weakened. Beyond that no trend is clearly discernible, at least by me.

In a 1980 vice-presidential address to the Society for Music Theory, Wallace Berry urged the assembled members to mend their ways and shun 'Babelism', obscurantism, Philistinism, dogmatism, myopia, monism ('disparate approaches and findings are essential, not merely admissible, in any effort toward comprehensive understanding'), and 'harlequinism', by which he meant a sort of cryptic, subversive juggling of paradoxes without any real intention of trying to resolve them.[4] It will surely be a good thing if this rather astonishing sermon is taken to heart. It will be good not only for theorists, but also for musicologists who look to theory and analysis for tools to help them with their own work. They are likely to be even more confused by Berry's long list of isms than the theorists are. That I myself have been confused may well appear from some of the observations in the following overview of the theory that has seemed relevant, promising, or unavoidable to a musicologist who has tried to orient his work towards criticism. Although this overview is devoted largely to what Meyer would call music theory's older paradigms, it extends some way beyond Benjamin's two unduly swollen central streams.

2

The historical moment at which music theory turned to a preoccupation with musical form is one we have paused at before, in connection with the history and ideology of musicology. In 1802 Forkel published his adulatory Bach biography, symbol of music's new sense of its own history; around the same time the instrumental music of Haydn, Mozart, and Beethoven emerged as the embodiment of a new aesthetic ideal. It was quintessentially a Romantic idea – and E. T. A. Hoffmann, a key figure in the aesthetics and theory (and composition) of music in those years, called those three composers 'Romantic'. The new interest in music's history went together with its new position in the hierarchy of the arts under the recently minted term 'aesthetics'. Music was considered on its own terms, as an autonomous structure in sound, rather than as an adjunct to dancing or liturgy, or to lyric or dramatic texts.

And music was valued not (or not only) because it was pleasing and moving, but because it was felt to offer presentiments of the sublime.

For us the significance or novelty of this may not be easy to grasp at first, accustomed as we are to a pantheon of great music including purely instrumental works of much earlier times, from Byrd's pavans and galliards for the virginals to Bach's preludes and fugues for the organ. This was music the Romantics did not know. What was new was their conviction that autonomous instrumental music, exemplified first and foremost by the symphonies of Beethoven, could penetrate into what Hoffmann called 'the spirit realm', the sphere of the highest human signification. Music became the paradigmatic art for the Romantics because it was the freest, the least tied down to earthly manifestations such as representation in painting and denotation in literature. When Pater said that all art aspires towards the condition of music, he meant the condition of symphonies, not the condition of hymns or waltzes or cantatas.

It should not be thought that this 'metaphysics of instrumental music' committed the listener or critic to bouts of enthusiastic reverie far above the particulars of the music at hand.[5] Hoffmann's special insight was to associate the metaphysical sources of the sublime in Beethoven's music with the technical sources of its unity – which, not surprisingly for his time, he likened to that of an organism. None of the arts has been affected more deeply than music by the ideology of organicism; its baleful influence is still very much with us.[6] A remarkable two-sided programme is manifest in Hoffmann's famous Beethoven reviews, which interweave Romantic rhetoric worthy of Kapellmeister Kreisler with detailed, indeed prosaic technical analyses of musical structure, pointing to internal features which Hoffmann thought contributed to the music's organic unity and power. It was only in the nineteenth century, then, that theory became wedded to analysis: the process of subjecting musical masterpieces to technical operations, descriptions, reductions, and demonstrations purporting to show how they 'work'. 'Theory and Analysis' became a standard joint item in the conservatory curriculum. It still occupies a place of prestige in university music curricula today.

The point of this historical excursus is to effect a reversal and turn tonal theory and analysis around in terms of their primacy: as in the title of this chapter. To understand the ideology of musicology it is necessary to know something about its history, and the same is true of modern theory. The impetus behind tonal theory was the technical demonstration of the merits of a body of music which was in fact valued on grounds that were far from merely technical.

This is what William Benjamin was getting at, I take it, by his remark about the 'mutually contradictory values' represented by the two strains into which he divided today's (or yesterday's) discipline of theory. Avant-garde theory is practised quite frankly as an aid to – even as an aspect of – avant-garde composition. Tonal theory – what Benjamin invidiously called 'the Schenkerian tradition' – is practised rather less frankly as a type of criticism. Theories of tonal music were not constructed and are not adopted for the theories' sake, usually, with analysis assuming a heuristic role in validating theoretical conclusions through examples drawn from the repertory. What was and is primary is the validation of a body of treasured musical compositions.

While some sort of theory has to support the analysis, it is significant that this can be of the most informal sort. It can be so informal as to practically dissolve out of the usual range of reference of the word 'theory'. Only in our own time has the demand arisen in some circles for music theory that will be systematic in a strictly scientific sense – and only from this standpoint does it seem altogether impossible to characterize Hoffmann, for instance, as a theorist.

For Hoffmann had his guiding 'theoretical' idea. He was the first to write about Beethoven's Fifth Symphony in terms of an organic unity projected at least partly by means of the affinity of themes and motifs recurring within and among different sections and movements. This simple but seminal idea has not yet lost its resonance. Associated in an extremist form with the work of

Rudolph Reti and his English followers, in a less extreme form it has long been accepted by a great variety of critics. / ᖯ ρ 67

I would not begrudge Hoffmann the title of 'theorist', then, though I think he can be more handsomely described as a critic. I think the same of theorists today whose main work seems to consist of analysing compositions from the standard repertory. Most of them make no more than token additions to the theory of tonal music in a general sense. Indeed, beyond a certain amount of refinement, one wonders how much more there can remain to do in so sharply delimited an area – though there is certainly plenty to do in the way of analysing particular pieces of music. In literary studies, the plethora of critical readings of canonical poems and novels has caused writers such as Jonathan Culler to call for an end to interpretation. This is not a problem afflicting music. On the contrary, there are major works in the canon for which no sustained analytical studies of the kind that is expected today have ever been published at all: Beethoven's 'Ghost' Trio, Schubert's 'Great' Symphony in C major, Berlioz's *Harold in Italy*, dozens of Bach cantatas . . .

No doubt those who practise musical analysis will remain resistant to the idea that what they are doing is a limited form of tacit criticism. (The word 'criticism' was never mentioned in a symposium on 'Music Theory: the Art, the Profession, and the Future' conducted by six leading American theorists in 1976, though they spoke hopefully of the relations of their art or profession with linguistics, psychology, mathematics, logic, acoustical science, and other 'hard' disciplines.[7]) All the same, that would be the immediate formulation of an observer from some other field of the humanities who might be asked to report on their activities. What you call analysis, that observer would say, we call formalistic criticism. And he might add some words of admiration and envy for the technical expertise with which such criticism can, in music, be carried out. ·

Some light was shed on this question in a relatively un-obtrusive exchange in the pages of the journal *Perspectives of New Music* some years ago, between two musicians who have in fact made more than token contributions to general theory (as well as to composition, analysis, and criticism). David Lewin, in response to what he took to be disturbing confusions in Edward T. Cone's article 'Beyond Analysis' of 1967, undertook to define and distinguish theory, analysis, and criticism.* Theory, he remarked, makes appeals on several different levels in attempting to formulate 'general sound-universes' of various kinds of music. It may appeal to divine or natural law, or to the intellectual consistency of a system, or else empirically to the practice of great composers. In the latter case, the theorist 'is naturally going to point out passages from the literature as support for the putative pertinence of his notions. He may, indeed, dig pretty hard at such passages.' But if the theorist probes pieces with the primary end of validating his theory he is not, according to Lewin, truly analysing them. Analysis must be directed to the explication of the work of art as an individual entity, not to the demonstration of general principles. Analysis must 'always reflect a *critical* attitude toward the piece'.[8]

Cone objected sharply to Lewin's hard and fast distinction between theory and analysis, as well as to much else in his response that has not been summarized here. But he did not disagree with him about criticism.

> Lewin's discussion of the relations between analysis and criticism is unexceptionable. I wish he would expand it. For he is quite right when he says that 'the important word is "criticism"'. The artist must be a critic. The observer must be a critic. . . . We should recognize the limitations of both theory and analysis, and . . . should call upon all modes of knowledge, including the theoretical, the analytical, and the intuitive, to help us achieve a proper critical response to a piece of music.[9]

Cone's wish, I might remark parenthetically, and even wistfully, is one I certainly shared at that time, when I myself was speaking up in what felt like a rather solitary way about the importance of criticism. Still, it was gratifying to find such firm agreement on the matter between two charter contributors to *Perspectives*.

As to the point of issue between them, I certainly agree with Lewin on the difference in principle between analytical exercises performed in aid of theory, and 'true' analysis done in aid of criticism. This is the kind of analysis that matters to historians, as well as to critics. In practice – here Cone is obviously right – one cannot always draw sharp distinctions. An incidental demonstration in a theory treatise may illuminate a work of art, just as a critical essay may incidentally illuminate a point of theory. (This is, I think, the strategy in many essays by Cone.) The most acute theorists are not usually the most sensitive critics, however, and sooner or later the basic impetus of any writer's work makes itself felt. Either theory or criticism suffers.

3

Another historical moment of great importance in the history of theory was the advent of modernism in the years around 1900. Most obviously, the experience of modernism stands behind Schoenberg's development of the twelve-tone system, which was the starting point for today's avant-garde compositional theory. But that experience also coloured the basic orientation of tonal theory, in particular the relation of theory to analysis and of analysis to criticism. For the full articulation of tonal theory occurred only at the time when the principles underlying tonal music seemed to be under attack. The work of two major figures in the development of modern theory and analysis, Heinrich Schenker in Vienna and Donald Francis Tovey in London, first appeared around the turn of the century and was obviously conceived of as a defence of the old order.

The menacing figure after 1890 was perceived to be Richard Strauss – and after 1910, Arnold Schoenberg (in German and English musical circles, Debussy and Stravinsky seemed to present less of a threat). Theory and analysis were deployed to celebrate the virtues of the music that the theorists treasured. And in those days, theorists were explicit enough about their values – Schenker with his great German tradition villainously halted by Liszt and Wagner, Tovey with his no-longer-navigable 'main stream of music'.[10] It seems clear, as I remarked earlier, though it may not be easy to substantiate, that the crisis of modernism sent many musicologists on twelfth- and thirteenth-century crusades. It is easier to see how it drove analysts into nineteenth-century bunkers, bunkers lined with the masterpieces of the traditional canon extending from Bach, whom the nineteenth century had made its own, up to Brahms and no further. If it can be said that modernism turned many musicologists into musical conservatives, it must also be said that modernism turned many theorists into reactionaries.

The canon itself was a characteristic creation of the nineteenth century. Up to around 1800, as we have seen, the repertory consisted largely of contemporary compositions; it had scarcely any historical dimension. But after Hoffmann's generation had learned to venerate the music of Haydn, Mozart, and Beethoven, it was automatically assumed that the canon would continue to grow in the future – and indeed that sturdy roots for it could be discovered in the past if only musicologists would dig for them. (Thus once Bach had been restored to the canon, the great Bach scholar Spitta devoted a major effort to Bach's seventeenth-century precursors, Scheidt, Schütz, and Buxtehude.) It is as though Hoffmann's powerful idea about the Fifth Symphony growing from a single motivic cell was carried over to the canon itself. Great music grew as though from some mysterious gene-pool of German origin; historicism, organicism, and nationalism were all stirred into the musical ideology of the time. When, after Schubert, Mendelssohn, and Schumann, a dispute arose about the authenticity of the branches represented by Wagner and Brahms, the issue was settled finally not by Tovey or Schenker but by Schoenberg, when he traced his own lineage to the latter. Almost until our own time, indeed, the continuing organic evolution of the canon of great music remained for many musicians an unconscious dogma.

As the embattled defenders of the traditional canon of Western art music in a world echoing with music of all categories, classes, eras, tribes, and cultures, the analysts seem to want to look more and more closely at less and less music. Schenker revered J. S. and C. P. E. Bach, Handel, the Viennese classicists, Mendelssohn, Schumann, Chopin, and Brahms, rejected Berlioz, Liszt, Wagner, and Verdi, ignored all music earlier than Bach, and vilified all later than Brahms. The subjects of his main analytical studies were drawn mostly from the stable of symphony orchestra warhorses and the piano teacher's rabbit hutch (opera he did not touch). A far from unintelligent primer on analysis by a young American theorist, Jeffrey Kresky, may be cited as one example among many others of similar conservatism on the part of recent writers.* From the straight and narrow path lined with the obligatory Bach invention, Schubert song, Chopin prelude and mazurka, Brahms intermezzo, and sonata movements by Mozart and Beethoven (the *Pathétique*), Kresky ventures no further than to Debussy's *La Fille aux cheveux de lin* and a fifty-five-bar passage from *Die Walküre*.

In his Conclusion, Kresky does have a few words about Schoenberg, and a brief demonstration with a musical example. Some tonal theorists have been able to extend their activity with considerable power to the music of Schoenberg, Stravinsky, Bartók, and beyond. With trivial exceptions, however, they have not – nor have theorists of any other school – devoted attention to music earlier than Bach. In the last fifty years or so, older music has been widely published, played, broadcast, and recorded; it has become a part of every listener's experience. To ignore it is to bury one's head in the sand. Nobody, I take it, will care to argue that the music of Dufay, Josquin, Byrd, and Monteverdi is all too weak – too primitive for analysis, or too inartistic to promote the aesthetic response which, as I have insisted, almost always stands behind analysis. As we shall see, avant-garde theorists have argued that preoccupation with the traditional canon and its standards on the part of the tonal theorists has distorted their view of more modern music. However this may be, it does appear to have shut them off almost completely from more ancient music.

This neglect of music from the more or less distant past – the same past that produced Dante and Donne, Botticelli and

Velázquez – seems to me a fairly serious charge than can be laid at the door of theory today. It is spoken of less often than the parallel charge, which is possibly, though not certainly, more serious – that of musicology neglecting music of the present.

4

In their attitudes towards the traditional canon of music, the analysts can be distinguished sharply from those musicologists who are occupied with the same material (or from musicologists in general, if the issue is conceived on broader ideological grounds). Musicologists strive to view this music within its full historical context: a context flooded with lesser music which the theorists ignore, coloured by historical performance conditions different from those we now accept, informed by complex economic, social, intellectual, and psychological forces, and cross-hatched by intertextuality – by the references composers make in one work to another as acknowledged model or un-acknowledged influence. Such, at least, is the musicologists' ideal. Even if for them the historical context confirms the centrality and value of much of the analysts' canon, there is a basic difference in focus. Where the analysts' attention is con-centrated on the inner workings of a masterpiece, the musicologists' is diffused across a network of facts and condi-tions impinging on it.

To be sure, there has already been occasion to see how far musicologists have, in general, fallen short of this ideal. That is the trouble. Especially in the postwar years, their concentration on limited positivistic tasks had the decided effect of sidestepping 'the music itself'; too often their encounters with actual pieces of music seemed hasty and disappointingly super-ficial. That is why analysis, for all its patent limitations, has fascinated those who have tried to develop serious music criticism in our time. What analysis does may be limited, but it does it extremely well. Critics are, in fact, *too* fascinated by analysis. I am thinking of the work of Edward Cone, Charles

Rosen, and Leonard Meyer, and with some reservations I am thinking of my own work also.

For if the musicologists' characteristic failure is superficiality, that of the analysts is myopia. Their dogged concentration on internal relationships within the single work of art is ultimately subversive as far as any reasonably complete view of music is concerned. Music's autonomous structure is only one of many elements that contribute to its import. Along with preoccupation with structure goes the neglect of other vital matters – not only the whole historical complex referred to above, but also everything else that makes music affective, moving, emotional, expressive. By removing the bare score from its context in order to examine it as an autonomous organism, the analyst removes that organism from the ecology that sustains it. It scarcely seems possible in this day and age to ignore the fact of that sustenance.

In the postwar years, however, a powerful appeal was exerted by analysis – and by exactly those strains of analysis that relied most dogmatically on a single principle, a monism or (as it was sometimes revealingly put) a 'secret' of musical form or musical coherence. Analysts who differed fundamentally in their actual analytical systems were nonetheless monists in this sense. One thinks of Schenker, pre-eminently; also of Rudolph Reti, the most influential though by no means the first exponent of 'thematicist' analysis; and also Alfred Lorenz, author of the quintessentially named *Das Geheimnis der Form bei Richard Wagner*, an immense and immensely involved study from the 1920s which enjoyed considerable prestige for years before being debunked by recent Wagner specialists. And while musicology and analysis can be viewed as contradictory, even as rival approaches to music, both were well calculated to thrive in the intellectual atmosphere of neopositivism. The appeal of systematic analysis was that it provided for a positivistic approach to art, for a criticism that could draw on precisely defined, seemingly objective operations and shun subjective criteria (and that would usually not even call itself criticism).

This was as true of thematicist analysis in the hands of Reti's followers Hans Keller and Deryck Cooke in London as it was of

Schenkerian analysis in the hands of Schenker's disciples Felix Salzer, Ernst Oster, and Oswald Jonas in New York and Chicago. It was also true of the psychologically based analytical system adumbrated in Leonard Meyer's *Emotion and Meaning in Music* of 1956, later of Allen Forte's 'set-theoretical' analysis, and later still of Jean-Jacques Nattiez's semiological analysis.[11]

Someone who was not a systematic analyst and not a monist, despite his frequent bursts of Johnsonian dogmatism, was Tovey. It is hard to know which of his traits exasperated theorists of the 1950s most – his breezy empiricist approach to analysis, his impatience with systematic theory, his ostensibly populist yet somehow suspect appeals to the 'naive listener', or his unabashed and unceasing use of frequently extravagant metaphors for the evocation of music's affect. Tovey's work could be ignored in the United States, where it was not widely influential. In Britain, where it was, it had to be repudiated.

Positivism in scholarship was originally a nineteenth-century movement, a movement which put its ineradicable stamp on early musicology. Schenker, editor of an admirable critical edition of Beethoven's piano sonatas, had no quarrel with positivistic musicology. But one prominent early musicologist, Hermann Kretzschmar, harkened to another nineteenth-century drum and developed a system of musical 'hermeneutics', and this provided Schenker with the source of an extended polemic after the turn of the century. Had it ever occurred to Schenker to peer across the Channel, he would have reacted with equal vigour against Tovey, with his reference to 'dark' and 'bright' keys, his 'purple patches' of prolonged harmony, and his madcap metaphors by which dominant chords 'whisper', motifs 'stagger', phrases are 'caught in the momentum of a planet in its orbit', and so on and so on. Tovey published his own latter-day analogue to Kretzschmar's notorious *Führer durch den Konzert-Saal* (1887–90) under the title *Essays in Musical Analysis* (1935–44); this unlucky title, which has probably militated seriously against the diffusion of Tovey's viewpoint in our time, would certainly have driven Schenker apoplectic. Music as expounded by Schenker is never concerned with metaphors of 'feeling' or 'expression' but only with the internal relationship of musical elements. Music is structure. Musical discourse must be purely musical.

No one has picked up on this theme more insistently than Milton Babbitt, who has seldom missed a chance to ridicule the use of 'incorrigible' statements about music. The language is that of the logical positivists, from whose doctrine Babbitt has never been able to escape. In Chapter 1 we have seen how under Arthur Mendel Princeton took an explicit lead in positivistic musicology. It also became a centre for the propagation of Schenker's system; this in turn provided an important ideological spur to avant-garde compositional theory, which was the real creation of Babbitt and the group around *Perspectives of New Music*. Yale under Allen Forte became another such centre. The rediscovery of Schenker at Princeton and Yale in the 1950s represents a true underground link between American neopositivism in music and the original nineteenth-century German movement.

5

The first strain of tonal theory that we will examine, however, is one that never gained official foothold in the American academic establishment. Rather it has pursued a circuitous route from Europe to America to Britain, and perhaps now back to America again.

The long *nostra culpa* recited by Wallace Berry to the Society for Music Theory (the one about Babelism, harlequinism, dogmatism, and so on) ended with the sad admission that theorists do not read each other's work very much. This may be so, but things cannot be nearly as bad as they were in 1951, when Rudolph Reti, a sixty-six-year-old Austrian refugee living in Montclair, New Jersey, published *The Thematic Process in Music*.* Theories of form depending on the fundamental affinity of the thematic and motivic material in a piece — what the Germans call *Substanzgemeinschaft*, and what I shall call 'thematicism' – had been around for a very long time. In Hoffmann's hands, as we have already seen, this idea was the basis for the first quasi-analytical demonstrations of music's organic structure. Particularly under the impetus of Gestalt psychology, such theories proliferated in studies by many German theorists of the 1920s and 1930s. Indeed, the writings of Schenker from the 1920s show strong thematicist leanings. But Reti seems not to have read any of this material. And even though he was on the fringes of the Schoenberg circle in the years around the First World War and still admired the composer's music, he does not cite Schoenberg either. It remained for later observers to draw a connection between Reti's ideas and Schoenberg's well-known discussion of the principle of 'developing variation' in Brahms, whereby a 'basic shape' or *Grundgestalt* suffuses an entire composition.

In 1951, however, Schoenberg's ideas were not yet well known and *The Thematic Process in Music* attracted a great deal of attention. In Britain, the book seems to have touched off the one coherent flurry of music-theoretical activity of the postwar years. Its leader was Hans Keller, a critic who had already made his name in England as one of the most vociferous early supporters of Benjamin Britten and – significantly – Schoenberg.

The most rigorous of Keller's analytical articles* was evidently the response to a kind of challenge, when he was invited by the editor of the *Music Review* to write on the same Mozart piano concerto (the C-major, K. 503) which Tovey had treated in a classic essay fifty years earlier. Somewhat unfairly – though he did have a point – Keller branded Tovey's writing about music as merely 'descriptive', tautological in that 'description gives a verbal account of what you hear and is essentially unnecessary'. True analysis should show the implicit 'organic' unity behind explicit diversity, notably in the matter of thematic contrasts. By manipulating the themes and motives of Mozart's concerto in various ways – selecting parts of them and omitting others, changing the rhythms, reading the notes backwards, upside down or with the order changed – Keller had little trouble showing how they are all related, how they are all derived one from another. 'The one essential point about a contrast is its unity,' he claimed; and in the greatest music, indeed, 'the looser the manifest integration, the stricter the demonstrable latent unification'.[12] For Keller this was a demonstrable, objective analytical criterion of evaluative criticism.

Keller's methodology drew specifically (if not very deeply) on serial operations as developed by Schoenberg, and his philosophy appealed to the '*latent* content of the *manifest* dream' as expounded by Freud. But whatever their intellectual superstructures or lack thereof, all strict thematicist theories are alike in their tendency to exaggerate the importance of the thematic and motivic shapes that are conceived of as the essence of music's organic unity. Harmony, rhythm, phrasing, proportions, even the order in which the related themes are presented — all these elements are slighted. Keller's model for a Mozart concerto seems to have been a sort of static, or at least undirected, relational field. Tovey's model was a narrative or, rather, a drama: which was why contrasts mattered to him as much as unity, and why he at least attempted to deal with all those other elements. I say 'as much as unity', for Tovey's organicist instincts were every bit as strong as Keller's — or Schenker's; he just had a different ideal of musical unity. 'There is a B in both,' he used to say, making sport of the thematicists of his own day. As far as he was concerned, they were fashioning their own kind of gigantic tautology out of music itself.

Keller himself was a not entirely unsportive critic who drew attention to his ideas as much by the abrasive style in which he presented them as by their intrinsic content. *Epater les Anglais* might have been emblazoned on the shield of this foreign-born controversialist, who hectored the English about Elgar and Britten (and soccer) while spearing their musical sacred cows. As a logical outcome of his disgust at tautological prose masquerading as musical discourse, Keller developed an entirely non-verbal style of presentation for his analytical ideas. Fragments of a composition were played next to other thematically related fragments and specially composed 'in-between' versions which were supposed to lead the ear wordlessly from the manifest to the latent. Some samples of this 'Wordless Functional Analysis' were broadcast on the BBC (where Keller worked) and one was published.[13] And as a further logical outcome of this step, Keller more or less gave up writing about music and never produced the comprehensive book on analysis and criticism that he had once contemplated. Two short books of this kind were published in the 1960s by a follower of his, Alan Walker: *A Study of Musical Analysis* and *An Anatomy of Musical Criticism* (this last apparently without reference to Northrop Frye).

'The British are at their most anti-Teutonic in their suspicion of far-reaching theories about music,' wrote Arnold Whittall in a very downhearted survey of musical analysis in Britain as of a few years ago.[14] And 'the British concern has, certainly, been much more with foregrounds than backgrounds, with themes and motives rather than with tonal or harmonic structure'. But Germans and Americans as well as Britons have been dismissive, not merely suspicious, of thematicists who have reached as far and as greedily as Reti, Keller, and Walker. On the other hand, if thematicism is taken in a non-dogmatic spirit as one analytical technique among others, it can yield important results; and one can probably say that British analysts have capitalized on this more than Americans, many of whom have been prejudiced against thematicism as a result of their concentration on the rather different organic vision of Schenker. Emphasis on themes and motifs is evident in such diverse works as the Jungian study *Wagner's 'Ring' and its Symbols* by Robert Donington and the ethnomusicological polemic *How Musical is Man?* by John Blacking.* Both authors pay specific tribute to Deryck Cooke, who wrote a much-criticized but widely influential tract on musical expression, *The Language of Music*, in 1959 (he is famous also for completing the unfinished draft of Mahler's Tenth Symphony). Cooke believed that thematic types provide the basis for a vocabulary, which he tried to compile, of the emotional states that are expressed in music.

A striking if possibly somewhat unexpected example of sensitive thematicist analysis can be seen in *The Consort and Keyboard*

Music of William Byrd (1978) by Oliver Neighbour.* The reader's first instinct would be to pigeonhole Neighbour's work as musicology, not only because he deals with a historical period which the analysts have neglected in such a pointed way, but also because it takes up characteristic musicological problems which they have always skirted, such as the sources, authenticity, chronology, and revision of works, influences on the composer, and his diachronic development. But Neighbour, lacking the blessings of a formal musicological training, like most of his generation in Britain, has had to rely for his 'theory' on what he has learned over many years from his studies of Schoenberg. In Byrd's fantasias and those of his predecessors, such as Robert White, Neighbour shows how the large periods of seemingly diffuse sectional works are held together and shaped by the subtle successive transformation of motivic shapes. It is a classic if restrained example of 'developing variation' which might have surprised the inventor of the term, though one would like to think it would not have displeased him.

In addition, Neighbour does not hesitate to treat Byrd's fantasias, pavans and galliards, In Nomines, and other instrumental compositions in 'descriptive' prose, nor to characterize and evaluate them. *The Consort and Keyboard Music of William Byrd* is, in fact, one of the most impressive models we have in English for modern historical criticism.

6

Whereas for the thematicists the unity of a musical composition depends on the way its parts (mostly motifs and themes) are related to one another, for Heinrich Schenker this depended on the way the parts are subsumed under the whole. Whether or not such a theory better deserves to be called 'organic', in this age when we are learning more and more about how organisms actually function, it clearly enjoys an advantage in the richness of the relationships envisaged. Add to this superior articulation, comprehensiveness, and systematization, and it is not hard to understand why Schenkerian analysis has had a greater effect than thematicism in the United States and, latterly, in Britain also. On the other hand, Schenker has made no appreciable headway at home, that is, in Germany or Austria ('partly due to certain follies of which he was guilty and partly due to his vulgar nationalism', according to Adorno[15]).

In Schenker's case, as I have already suggested, the fetish which he shared with Reti and Keller about music's unity is best understood in terms of his antipathy to modernism, which had brought the spectre of disunity in music to the fore. It would be interesting to learn something about Schenker's personal experience with composition, before he gave it up early in life, but the extensive Schenker bibliography includes virtually nothing about his biography. The bibliography, too, is 'purely musical'.

While Keller sought the implicit unity behind seemingly contrasted themes, Schenker went behind the very level on which themes are manifested. Levels or hierarchical layers are fundamental to his analytic method. This begins by abstracting or reducing explicit 'surface' phenomena such as themes and musical phrases and periods to their underlying harmonic areas (perhaps the best English term for Schenker's *Stufen*). It then goes on to reduce the *Stufen* to a simple, invariant pattern that Schenker was able to find at every level of every tonal composition. This is the *Ursatz*, a sort of vastly expanded cadence formula. The melodic, top part of the *Ursatz*, the *Urlinie* or 'basic line', proved to be the 'horizontal' unfolding over a period of time of the notes of the common chord or triad, notes which in the triad itself are ranged 'vertically' – that is, sounded simultaneously as a chord. The major triad Schenker believed to be 'the chord of nature'. We recall Lewin's observation about the appeal of theory to natural law.

Hence a single 'principle', that of the triad, governs both the vertical and the horizontal pitch dimensions of music, both the simultaneous and the successive, both the detail and the whole. That the vertical dimension (harmony) is in a sense 'governed' by the triad is a traditional enough idea, though Schenker did not formulate it traditionally. All chords assume their function or harmonic meaning referentially to the tonic triad of the key (which is the last chord, the chord of rest, in the final cadence of a piece). That the horizontal dimension (melody, or line) is also governed by the triad was a more radical concept. In Schenker's theory, all the notes of a melody can be explained as diminutions, ornamentations, 'neighbour tones', prolongations, and various other technical categories in between the 'structural' notes of the *Urlinie* which unfold the tonic triad in time. Indeed, all the thousands of notes in a piece can be explained as elements of multiple lines unfolding on one hierarchical layer or another. What is more, the *way* in which the unfolding takes place – by means of the linear voice-leading rules of strict counterpoint – is the same in the *Ursatz* as in all the structural layers, from background to foreground. The layers are symmetrical.

A simple example may be found useful. In the tune for the 'Ode to Joy' in the finale of Beethoven's Ninth Symphony, the *Urlinie* $\hat{3}$–$\hat{2}$–$\hat{1}$ (F sharp–E–D in the key of D major) may be heard on the surface at the words '[sanf]ter Flügel weilt' – that is, at the tune's actual cadence; on a slightly deeper structural level at 'Alle Menschen . . . Flügel weilt'; and on the level of the tune as a whole at 'Freude, schöne Götterfunken . . . Deine Zauber . . . Flügel weilt'. Deepest of all, over the span of the entire twenty-minute finale, there are three structural tones which mark the *Urlinie* on the ultimate background level. All other notes of the piece, all tens of thousands of them, can be ranged systematically on many, many layers in relations to these three. All parts are thus organically subsumed under the whole.

This little example from the 'Ode to Joy' can also serve to introduce three standard criticisms of Schenker. First, a note such as the low A on '[streng Ge]teilt', which any listener will sense as vital for the shape and character of the tune, is accorded no special place in the analysis (though of course it is accorded *a* place). Schenkerian analysis repeatedly slights salient features in the music. Second, the very next note, F sharp, on 'Al[le]', gains special emphasis from its rhythmic placement in syncopation, as well as from its association with the one word that Beethoven wanted, apparently, to stress above all others. Schenkerian analysis ignores rhythmic and textual considerations. Third, the second couplet, beginning 'Wir betreten, feuertrunken', set to nearly the same music as the fourth and final couplet, 'Alle Menschen', is nonetheless treated differently in the analysis. Why, when this couplet makes its cadence at 'Heiligtum', must we interpret this as structurally different from the identical cadence at 'Flügel weilt'? In the crucial matter of the placement of the structural tone on the various layers, on which so much else depends, Schenker lacks persuasive criteria and seems arbitrary again and again.

This is not the place for an extended discussion of the Schenker system. The above criticisms have never been powerful enough to counter the very real attractions it can offer to a certain kind of mind. It offers a proto-structuralist aesthetic that seems logical and even elegant, whatever dark suspicions may arise from time to time that Schenker, like the thematicists, is making all tonal music into a giant tautology. And it offers a clear method with an objective feel to it. Schenkerian analysis is not easy – it requires a lot of work and the constant exercise of musical judgment – but it is eminently doable. It shows you how to get on with the job and how to pinpoint every note in a composition either on or in the interstices between the graphs of this or that hierarchical layer. Schenker's famous graphs, using mainly musical notation, preclude the necessity for much prose in the analysis; indeed one of his last publications was a tiny booklet containing only *Fünf Urlinie-Tafeln*. The analogy with Keller's Wordless Functional Analysis has been noted by Whittall and others. Both men yearned to make their analyses 'purely musical'. Both thematicism and Schenkerian analysis, as I have said, were well calculated to flourish in the positivistic atmosphere of the 1950s.

When the young theorist Allen Forte was appointed at Yale in

1959, he proclaimed an ideological commitment to Schenker and a programme of work which was to make that university into the world centre for the dissemination and extension of the Austrian theorist's thought. 'Schenker's Conception of Musical Structure', an essay which Schenkerians regard as a classic, was published in the *Journal of Music Theory*, a publication founded at Yale in 1957 and edited by Forte in the 1960s.* The example chosen in this essay to exemplify Schenker's analytical method is in my view not only a weak analysis in itself, but also one that is open to the same three standard criticisms mentioned above in connection with the 'Ode to Joy'.[16] However this may be, the analysis – it is of Schumann's tiny song 'Aus meinen Thränen spriessen' from *Dichterliebe* – has apparently impressed many musicians, and Forte's incisive formulation of five 'unsolved problems of music theory' to which Schenker's methods might profitably be applied was certainly taken to heart by many American theorists. They are, in his words, (1) Constructing a theory of rhythm for tonal music, (2) Determining the sources and development of triadic tonality, (3) Gaining information about compositional technique, (4) Improving theory in-struction, and (5) Understanding the structure of problematic modern works.

Twenty-five years later, after a good deal of work along these five lines, the results are mixed. Doubtless much has been accomplished under (4); as usual, yesterday's orthodoxy is en-shrined in today's textbooks. The important work of Forte himself has been directed to problem (5), though the path from his *Contemporary Tone Structures* (1955) to *The Structure of Atonal Music* (1973) and *The Harmonic Organization of 'The Rite of Spring'* (1978) is away from Schenkerian methods towards his own individual method of 'set-theoretic analysis', which has been influential in its own right. A good deal of light has been shed on problem (3), as we shall see at some leisure in the next chapter. But this has happened in spite of the Schenkerians' interest in the matter, I believe, or at least only indirectly as a result of it. As for problem (2), one or two tendentious articles on pre-tonal music have done very little to lighten the charge which I have entered above about analysts' conservatism in the matter of repertory. They are simply not serious about any music earlier than that of the traditional canon. While the *Journal of Music Theory* has always carried articles about past theorists and theory, those articles have been written by musicologists – historians of theory – and not by Schenkerians.

And problem (1) remains a major issue for the Schenkerians. It is hard to get around the fact that even though a certain dynamism is built into the idea of the 'unfolding' of the *Ursatz*, Schenker says virtually nothing about rhythm, durational proportions, or any other temporal questions. Basically, and despite various protestations to the contrary, his model of music is as static as that of the thematicists. And the idea of constructing a theory of rhythm by analogy with Schenker's theory of pitch seems altogether too pat, too obviously beholden to the postwar avant garde's idea of deriving serial procedures for durations, dynamics, and so on by analogy with Schoenberg's twelve-tone system for pitch. The strictly hierarchical (though scarcely Schenkerian) theory of rhythm enunciated by Grosvenor Cooper and Leonard Meyer, in *The Rhythmic Structure of Music* (1960), never satisfied the theory community.

The most stubborn problem of all is rooted in Schenker's idealism, in his determination to seek the essence of all tonal music in an invariable abstract formula rather than in its infinite, concrete, magnificent variety. As Charles Rosen has remarked,

> his method takes the form of a gradual reduction of the surface of the music to his basic phrase [the *Ursatz*], and the analysis moves in one direction, away from what is actually heard and toward a form which is more or less the same for every work. It is a method which, for all it reveals, concentrates on a single aspect of music and, above all, makes it impossible to bring the other aspects into play. The work appears to drain away into the secret form hidden within itself. That is the impasse of every critical method which places the source of its vitality in an implicit form. . . .

Criticism is not the reduction of a work to its individual, interior symmetries, but the continuous movement from explicit to implicit and back again. And it must end where it started – with the surface.[17]

Highly sensitive to the charge of reductionism, Schenker's followers, though they are not prepared to come all the way up to the surface, nevertheless claim that what counts in his and their analyses is not the 'background' but the 'middleground' and in particular the process of transformation between the various layers. But their disclaimers leave Rosen unmoved, apparently: and he is not the only one.

In the service of his idealistic vision, Schenker was ready to strip away not only salient details of individual compositions, but also distinctions between compositions, composers, and periods. The form of a Bach prelude is in principle the same as that of a Brahms sonata movement. Indeed, he was ready to strip away most of music history, as we have seen; for musicologists, the most baffling and irritating aspect of Schenker's thinking is his view of music history as an absolutely flat plateau flanked by bottomless chasms. All this makes him a very difficult figure for the historian or the critic to get much out of. Such, at least, is my experience. There are (a few) musicologists who profess to admire Schenker, but I cannot think of any major study in historical criticism that draws on his work in a substantial way. James Webster's important study of 'Schubert's Sonata Form and Brahms's First Maturity', for example, which uses greatly simplified Schenker graphs to good effect, uses them to enlarge on an insight of Tovey's which owes nothing to Schenker.*

7

In discussing musical theories, as other theories, there is always a temptation to pay too much attention to the monists. For it is in their nature as monists to develop highly articulated theories which one can easily get hold of and either criticize or embrace.

It is also in their nature to attract disciples, and disciples tend to issue noisy but unrealistic assessments of the status of their creed. Now it is conspiratorially rejected, now it is accepted by everybody in the know.

The temptation ought to be resisted, for there are relatively few disciples as compared to unattached analysts: analysts who will readily acknowledge a debt to one or more theorists without feeling any necessity to follow them rigorously. One cannot help feeling a sense of overkill about Eugene Narmour's full-scale attack on Schenker in his *Beyond Schenkerism* (1977), with its elaborate logical demonstrations, refutations, and polemical thrusts and parries.* Narmour scores a number of powerful points against Schenker's theory, notably as regards the patently vulnerable concept of the *Ursatz*, but it is disturbing that he has so little to say about Schenker's practice. There is much to learn from Schenker's analytical insights on a detailed level, considered apart from his theory, as for example in his studies of the late Beethoven piano sonatas, written before the concept of the *Ursatz* was even developed. (It was the last major element of Schenker's theory to fall into place.) In the words of a musicologist who is deeply concerned with theory and who is a not uncritical admirer of Schenker, 'The collection of analytical tools at his disposal for conceptualizing the smaller- and lesser-scale procedures of tonal music must be impressive to anyone, whether one is inclined to love or to leave it, whether one is prepared or not to follow him from foreground to more background layers, and whether or not his particular analyses seem convincing.'[18]

Narmour draws a useful distinction between two classes of Schenker's followers, one that points to a further attraction, on a more sophisticated level, that Schenker's work has exerted on another type of theorist. The distinction is based on their view of the *Ursatz*. 'Schenkerians', who include Schenker's direct and indirect disciples, view the *Ursatz* as an empirical 'deep structure' perceived in all tonal music, whereas 'neo-Schenkerians', who include leading theorists of avant-garde music, view it as an *a priori* axiom in a more or less formal system. According to

Narmour, there is a basic confusion between these incompatible views in Schenker's own thinking. Narmour is fascinated by the neo-Schenkerians, and with good reason: he has his own theoretical 'model' to propose for tonal music in place of their 'system' – an 'implication-realization model' derived from the work of Meyer. Beyond Schenkerism lies a new monism, Narmourism: hence the overkill. We shall get to Narmour's neo-Schenkerians in just a moment.

More than any other group in music, it will probably be agreed, Narmour's Schenkerians see themselves as the only true believers and keepers of the faith. Other, less monistically inclined theorists come to the Master in an undogmatic spirit; his thought has sustained and stimulated work of many different kinds with various problems, musical elements, and repertories. It is much more suggestive than Reti's thematicism, for example, which seems to have, in intellectual terms, no place to go. Theorists and analysts of all complexions have been able to make use of ideas and techniques such as prolongation, the reduction of complex passages to basic *Stufen*, of long-range linear connections, the concept of hierarchical layers, and others.

Such theorists are certainly not neo-Schenkerians, in Narmour's sense. Narmour would not even call them Schenkerians. David Epstein might perhaps be called an ecumenical Schenkerian, for in his *Beyond Orpheus* (1977) he attempts to accommodate Schenkerian analysis with thematicism and bind them both by an overarching theory of rhythm (a non-Schenkerian theory of rhythm, so far as I can judge).* Given this bold, possibly even naive ambition, it is not surprising that while Epstein comes up with many valuable insights about tonal music, he also leaves many questions unanswered. Indeed his whole argument is put together loosely, even sketchily; his *modus operandi* could hardly differ more from that of a systematic theorist such as Narmour. But that is one of the recommendations of a study which can perhaps be taken as symptomatic of a new flexibility in today's music theory. Epstein's chosen mentor in thematicism is not Reti or Keller but Schoenberg – a more fashionable name, to be sure, though I think it would be unfair to attribute the choice solely to fashion. What really attracted Epstein to Schoenberg was, more likely, that the latter's idea of the *Grundgestalt* and its 'developing variation' amounts to little more than a brilliant suggestion. It was never developed into a full-fledged thematicist theory. It therefore remains as a flexible tool, not a dogmatic system, for others such as Epstein to use in their own ways. (And a few years later the young musicologist Walter Frisch used it in another way, in *Brahms and the Principle of Developing Variation*,* to trace the evolution of Brahms's method of coordinating that local technique with the larger demands of classical form.)

Of interest to musicologists is a small appendix in Epstein's book, 'Middle-Period Beethoven: Motive Form and Tonal Plan', which in effect sets out to localize a certain musical procedure within a limited historical repertory, namely the symphonies, quartets, and sonatas of Beethoven's middle period. This is the sort of thing that previous analysts, habituated to look hard at a single work in isolation, have seldom attempted. Once again, the results of Epstein's demonstration leave one with many questions (including what Epstein understands as Beethoven's middle period); but once again, the effort seems symptomatic. It is also symptomatic, not to say ironic, that the most disapproving review of *Beyond Orpheus* should have come from England – from Arnold Whittall, who seems to regard Epstein not as an ecumenical Schenkerian but as a subversive one at best.[19] Thanks in part to the activities of some American émigrés, Schenker's prestige and influence are rising in Britain at the very time they are sinking, though not without dignity, in the United States. Whittall's show of bristling orthodoxy would seem to be a passing phase among British theorists, however, if one may judge from the first issues of a new journal, *Music Analysis*, which he has helped to found. The coverage here is wide and enterprising, and the intellectual tone notably undogmatic.

Also new, as I write, is *A Generative Theory of Tonal Music* (1983) by Fred Lerdahl and Ray Jackendoff, a composer-linguist team whose articles since 1977 have been in the forefront of music-theoretical work drawing on concepts and methodologies from linguistics.* Like Epstein, but in a very different style, Lerdahl and Jackendoff seek a comprehensive theory of tonal music accommodating both pitch and rhythm. But these men actually distance themselves from Schenker – though they are the first to admit that their reductive pitch system ends up being very close, at least in form, to his. The point is that instead of starting with Schenker, like Epstein or Forte, they develop their own careful series of rules of musical reduction *de novo*, expressed in tree-diagrams inspired by the phonological and syntactical tree-diagrams of linguistics.

On short acquaintance, their theory can be seen to avoid – or perhaps the word should be 'correct' – many dubious aspects of Schenker's theory. To begin with, while their reduction of pitch elements ('prolongational reduction') is no less relentless than his, they are not concerned to isolate middleground or background layers. The emphasis remains on the foreground, so there is no inclination to slight 'surface' features of the music. They posit no *Ursatz*, no 'chord of nature'. They also go to great trouble to rationalize and systematize criteria for determining the hierarchical status of tones – for determining which tones are structural; and the touchstone for this is always what the listener intuitively perceives (hence the un-Schenkerian regard for the foreground). An important class of these criteria is derived from a fully articulated, partly hierarchical theory of rhythm (involving 'metrical reduction'). This theory, clearly an improvement over that of Cooper and Meyer, may well prove to be Lerdahl and Jackendoff's most powerful contribution.

Detailed analysis of their intricate and elegant argument would obviously take us too far afield here. Much else is refreshingly unconventional about this impressive book. The authors are always ready to point out large areas of music and experience that they have deliberately chosen to omit from their theory, and say why; in the process they have interesting (if sometimes breezy) things to say about serialism, innate response to music, cognition, affect, and many other topics. They are conventional, as theorists, only in saying nothing whatsoever about history. Which brings one up short. After all the omissions have been admitted, even paraded, one is bound to observe that what we have here is still only a theory of musical structure, and a carefully delimited one at that. Less aggressively than Narmour, Lerdahl and Jackendoff offer their theory as a replacement for Schenker; we shall see whether it is widely accepted. If it is, it will simply be a better account of tonal music of the less problematic sort – that is, music constituting a fraction of the Western tradition. It treats structure alone, and treats it as an absolute, outside of any historical context. It is hard to see, at least so far, how much more historians are going to get out of it than out of Schenker.

8

The historical moment that focused and clarified the work of tonal theorists such as Schenker and Tovey also provided the starting point for modernist compositional theory. This is the other stream of William Benjamin's mixed metaphor, cited above, the stream sharing space with Schenkerism (or neo-Schenkerism) in the minds of modern theorists.

The first stirrings of this theory were hardly to be distinguished from the retrenchment activities of the conservatives. Schenker published his *Harmonielehre* in 1906, destined by venerable German pedagogic tradition to constitute the first member of a great theory trilogy; his *Kontrapunkt* appeared in 1910–22 and *Der freie Satz* (Free Composition) in 1935. Tovey, ever disorganized, nonetheless pulled himself together to write the series of music articles for the *Encyclopaedia Britannica*, eleventh edition, of 1911. At around the same time another *Harmonielehre* was published, that of Schoenberg.[20] Schoenberg, of course, came to the crisis of modernism from a standpoint diametrically opposed to that of Schenker and Tovey: not with his finger in the dyke but with his whole frame spreadeagled on a board swept along by the surf of history. Yet paradoxically, his need to write a theory text based on traditional models (which is not to say a traditional theory text) was no less urgent than theirs. So, at least, begins what may be called the official history of the long and remarkable involvement of theory with avant-garde composition in this century.

This history is recounted succinctly in the Introduction to an exemplary collection of essays published in 1972, *Perspectives on Contemporary Music Theory*, edited by Benjamin Boretz and Edward T. Cone.* The voice sounds more like Boretz than Cone:

> The demand of contemporary composers has been for the formulation of *adequate* theoretical principles, principles in conformity with what they know they need empirically. . . . That such a demand should be the particular child of our century is plausible, in view of the musical crisis precipitated by the appearance of extraordinary compositional events following a long habituation to a stable and powerful tradition. For the very inexplicability of these events at the moment of their appearance exposed brutally the inadequate conceptual and empirical scope of existing traditional theory, by revealing its powerlessness to render them explicable, to account for them as departures by extension rather than discontinuity. . . . Schoenberg in particular, and by his own account, felt himself utterly abandoned to conceptual isolation and empirical self-reliance by the failure of any available account of traditional music to provide a coherent reference for the developments taking place within his own work (pp. vii–viii).

Schoenberg, according to this history, was the first composer fully to experience the anguish of modernist alienation – 'conceptual isolation'. He was driven to reformulate traditional theory before he could work out a modernist, compositional theory of his own. This was the twelve-tone system, developed in the early 1920s.

In Schoenberg's theory as well as in his music, forward-looking tendencies always maintained a fascinating tension with backward-looking ones. The traditionalism of his music was stressed harshly enough as long ago as 1952, in Boulez's notorious tract 'Schönberg is Dead', which called for its explicit renunciation as a compositional model in favour of the music of Webern.[21] In music theory, Schoenberg's traditionalism meant simply that radical new theory had to be relatable to theory of the past.

Not surprisingly, this demand continued to find an echo in the minds of those who wrote and wrote about contemporary music in the post-Schoenberg generation. Important figures in the United States were Roger Sessions, a major composer and also a very influential writer on music from the 1930s to the 1950s, and Edward Cone, a devoted student of his. And whether surprisingly or not, many – perhaps most – young theorists are apparently still thinking along the same broad lines.

Cone's work is exemplary, even though the greater part of it deals with the classics of tonal music, and only a lesser part with the twentieth-century masters. Not subscribing to any doctrine (such as Schenker's) which prohibits him from appreciating or analysing the music of these masters, Cone has sought ways to apprehend them comparable to his apprehension of Bach, Schubert, Berlioz, and Brahms. Thus in his early article 'Stravinsky: the Progress of a Method', published in 1962, the 'progress' in question presupposes a continuity between the tonal Stravinsky of *Symphonies of Wind Instruments* (1920) and the serial Stravinsky of *Movements* (1959), not a break.* And the 'method', Cone's formulation of a 'basic Stravinskian technique', is construed in terms applicable to earlier music.

Cone himself mentions the Brandenburg Concertos as a vague model for the first phase of this idiosyncratic technique, a phase that he calls 'stratification'. Stravinsky juxtaposes sections of music sharply differentiated in instrumentation, register, and so on, which alternate in complex ways, forming several distinct layers of music constantly interrupted by one another – sometimes very rudely – while always maintaining something of their original characters. 'Interlock', the association of the successive sections of each layer, and 'synthesis', the association of the different layers themselves, are further phases of the basic technique, employing such devices as motivic and long-range linear relationship (so Cone might be said to be drawing on concepts dear to Reti and Schenker, respectively, but in a way neither one of them would have allowed). Some aspects of what Cone described in Stravinsky had been adumbrated previously, but no one had formulated the theoretical concepts so incisively, or had written a more genuinely illuminating account of any single Stravinsky piece than Cone's brilliant pithy analysis, with its twenty-eight-inch foldout, of the *Symphonies*.

Around the time of his Stravinsky article Cone seems to have felt a need to enunciate and develop his position in a series of essays that are now classics – 'Analysis Today', 'Music: a View from Delft' and 'Beyond Analysis'.* In brief, Cone demands of any kind of music some recognizable transformation of or analogue to such categories as phrase, cadence, 'structural downbeat', unity, process, and teleology. All these are categories which have emerged from our experience of tonal music. He finds all this in Schoenberg, Stravinsky – both early and late Stravinsky – and of course Sessions; he is less sure about Webern; and he is sure he does not find it in most of what I have called the second phase of modernism, the avant-garde music of the postwar era. In a field where obscurity is frequent, obfuscation not unknown, and ostentation endemic, Cone's is a rare voice which seeks always to clarify and inform; but there is nonetheless a quiet polemic pulse behind his cool and elegant discourse. A composer and pianist, he was approaching his middle years before he started writing about music in earnest, and one suspects he would not have done so at all if he did not have strong feelings to vent about Cage on the one hand and Babbitt on the other.

We might speak of a traditionalist or, perhaps, a 'transformationist' wing of modernist theory, in which Cone occupies a place of honour. Its most substantial body of formal work is that of George Perle. The title of Perle's second book, *Twelve-Tone Tonality*, is emblematic of his traditional orientation: even though that book is his personal testament of compositional theory – that is, in effect a private reading of serialism on which he bases his practice as a composer – and even though it is indebted to the radical mathematical theory of Milton Babbitt. *Twelve-Tone Tonality* is a work of 'prescriptive' theory, to adapt (and neutralize) the terminology introduced by Cone in 'Analysis Today'. Perle's earlier book *Serialism and Atonality* I would call a work of 'descriptive' theory, like Cone's essay on Stravinsky, in that it codifies principles derived from the practice of other composers, in this case Schoenberg, Berg, and Webern. And Perle's most recent study, *The Operas of Alban Berg*,* is a work of criticism – a leaning towards criticism being not uncharacteristic of writers in the transformationist wing of modernist theory.

Volume 1 of this study, which treats *Wozzeck*, encompasses not only such standard theoretical tasks as the exposition of the opera's musical structure as a whole and its musical language in detail, but also unstandard ones: discussion of the antecedents of the work in Berg's early songs, for example, and of the representational and symbolic aspects of Berg's complex leitmotiv system. Elsewhere Perle has also involved himself with so unanalytical an endeavour as the decoding of this composer's extraordinary private musical cyphers in such works as the Lyric Suite and the Violin Concerto.[22] A lifetime's preoccupation with theory lies behind Perle's criticism, theory that he is now prepared to present not for its own sake, and not for his own use, but in the interest of explicating actual pieces of music in their historical context. Perle's *Wozzeck* is a work that musicologists may well admire – the American Musicological Society gave it a prize – and also ponder as a general model for work they are going to have to do sooner or later with twentieth-century music.

It stands to reason that a study like *The Operas of Alban Berg* will be read more than one like *Twelve-Tone Tonality* – and the reason lies deeper than their relative density of mathematical discourse. Criticism looks outward to the public world of the musical repertory, compositional theory looks inward to the private refuge of the composer's workshop. Unlike tonal theory, compositional theory is valued primarily for what it enables the theorist to do as a composer of new music, only secondarily for what it tells him or anyone else about music already composed. Therefore its relevance to anyone but the composer-theorist and his circle of associates is limited. This is as true of Schoenberg's twelve-tone theory – or, better, of what Perle and others have been able to formulate on Schoenberg's behalf on the basis of his practice – as it is of Perle's own 'twelve-tone tonality'. It is equally true of the modernist theory of Milton Babbitt and the Princeton School.

The discussion of this that follows is something of an excursus, then: the reader may even wonder why I take up compositional theory at all. Our concern here with theory and analysis is in what they contribute to the knowledge, not the creation, of music. One reason for the excursus is a prudent hedging of bets about those 'primary' and 'secondary' values, of course; it is not likely that something that aids creation will prove to be entirely useless in elucidation. Another, perhaps less good reason is that in America in the 1950s and 1960s, practically nothing in the whole music-intellectual sphere stirred up as much interest and controversy as the ideas and activities of Babbitt.

9

Babbitt, like Cone, was also a student of Sessions and a colleague of both men at Princeton. He has opposed their transformationist position vis-à-vis Schoenberg from the start. For him tonality and serialism are radically different musical systems and analogies between them are fallacious.

He has exchanged some sharp words on this subject with his old friend and long-term fellow-serialist Perle.[23] One typically sensitive issue (remember the title *Twelve-Tone Tonality*) concerns the structural organization by means of harmonic areas – Schenker's *Stufen* – which is at the heart of all theories of form in tonal music. In Schubert's 'Great' Symphony in C major, for example, the main theme of the finale – which is put together, as it happens, out of the seven notes of the C-major scale, and no others – comes back at the recapitulation in E flat major. This unusual transposition contributes not only to the unique expressive effect of the music but also to its unique structural coherence. Could not something analogous transpire, at least in terms of structure, in a twelve-tone work beginning with a row whose first note is C, and using at its recapitulation (or at some point comparable to a recapitulation) the same row transposed so that its first note is now E flat?

No, Babbitt has said again and again. For what is *essential* about Schubert's transposition of the theme from C to E flat is the fact that three new pitches (B flat, E flat, and A flat) are brought into play in a functional manner, while three of the original seven (B, E, and A natural) are set aside. In the hypothetical twelve-tone example, on the other hand, since all twelve pitches of the chromatic scale are already there in the original row, no new 'sounds' can be added in the transposition. 'The analogy between the transposition of a [twelve-tone] row and those of a major (or minor) scale is untenable.'[24] Transposition of a row is in itself ultimately trivial as far as structural organization is concerned.

Benjamin Boretz, one of Babbitt's most influential students, followers, and expositors, calls Babbitt (as a theorist) a relativist because he insists on the plurality of musical systems and postulates that any self-consistent system may have its own limited applicability. In practice, the systems in question come down to two, serialism and tonality, though it may be mentioned parenthetically that Babbitt's position would also admit non-Western musical systems (and so it is less odd than it might seem to find a specialist in Indian music contributing to Babbitt's *Festschrift* in 1976).[25] What it does not admit is any other post-tonal music that is not 'systematic'. The inflated prestige of serial music in American academic circles in the 1950s and 1960s was a direct result of this 'relativism', and here the example of Babbitt's work as a composer went hand in hand with his teaching as a theorist.

In reference to Schoenberg's famous lecture 'Composition

with Twelve Tones', the one place where the inventor of the twelve-tone system discussed it at any length, Babbitt remarked more in wonder than in regret how defensive Schoenberg seems to be here about the system *qua* system, spending most of his energy justifying it on historical grounds and practically apologizing for not using tone rows transposed by the 'traditional' interval of the fifth. The system's demonstrable consistency, Babbitt concluded,

> is an astounding fortuity.... Schoenberg, like many other great innovators, was not, at least at this point, entirely aware of the implications of his own discovery. This is, in no sense, to minimize his achievement; on the contrary, it makes the achievement appear all the more remarkable.[26]

At the same time that Boulez was concerned to emphasize the traditional aspects of Schoenberg's music, Babbitt was concerned to emphasize the radical aspects of his theory.

Babbitt's mission as composer and theorist was to lay bare those implications of the twelve-tone system that even Schoenberg may never have grasped fully. Himself a mathematician as well as a composer, he early developed a formulation of it in terms of numerical group theory. This allowed him to investigate the properties of twelve-tone rows – or 'sets', as they are now called in deference to his work – in the abstract: such properties as the way certain kinds of sets divide into complementary segments ('combinatoriality'), the categories of pitches that will remain invariant when sets are transposed at certain intervals, how sets can be made to generate 'derived' sets, and so on. All this he makes use of in his own compositions – instrumental, vocal, and electronic: not surprisingly, given his turn of mind, Babbitt became a pioneer of electronic music in the 1950s. His *Philomel* of 1964, for soprano and electronic tape, is a classic of the genre.

As I remarked at the beginning of this chapter, music theory in this century is mostly concerned with the problem of musical form; avant-garde compositional theory is no exception. The main problem for Babbitt and his students such as Boretz is to derive principles for the structure of serial compositions – for their extension over long periods of time – from the original set itself which also determines the bar-by-bar details. Particularly in this area they could draw inspiration from Schenker, who showed how the structural articulation of a tonal composition could be derived from the same *Ursatz* which also determines its details.

This is the importance of Schenker to avant-garde metatheory. Schenker provides, if not a fully rigorous model, at least the vision of such a model for a genuinely systematic theory of tonal music. The idea that new 'systems' can be generated for avant-garde music is after all a slightly crazy one, some intuition of which fact on the part of Schoenberg (who was only crazy north-north-west) may well account for his defensive tone when talking about twelve-tone music. Reference to the world of established, accepted music is required to make the idea seem plausible. This Schenker's theory supplied, at least to the extent that it could be construed as or developed into a formal axiomatic theory. And this is certainly one major reason for its continued cultivation, and one reason why, in William Benjamin's words, neo-Schenkerism (as Narmour defines it) and avant-garde compositional theory 'have entered into a curious marriage of convenience'. Benjamin claims that the two must drift apart because of their conflicting values, and perhaps in the 1980s they must, if consistency of values comes back into fashion. In the positivistic climate of the 1950s, however, the consistency of logic, not of values, was all that it was possible to talk about in ways that Babbitt would not dismiss as 'literally meaningless'.

If we once again recall Lewin's three authorities to which music theory may appeal, Babbitt can indeed be seen to appeal to the practice of great composers, by means of his analyses of works by Schoenberg and Webern in particular. He does *not* appeal to natural law. But the most explicit appeal of his theory is to the intellectual consistency of the system; hence the technical talk about systems, models, hierarchies, and so on which deadens so much theory (both serial and neo-Schenkerian) of the 1960s. Folk wisdom attributes similar habits of mind to musicians and mathematicians, but few musicians can comfortably thread their way through Babbitt's more difficult papers or those of certain of his students. No branch of music theory since the Middle Ages has given so strong an impression of curling away from the experience of music into the far reaches of the theorists' intellects. The impression is deceptive, of course, because the theory is intimately implicated with music that is composed – some of it music of unquestioned stature. That is the strength of the theory, and the source of its prestige. Even though the 1970s and 1980s have witnessed a reaction against avant-garde serialism, there are few serious critics who are inclined to write off Babbitt's own music.

On the other hand, the unequivocal claim that 'the invention of musical systems is in itself to be part of the creative process' – which Boretz attributes to Babbitt[27] – has not been received kindly by critics or by all composer-theorists, even at Princeton. This claim is as fundamental as it is bold. 'Maybe it just is a fact about modern art that coming to care about it demands coming to care about the problems in producing it,' Stanley Cavell has written in a subtle and sceptical extended meditation on this whole problem.[28] But most composers (and listeners) still hold to the position of Schoenberg, the paramount transformationist, who discouraged discussion of the twelve-tone system and wanted his music to stand or fall irrespective of any appreciation or even knowledge of the technical problems he had to solve in producing it. Indeed, in the exchange about 'Beyond Analysis', mentioned above, what disturbed Lewin were not so much Cone's views about theory and analysis vis-à-vis criticism, which were by then an old story, as Cone's 'hidden' message that young composers should stay clear of theory altogether. Lewin would presumably side with Boretz when he enlarges on Babbitt's claim in his *Perspectives on Contemporary Music Theory* introduction:

The vitality and diversity of contemporary music theory is comparable to, and – more pertinently – closely aligned with, that of composition itself. And while much of this theory has revealed, retrospectively as it were, the extent to which our experience of traditional music itself would have been impoverished in the absence of an adequate theoretical-conceptual framework, it has even more crucially revealed how our experience of and within contemporary music would, in such an absence, have been virtually inconceivable (p. x).

It is very unlikely, however, that experience of most of the music Boretz has in mind is conceivable, even in the presence of such theory, to many people who are not 'within' that music. And conversely, it is likely that more people have got something out of Babbitt's music than have got anything out of his theory.

10

From the above paragraphs the reader may have received the impression of avant-garde compositional theory as an elevated dialogue conducted mainly at a small rural university in New Jersey. This impression was not dispelled when in 1962 the Princeton University Press began publication of *Perspectives of New Music* on behalf of the Fromm Foundation, the creation of a very emphatic and intelligent patron who had already funded various projects to encourage contemporary music. The most ambitious of these was to be a journal dedicated to 'the perplexing problems' facing young composers, the problems of compositional theory. I do not know whether Babbitt or Boretz were consulted about this – Paul Fromm was quite capable of making his own decisions – but if not it must have struck both composers rather in the way that King Ludwig's famous invitation struck Richard Wagner. Boretz had long been trying to start a journal about contemporary music. Babbitt's aims were more comprehensive.

His writing of the 1950s had developed into a strange

amalgam. Conjoined with a fanatical scientism, a search for quasi-logical precision of reference which tortured his syntax into increasingly Jamesian spirals for very un-Jamesian ends, there was an undertone of distress, even rage, erupting into repeated assaults and innuendos directed against various predictable targets. This scarcely contained emotion issued obviously (and openly enough) from the same sense of modernist alienation as was expressed very differently by Schoenberg or, to take an even more extravagant case, Adorno. But while Adorno was telling anyone who would listen at Darmstadt and Donaueschingen that modern music was decisively cut off from decadent bourgeois culture, Babbitt at Princeton was pointing out that avant-garde music could find its niche after all – though only by retreating from one bastion of middle-class culture, the concert hall, to another, the university. Like pure science, he argued, musical composition has a claim on the university as a protector of abstract thought. (The complicity of composition and theory, it will be seen, was crucial to this argument, the complicity of theory and mathematics extremely helpful.) Instead of lamenting the no-doubt irreparable breach between avant-garde music and the public, composers like mathematicians should turn their backs on the public and demand their rightful place in the academy. Otherwise 'music will cease to evolve, and in that important sense, will cease to live'.[29]

As a matter of fact, American composers were already in the academy, well in, but apparently further commitments and perquisites were expected. So Princeton actually set up an academic programme for the PhD degree in musical composition, for which the final exercise consisted of a musical composition plus a theory dissertation or essay. The marriage of theory and composition was legitimitized by graduate councils around the country; the avant garde was house-broken into the academy. And *Perspectives* provided the organ in which the new PhDs might hope to get both their music reviewed (or analysed) and their theory articles published in an unexceptionably imposing format. For a number of years the journal was quite brilliant; but it did not unperplex young composers. Alas, they wrote more and more theory and less and less music. And the theory they wrote, it seemed to many who read it or tried to read it, was calculated to perplex as much as to inform and illuminate.

It is natural to think of *Perspectives* as a sequel to *Die Reihe*, which from 1955 to 1962 had carried the writing of Boulez, Stockhausen, Krenek, Pousseur, Ligeti, and the other postwar avant gardists in Europe. Serialism was the main subject and mathematics the main mode of both journals, and there were ample areas of agreement between the two schools of theory they represented. Yet *Perspectives* was also conceived of as an American answer and corrective to its European counterpart. The first issue of *Perspectives* contained, among other polemical pieces, including one by a pianist attacking musicology, a review of four English-language issues of *Die Reihe* by a professor of physics.[30] He demonstrated that the scientific terminology that is so prominent in all the articles – including those by the editors, Eimert and Stockhausen – was used without the least understanding of its actual scientific meaning. The American demand was for a rigorous (or at least a correct) scientism, then, instead of a fraudulent one. While there was no argument with Eimert and Stockhausen's basic assumption as to the essential complicity of theory and avant-garde music – that was a shared ideal across the Atlantic – the Americans proposed to get it right.

At the risk of seeming to overpolemicize *Perspectives of New Music*, it may be suggested that another impetus for its foundation was to provide an alternative to the *Journal of Music Theory* as a platform from which to disseminate specifically compositional theory. For while numerous contributors to the Yale publication were indeed composers, Allen Forte, who then edited it, and the musicologists who wrote occasional articles on the history of theory for it were not. More overt was the polemic stance against John Cage and the alternative tradition in American music which he symbolizes, what Leonard Meyer calls 'transcendental particularism'. The second issue of *Perspectives* contained a review of Cage's much-discussed first book, *Silence*, by a professor of English.[31] Now Cage is an exasperatingly slippery figure to wrestle with, because if you are profoundly serious about art, as everybody around *Perspectives* certainly was, there are not too many ways of dealing with someone who is profoundly unserious about it. You can try to match him by assuming an attitude of unseriousness which must, however, be taken as seriously ironic; only a poet (which the professor is) could have carried this off, perhaps. Or you can try to ignore him altogether. This was tried subsequently.

Cage made more of a problem for the Princeton School than they ever really wanted to acknowledge, I think. It was not so much that European composer-theorists had taken him up and were incorporating his *I Ching* mushroom dreams into their crypto-mathematical fantasies. It was rather that in *Silence*, and elsewhere, Cage projected thought about music — call it 'theory' or not — effectively, repeatedly, and to a wide audience, and that that thought was reflected only too triumphantly by his music. He offered, in fact, a rather forceful example of the complicity of theory (of a sort) and avant-garde music (of a sort). This was the very complicity that provided *Die Reihe* and *Perspectives* with their mutual *raison d'être*.

By 1972 the editors of *Perspectives on Contemporary Music Theory* (which was little more than a book-length spin-off of *Perspectives of New Music*) were ready to acknowledge a 'spectacular' mode of avant-garde theory — this was apparently a euphemism for irrational — extending in Europe from the Futurists and the Dadaists to the ideologues of total serialism who had bluffed their way through the pages of *Die Reihe*, and in America from Ives to Cage and his followers. They did not actually print any such writing in their book. But all of it, they remarked rather stiffly, is 'defensibly "theoretical" in the sense being employed here, for the reflection of its explicit compositional concerns to correlative characteristics of musical surface and structure is undeniable'.[32]

Exactly: and while naturally one would prefer to have one's mathematics correct rather than incorrect, it does not greatly matter in the long run since almost everyone agrees that compositional theory can only be judged by its reflection in actual music. That is theory's ultimate appeal, its ultimate source of relevance. Ultimately Babbitt's prestige rests on his compositions, not on his theory; nobody would ever have paid him any heed if they had not been impressed by his music. The same is true of Stockhausen. If bad theory can lead to convincing music, the need for good theory is less than overwhelming.

Music 'will cease to evolve' if it is not taken into the academy, wrote Babbitt, 'and in that important sense, will cease to live'. This statement has been often pounced upon. The academy has become a sort of greenhouse; even a writer so contemptuous of the use of metaphorical language in reference to music as Babbitt cannot avoid sometimes succumbing to the organic fallacy. And the distinctive logo chosen for *Perspectives* in 1962, a twelve-pointed line diagram once doodled by Stravinsky, recalled that Stravinsky was now writing serial music, to be sure – but what it recalled more importantly, I think, was that he was still alive and still writing. Stravinsky was understood to be that last Grand Master of music. Music's organic growth extended from Bach to Mozart and Beethoven, from Brahms to Schoenberg, and now – as a result of some hasty rearrangements – to serialism's most distinguished recent convert. By 1971, when Stravinsky died at the age of eighty-nine, it was clear there was no credible successor. Something died at the centre of the ideology of organicism.

So in a deep sense, perhaps, *Perspectives* and all it stood for could not survive much longer. By that time Fromm had withdrawn support from the journal and it was turning into something of an embarrassment at Princeton. Under Boretz's continuing editorship it now became in everything save bulk a typical avant-garde little magazine replete with amateur graphics, wildly fluctuating typefaces, spectacular personal effusions and – a fascinating new feature – poems in *vers libre*, generally printed a dozen lines or so per page, commenting on a few bars of some composition. It was a full swing of the pendulum. Keller's Wordless Functional Analysis and Schenker's near-wordless *Urlinie-Tafeln* had given way to an impressionistic criticism which would have left Kretzschmar and Tovey themselves, with all their purple rhetoric, speechless.

The avant garde has extricated itself from the academy (leaving behind PhD programmes for composers who no longer care for theory or for very much else in the academy). Among young composers in the last dozen years there has been a noticeable disillusion with what they tend to refer to as 'ideology' or 'dogmatism'. The end of modernism has been proclaimed only too eagerly on many occasions – even once in the pages of *Perspectives*, back in 1965[33] – but seldom more vehemently than in the article cited at the beginning of this chapter. The author is one of the most highly regarded of recent Princeton composer-theorists:

> Composers everywhere, and particularly in the United States, are turning away from the much-trumpeted innovations of the last thirty years, from the systems, the technologies, the ideologies, and the strategies for audience manipulation. . . . The music of the post-war avant-garde is not, as commonly supposed, a music in which theory precedes practice; it is the first music in history which is not preceded by an unconscious theory. It is, therefore, the first music which cannot, in principle, be taught or learned, the first music which cannot be improvised, precisely imagined, embellished, simplified, or played with in any creative sense. . . . [I]t is hardly music at all.[34]

Nor is the music of the first phase of modernism – Schoenberg's phase – excluded from this indictment; William Benjamin's vision is of a return to tonality, to 'tradition', to some extended form of Schenker's theory. (The article was written to celebrate the publication of the English version of Schenker's *Der freie Satz*.) The idea seems to be that Schenker makes conscious that 'unconscious theory' on which the true tradition of music rests. Schenker too stoutly prophesied that tonality would return.

'Fluctuating stasis' – this is the much-discussed formula promoted by Leonard Meyer to describe the situation in the arts when he surveyed them in the 1960s. 'Traditionalism', 'transcendental particularism' – the music of Cage and his school –

and 'analytic formalism' – the music of Babbitt and so-called total serialism – were likely to coexist in a steady state for the foreseeable future, he predicted. Now one system, now the other will rise in prestige, influence, and vitality, as opposed to the heretofore accepted expectation by the Western historical consciousness of stylistic growth, development, progress, and teleology. When Meyer wrote, transcendentalism and formalism were major forces. In the 1980s they are in decline; and the traditionalist attitudes articulated by Benjamin, as well as the direction of his work as a theorist, are symptomatic of this new situation. The same would seem to be true, incidentally, of another slightly less young Princeton composer-theorist whom we have mentioned, Fred Lerdahl, who spent the years around 1980 developing *A Generative Theory of Tonal Music*. Older members of his *école*, around 1960 or 1970, would have worked on serialism.

Certainly for someone who has concluded that avant-garde music is 'hardly music at all', avant-garde theory is not worth a moment's further consideration. Benjamin holds back from any direct reference to compositional theory from Schoenberg to Babbitt to Boretz, but there can be no question what he means by systems, technologies, and ideologies. If Meyer is right, however, there will be a time when formalism attracts new interest, and then the serial music of the postwar decades will seem like music again. At such a time, avant-garde theory will be looked at again, if not by composers and theorists, by critics and musicologists (assuming that by then musicologists will have worked their way into the twentieth century, which seems a safe assumption).

Musicologists will read this theory selectively and critically, paying attention not only to the difficult texts themselves but also to the possibly even more difficult subtexts. They will read avant-garde theory for what it reveals about the music itself, even though they know it was generated in order to create music, not to elucidate it. Musicologists, some of them, know how to read for subtexts. They have learned it from long bouts of wrestling with older theory.

11 p.

Meyer is one theorist who has never shared the anguish of alienation expressed in one way by Schoenberg, in another by Babbitt, and in another by William Benjamin. That is because he is the first figure considered in this chapter since Tovey whose stance is, as I shall suggest in a moment, basically populist rather than elite. Adhering to none of the standard orthodoxies, Meyer has always kept his distance from other theorists, and vice versa – Benjamin does not even mention him as a force in modern theory – though as I shall also suggest, he is closer to them than they think, or used to think. The stand-off may be due in part to something as simple as the fact that Meyer shuns the theory journals (or any other music journals, as a rule), preferring to address his work to the lay intellectual community at large. A genuine polymath of music, he has more or less systematically worked his way through the central problems of aesthetics, theory, modernism, criticism, history, and a great many of the attendant peripheral problems, in a series of patiently argued treatises.

Anyone who tries to measure out the universe is bound to reveal the limitations of his mental calipers. Within these limitations, though, Meyer is a tireless, ingenious, good-humoured, and very wide-ranging thinker who really seems more interested in fishing up and facing up to all problems, big and small, than in proving himself right. This was at once clear from his doctoral dissertation, a vintage University of Chicago study published in 1956 as *Emotion and Meaning in Music* and still his most influential book.*

It starts like a formal contribution to aesthetics, as Meyer develops what he calls the 'absolutist' or 'absolute expressionist' view of music's meaning from his own new standpoint. This view – well-nigh universal in the 1950s, as I hardly need to reiterate – holds that meaning must be found in the internal workings of the music itself. But Meyer also appended a chapter on the 'referentialist' position, not in order to counter it, but to elaborate briefly such categories as 'image formation', 'mood', and 'connotation', categories that may suggest how music also communicates meanings referring to the extra-musical world of concepts, actions, emotional states, and character. As for music's autonomous import, Meyer's first root idea about this is that it must be understood in terms of learned responses within some established musical style. His second root idea defines a psychological mechanism for such responses. Within a culturally determined stylistic norm, one musical event implies others, and emotion and meaning result when the listener's learned expectations are satisfied, delayed, or frustrated.

This resolution of the problem of meaning in music has not been embraced, to put it gently, by philosophers (why should expectation be equated with *meaning*?). However, they have been at something of a loss to deal with the rest of the book, for except for the two opening chapters and the final chapter on referentialism, already mentioned, this is given over to a fairly detailed and technical musical analysis of the various categories of expectation that are set up in various kinds of music. Musicians, on their part, though they have often found the analysis partial or even simplistic, have been genuinely impressed by the comprehensive scheme in which that analysis is embedded. For while Meyer's system claims to be as objective as any positivist's —

> once the norms of a style have been ascertained, the study and analysis of the affective content of a particular work in that style can be made without continual and explicit reference to the responses of the listener or critic. That is, subjective content can be discussed objectively (p. 32)

— it takes careful account of whole areas that are almost always passed over. One, of course, is 'referentialism'. Another is communication. Whereas other theorists deal with scores in the abstract, Meyer deals with music as perceived by listeners. His theory is oriented towards the receptor rather than the stimulus, to the listener who experiences 'emotion and meaning' rather than the composer who puts them in.

It may be stretching a term to call him a populist on this account, especially in view of the later direction of his work. But Meyer, more than any other modern theorist, has spoken up from within the profession for those outside it. By starting not with composer strategy but with listener psychology, he abumbrated what it is now fashionable to call a phenomenological theory of musical form. (The only other, more recent, comprehensive theory to give listener perception so central a place – though it is a different place – is that of Lerdahl and Jackendoff, who have read Meyer with care.) A further attraction of Meyer's approach is that it rests on the idea of culturally conditioned styles. This means that his analysis allows for historical discrimination; it should be applicable with due modifications to Gregorian chant, Machaut, Handel, and Debussy. Indeed, for its time *Emotion and Meaning in Music* was remarkable in drawing a good deal of its material about expectation in established styles from non-Western music – and gained some of its warmest responses from ethnomusicologists as a result.

Meyer returned centrally to the themes of *Emotion and Meaning* three books and seventeen years later. *Explaining Music* (1973) represents refinement on one front and regression on others.* Much of what was innovative in the earlier book has fallen away to leave yet another celebration of music belonging to the traditional Western canon, another *explication* of melodies by Bach, Haydn, Schumann, and Dvořák. For Meyer here refines the analysis of the central chapters of *Emotion and Meaning* into an elaborate and implicitly value-laden theory of tonal melody. There is not much talk about emotion or meaning – concepts hardly developed even in the earlier book, which in retrospect can be seen also to have been directed principally towards theory and analysis, rather than aesthetics. Nor is there much talk about referentialism; Meyer repeatedly begs off from addressing what he now calls the 'ethetic' aspects of music. The network of relationships traced in tonal melodies is now seen essentially as an explanation of musical 'logic', of the way tonal melodies 'work'.

Meyer's position has slipped, in his own terms, from absolute expressionism to formalism. His model for music, as compared to Schenker's, is empirical rather than idealist, foreground- rather than background-oriented, populist rather than elite, and mechanistic, perhaps, rather than organic. This thought is inevitably suggested by his recourse to the language of information theory to account for musical communication (redundancy, feedback, noise, and so on). Meyer began with concepts from Gestalt psychology, but his final vision is of an intricate complex of interlinked implications, delays, realizations, and non-realizations all operating on multiple hierarchical levels. It has all the immediacy of a big computer program.

After carrying out his theoretical investigations to the provisional terminus marked by *Explaining Music*, Meyer moved on to other things. It was his student Eugene Narmour who in 1977 published a preliminary essay 'Toward an Implication-Realization Model' and promised a full-scale treatment in a book to come. This preliminary essay, as we have seen, Narmour felt it necessary to frame in a sharply polemical context; *Beyond Schenkerism* predicts, nay demands a radical, paradigmatic shift. But besides polemicizing Meyer's theory, Narmour has already tightened up its psychological and metatheoretical underpinnings. It may indeed attract more interest from systematic theorists in this form than in Meyer's more informal and populist original version.

Music, the Arts, and Ideas,* whose subject is modernism as it looked to Meyer in the mid-1960s, occupies the position of a large parenthesis between the two other studies of his that we have touched upon. It also marked the beginning of a new line of thought which will be picked up again in another typically far-reaching study, now nearing completion, of musical style and history. Its central idea, that of 'fluctuating stasis' in the contemporary arts, has been referred to above. The novelty of this idea does not lie in the notion of different styles of art coexisting, which is self-evident, nor even in Meyer's sweeping classification of the whole range of contemporary art and ideology into his three categories traditionalism, formalism, and transcendentalism. The novelty lies in the hypothesis that this coexistence, far from being a confused or unstable situation that will sooner or later sort itself out into a new synthesis, in fact represents a permanent steady-state. This is not subject to proof, of course – it is in no present danger of falsification, either – but Meyer supports 'The Probability of Stasis' with a massive argument involving citations from authors on an impressive range of subjects and also, it must be said, much repetition. I have written above about musicians' dogmatic faith in the continuing 'organic' evolution of the canon of great music, and about its demise. Meyer in *Music, the Arts, and Ideas* performed its obsequies with more than adequate pomp and circumstance.

Music, the Arts, and Ideas is not music theory, of course, like Meyer's other books and the other material treated in this chapter. It is intellectual history, written on the assumption that music is a mirror of the intellectual life of our time. It is the sort of thing musicologists so very rarely attempt, and should attempt more often. Perhaps the assumption is Quixotic, Pickwickian, Pateresque; the effort – the ambition – was admirable all the same. I wish Meyer had dealt more clearly with an issue that touches closely on the concerns of the present book, and that I think was also important for his: namely the place of criticism (conceived for this purpose in the broadest possible terms, so as to include theory, analysis, and musicology) in his tripartite scheme. Meyer does not speak much about criticism in specific terms – does not, that is, separate criticism off from art and ideology in general. He does not say, for example, whether he considers musicology to be a genre of traditionalist criticism, nor even (in so many words) that analysis is the characteristic genre of formalism. He does not discuss the steady-state in criticism specifically, either. Presumably this will follow directly from the steady-state in art and ideology.

We must also presume, then, that three different categories of response to and appreciation, evaluation, and criticism of art will coexist, as they now coexist, and that individual critics will choose (by what mechanism?) among them. No scruples of ideological purity will prevent them from making mixed choices. Meyer himself expresses much nostalgia for traditionalist ideology and devotes himself to traditional music (his convoluted response to the music of formalism, which we need not take time to analyse here, seems in the end as negative as his attitude towards transcendentalism). But his brand of criticism — which in *Explaining Music* he chooses to call 'critical analysis' — is formalistic. This is consistent with his view of the centrality of formalistic ideology for now and for the future.

And if the three strains of criticism continue to coexist, traditionalist critics will continue to scold formalists (as in this book), formalists snub transcendentalists, transcendentalists taunt traditionalists, etc. —

Tu. Voi. Lor. Tutti e due! No, tutti e tre!

There will also be times when one or the other of them fluctuates to the top of the heap. When Meyer wrote *Music, the Arts, and Ideas*, as we said just a moment ago, formalism and transcendentalism were major forces, in art as in ideology and criticism. Meyer was part of the picture, part of the problem. If the period from the mid-1970s has been marked by an upswing in traditionalist ideology, one would expect to see a parallel tendency in criticism. It is in these terms, I take it, that Meyer would interpret the phenomenon we shall be treating in the next chapter. This is the growth in America of a kind of historically oriented criticism, a kind of criticism oriented towards musicology.

4. Musicology and Criticism

It is an odd fact that almost every new, young literary talent in music now makes a name for himself in some musicological sphere; or, to put it another way, the kind of serious critical talent that one would like to see working in daily criticism is employed, so to speak, in other centuries; the degree of seriousness with which the musicologist approaches his labour is rarely met with in the round of daily criticism. Indeed, the startling ascendancy of musicology in our time, its virtues apart, is very closely related to the decline of significant criticism. It is not a mere coincidence that the prestige, techniques and public recognition of the one have soared, while those of the other have become progressively more and more bankrupt. . . . The public rightly values, if it somewhat over-estimates, the musicologist's concrete and verifiable achievements in the field of textual 'authenticity', 'genuine' historical discoveries, and so forth. My quotation marks are not ironic but merely spotlight musicology's essential *positivity*. . . .[1]

This is how the situation in Britain looked to a young critic in 1955 – a critic who has since made his rather complicated peace with musicology. Donald Mitchell was writing from within what he saw as the solid framework of English music criticism, 'daily criticism' being his omnibus term for journalistic writing on various levels performed daily, weekly, or monthly. On the face of it, the scene he painted seems very different from that on the other side of the Atlantic. Here, as we have seen in the last two chapters, the equally startling ascendancy of both musicology and analysis was taking place within the academy – possibly at the expense of other areas of music study, but hardly at the expense of daily criticism. To speak of 'literary talent in music' being deflected to scholarship seems, to an American observer, an odd way of putting things.

Yet in both countries what was being observed was the ascendancy of positivism.

> When one realizes that the 'authenticity' of musicology functions as a kind of substitute for the value judgments that critics have given up making, it is easy to see why so many talents who might have become critics turn instead to historical, textual or pre-classical studies. Musicology offers, by way of relief, a potential series of positives (accuracy, authenticity, and the like) while at the same time not requiring of the practitioner the exercise of that very discrimination which is, or should be, the critic's *raison d'être*; 'authenticity' (of text or work) replaces evaluation. Small wonder then, that so many minds are attracted to musicology; it is the *vacancy* of present-day criticism which has contributed to its massive *extent* and still extending influence (p. 9).

Mitchell complained, not for the first time, that journalistic critics had begun to shirk evaluation, discrimination, and the making of value judgments. A few years later, I was to enter my own complaint that academic musicologists and analysts had not yet begun to face up to criticism. For all the differences between the situations in the two countries, the sources of our dissatisfaction were not all that different.

While musicology and theory and analysis can be viewed as rival, even contradictory thought-systems in music, both were well calculated to thrive in the intellectual atmosphere of the 1950s, as has already been remarked. The special confluence of the two at Princeton has also been noted. Babbitt was the leading avant-garde theorist and founder of the Princeton School which put its stamp on *Perspectives of New Music*. Mendel, who in the article 'Evidence and Explanation' and other writings assumed the role of spokesman for positivistic musicology, manned with one or two of his students an outpost of the New Bach Edition, the paradigmatic venture of postwar musicology in this tradition. These two foci of work were reflected, if less neatly and powerfully, at other major centres in America. Universities established or re-established music-theory departments to offer advanced work. In musicology, the preparation of editions and studies of a documentary, archival sort still make up the dominant tradition in doctoral dissertations. These dissertations with depressing frequency determine the type of work musicologists engage in for the remainder of their careers.

Yet it is not the only tradition; and the purpose of this chapter is to trace the movement of another current of musicology away from positivism, towards something rather new. Analysis and musicology have the capacity to influence one another for the better – and musicology, at least, has submitted to the influence. I have stressed sufficiently, I expect, the limitations of analysis. While one might wish also to see other influences, this is one that has been readily available to musicologists and that has moved them the farthest.

As a kind of formalistic criticism, analysis does not address all or even many of the problems that must be faced if music is to be studied in its integrity. But it does at least concentrate one's attention on individual works of art rather than on historical generalizations or bibliographical minutiae. Students of musicology enter the field, generally, because of a commitment to music as aesthetic experience, and when tasks of a merely mechanical or detective nature begin to dissatisfy them, it is natural for them to look across the street, as it were, to a discipline which promises closer engagement with the music. In many cases they draw back, dismayed by the analysts' narrow frame of reference. But the best students have always been able to take something from analysis without accepting all of its postulates or submitting to all of its bigotries. And this, I believe, has had a liberating or at least a liberalizing effect on musicology.

2

Before getting to this, we should perhaps say a little more about the musicology that Mitchell was responding to in postwar Britain. This period marked the beginning of a slow change-over – still not fully completed – from musicology as an 'amateur' pursuit or calling to musicology as an academic discipline. The most eminent musicological faculty was assembled at Oxford: Frank Harrison, F. W. Sternfeld, Egon Wellesz, Sir Jack Westrup. Yet the liveliest work issued from Cambridge, where Thurston Dart was lecturer from 1947 to 1962 and professor for what have been officially described as two 'strife-ridden' years thereafter.[2] A leading harpsichordist, Dart was as strong a force for the historical performance of music as he was for musicology. The foci of work at Cambridge were not musicology and theory and analysis, but musicology and historical performance.

In his brief, intensely packed career Dart issued about seventy-five recordings, produced about the same number of editions of old music, as well as putting in an immense amount of work as secretary of *Musica Britannica*, and published about the same number of scholarly articles.[3] He completed one book, a short but influential manual on *The Interpretation of Music* (1954).* What is striking about the articles is how many of them follow the same basic format: the description and analysis of a single source, generally of English music. Whereas previous British scholars had written historical surveys or life-and-works studies – Gerald Abraham's *A Hundred Years of Music*, Harrison's *Music in Medieval Britain*, Westrup's *Purcell* – Dart concentrated on individual manuscripts and prints. The thrust of his work was from the general to the particular.

Not (as Dart showed) that such work must necessarily be dry. Nearly all his articles include some ingenious deduction or, as often as not, speculation about provenance, ownership, scribal identity, relations with other sources, attribution of the anonymous contents, and the like. Audacious speculation became Dart's hallmark, in fact. In the last chapter I mentioned Wallace Berry's admonition about what he called 'harlequinism' in music theory; Dart was a musicological harlequin, and his motley caused much shaking of heads among his colleagues. The most famous of his *lazzi* was to propose that the two leading keyboard composers of the early sixteenth century, Antonio de Cabezón located in Spain and Marco Antonio Cavazzoni in Italy, were on account of the similarity of their names brothers. When this was refuted by archival evidence, Dart issued a not very shame-faced apology, slipping in suggestions that the French musical dynasties the Couperins and the Forquerays might have been related to the English Cowpers and Coopers and the Scottish Farquhars, respectively.[4]

This imaginative, speculative, and sometimes antic soul, firmly wedded to the concert stage and the recording studio, seems at first glance hard to reconcile with the traditional image of the positivistic musicologist. So does the stubborn, autocratic, radical educator who in the 1960s hammered out a curriculum at King's College, London, encompassing not only history and performance but also ethnomusicology and music of the avant garde. Only nineteenth-century music, it seems, was left out. Yet for all his unusual array of interests and activities in music, there were some things that Dart stayed strictly away from. One was history – history as an intellectual construction, as opposed to a loving assembly of past facts and old sources. Another was criticism. 'Look at the music,' he would say dismissively when people questioned his statements and his interpretations. It was the ultimate put-down: look but do not ask me to talk or write. The investigation of sources and performing practice was one area, musical response was another, and they were carefully to be kept apart.

It is a familiar separation. It has been lamented a number of times in this book. The first substantial chapter in Dart's *The Interpretation of Music* addresses, rather surprisingly, 'The Editor's Task'; but in fact this priority followed directly enough from his basic model for musicology. The flow-chart runs from source to edition to performance – with understanding and appreciation, history, and criticism left off to the side. The musicologist studies sources, makes editions from them, and performs the music thus edited. There is something agreeably down-to-earth about all this, no doubt, something we are perhaps too quick to characterize as typically British in its practical orientation. But one also catches a disturbing whiff of anti-intellectualism. In the last analysis Dart was not really serious about music history: that is what the harlequinism was about. As for criticism, he was not even interested in harlequinizing about that.

Musical experience and the historical nexus were areas that were off-limits to Dart's scholarship, which is why I post him ultimately with the positivists, though in some ways he does sit rather strangely among them. Less of a leap is required to place most of his followers in the same camp. After his death in 1971, a memorial volume was planned by his students and associates, with essays solicited in three categories which would presumably have pleased the deceased.[5] Twelve contributions came in under 'The Study of Manuscripts and Printed Sources' and 'The Use of Archives', and but four under 'Interpretation and Performance'. And of these four, Philip Brett's 'English Music for the Scottish Progress of 1617' is the only one that talks about a piece of music – a verse anthem by Orlando Gibbons – as though it were a work of art. The entrenchment of positivistic musicology is a task that British musicologists working with old music seem to have plunged themselves into with special enthusiasm.

At Cambridge itself, a don who is just too young to have studied with Dart (and who in any case studied at Reading and Birmingham), Iain Fenlon, has assumed a position of leadership in this movement. The yearbook *Early Music History*, which he is editing, 'aims to encourage the best British, American and European scholarship, whether in manuscript studies, analytical work, iconography, textual criticism or the relationship between music and society'.[6] Observe that no mention is made of criticism, even though the most glaring lacuna in early-music studies is here, as Brett and others have been saying for some time,[7] not in 'refining and extending traditional techniques . . . and developing new methodological ideas'. An anthology treating *Music in Medieval and Early Modern Europe* (1981) from the standpoint of 'Patronage, Sources and Texts' is another enterprise of Fenlon's. Again early-music studies are being consciously deflected away from a consideration of the music itself.

Fenlon's own intellectual profile is made graphic by one of those coincidences that occasionally enliven the course of learning. In 1980 his study of music in sixteenth-century Mantua* was published simultaneously with another rather similar study, by an American scholar, Anthony Newcomb, on neighbouring Ferrara.* Both Este and Gonzaga courts were centres of cultivation of the late madrigal – Giaches Wert and Claudio Monteverdi were at Mantua, Luzzasco Luzzaschi and (briefly) Carlo Gesualdo da Venosa were at Ferrara. Parallels between the two studies extend to such details as appendices containing eighty-odd archival documents in each case, plus extended inventories of the respective ducal libraries.

The difference is that Newcomb's interest is focused on the music; his climactic chapter is an attempt to trace the historical change in the Ferrarese madrigal by means of fairly close analysis of selected compositions. Fenlon's interest is in patronage, the patronage that also supported Mantuan painting and architecture, in politics, and in 'the relationship of music and society'. He deliberately eschews detailed discussion of any music. (Both studies are parallel, too, in providing a second volume devoted to music examples – though there was an amusingly symbolic time-lag between the publication of Fenlon's second volume and his first.) By Fenlon's standards, Newcomb deals with music in too purely 'internalist' a fashion, paying insufficient attention to the socio-political conditions that produced it. By Newcomb's standards, such 'relationships between music and society' as Fenlon is able to address without getting into the music itself must necessarily be superficial.[8]

In Britain, it seems, the reaction against criticism that worried

Donald Mitchell in 1955 has in thirty years simply deepened. In addition to patronage and social history, all branches of the higher bibliography – filiation, codicology, paper studies – are eagerly pursued. In a characteristic study for the Dart memorial volume, for example, editions by music's first printer, Ottaviano dei Petrucci of Fossombrone, are dated by minute analysis of the way his woodblock initial capital letters deteriorated from one exemplar to another.[9] Few (perhaps none) of these 'new methodological ideas' are new to humanistic scholarship at large, though some have not been applied consistently to musicology before, and are undergoing specialized refinement in the process. Certainly they are breaking no fresh ground. The ground was cultivated by Dart with his programme of sustained scrutiny of individual sources, a programme which has in any case a long history in German and American scholarship. They are, however, giving positivistic musicology a new lease on life.

In the United States, as I have already suggested, the coexistence of musicology and analysis and indeed the very tension between them has had the effect of deepening some musicologists' commitment to actual music. Analysis has also refined their techniques of dealing with music. One can of course also point to much recent American work that is just as resolutely positivistic as that of the new British school – so much, that those of Dart's students who have come to this country must certainly feel right at home. (In 1984 Margaret Bent, unsurpassed as an editor and sleuth of fifteenth-century music, was elected president of the American Musicological Society.) Fenlon's collections contain more American and Anglo-American than British contributions. But the most interesting work now being done in America is that which combines traditional musicological techniques with something approaching criticism, even if it is criticism of a formalistic kind still not far removed from analysis. The most interesting work, in fact, is generally not in Renaissance music. It is indicative that a scholar with Newcomb's inclinations should have turned his main energies, in recent years, to music of the nineteenth century.[10]

3

The two most explicit attacks on positivistic musicology were made in the mid-1960s by myself and Leo Treitler. The fact that our positions seem now to have converged is interesting, because in ideology, style, and logistics, the two attacks were at the outset so different.

The impetus for my short article of 1965, 'A Profile for American Musicology',* was dissatisfaction with the Palisca *et al.* report in the 'Humanistic Scholarship in America' series, which has been discussed at some length in Chapter 2. The article originated in a public address, and its starting point – as by now the reader will be not at all surprised to hear – was criticism. I did not follow up the polemic explicitly, though it had been adumbrated in an earlier piece and would rumble on dimly in some later ones. At the time, issuing examples of the kind of work I favoured seemed to me better for all concerned than talking about possibilities in the abstract. No doubt it was a double-edged tactic.

Treitler's impetus, or at least a part of his impetus, was dissatisfaction with Mendel's disquisition on 'Evidence and Explanation', which has also been discussed above. Treitler's polemic has proceeded as a leisurely series of essays from 1966 to 1984 which constitute a comprehensive ongoing critique of musicology and indeed of other strands of thought about music. His starting point was and still is the philosophy of history. Although Treitler has written impressive essays on a number of quite different musical topics, in addition to his main work on plainchant, he has not yet shown in a full-length study what kind of musicology it is that he really wants.

'A Profile for American Musicology' was written against the background of academic work in other humanistic fields – classics, the history of art, and especially literary studies. If *Opera as Drama*, which I had published in 1956, still seems like a rather unusual book, that is mainly because it combined two modes usually kept separate; each was handled in a conventional enough manner. The book's underlying premise was derived from dramatic criticism – from that of T. S. Eliot, Una Ellis-Fermor, and Francis Fergusson – and its subject matter was drawn from the received account of operatic history, for the most part. I was read by literary people, as well as by musicians, and I myself read literary criticism (as well as music). In American academic literary studies, of course, criticism occupied a major place, and had done so for some time. By 1965 the field was engaged in the long process of disengagement from the New Criticism and was wrestling enthusiastically with the work of Northrop Frye. Why was there no analogous recognition of criticism in music-academic circles?

Art history was not so clear a case, perhaps. Nonetheless the volume on *Art and Archeology* in the 'Humanistic Scholarship in America' series – the companion volume to *Musicology* – started out flatly with the assertion that 'the art historian must be a critic as well'. The author, James S. Ackerman, went on to explain:

> As long as the work of art is studied as a historical document it differs from the archival document only in form, not in kind. The art historian should be interested in the difference in kind, which is immanent in the capacity of art to awaken in us complex responses that are at once intellectual, emotional, and physical, so that he needs, in addition to the tools of other historians, principles and methods specifically designed to deal with this unique mode of experience. . . . I look on criticism not as an additional technique to be adopted by historians but as a challenge that forces us to re-examine the fundamental philosophical principles by which we operate.[11]

Now my article scarcely delved to the level of philosophical principles. It left unexamined and tacitly accepted the methodology of music history that was then current. All it did was propose that music history, conceived as ecumenically as might be wished so as to include the 'diachronic' history of musical events as well as the social history of music, should be valued not as an end but as a means. Likewise the detailed analysis of particular musical styles, a 'synchronic' historical activity which at that time was often given the place of honour in discussions of musicology, should be pursued not for normative evidence about an era, but for contextual evidence about the artistic character and individuality of particular pieces of music. When musicology is oriented towards criticism,

> Each of the things we [musicologists] do – paleography, transcription, repertory studies, archival work, biography, bibliography, sociology, *Aufführungspraxis*, schools and influences, theory, style analysis, individual analysis – each of these things, which some scholar somewhere treats as an end in itself, is treated as a step on a ladder. Hopefully the top step provides a platform of insight into individual works of art – into Josquin's 'Pange lingua' Mass, Marenzio's 'Liquide perle', Beethoven's opus 95, the *Oedipus rex*. These works cannot be understood in isolation, only in a context. The infinitely laborious and infinitely diverting ascent of the musicologist should provide this context.[12]

There was an extended riposte to the paper by Edward E. Lowinsky, one of the most sophisticated and wide-ranging of the older émigré scholars.[13] Having himself written that 'The beginning and end of musicological studies lies in the sympathetic and critical examination and evaluation of the individual work of art', Lowinsky was not one to question the importance I attached to a critical orientation for musicology, angered though he was by much of what I had to say besides that. He objected *inter alia* to the hierarchy that was set up among the various subdisciplines of musicology in the paragraph cited above, and he was impatient with my informal definition of criticism:

> the way of looking at art that tries to take into account the meaning it conveys, the pleasure it initiates, and the value it assumes, for us today. Criticism deals with pieces of music and men listening, with fact and feeling, with the life of the past in the present, with the composer's private image in the public

mirror of an audience. At worst criticism is one man's impressionism – like bad art – and at best it is an uneasy dialectic. Allen Tate says that criticism is a perpetual impossibility and a perpetual necessity; and he adds stonily that in this it resembles all our other ultimate pursuits (p. 63).

It is, no question, an uneasy definition. Today the ladder analogy also makes me uneasy, not because it misrepresents what still seem to me clear priorities, but because it implies that the steps are all entirely independent of one another. Both the nature of criticism, and also the delicate relation that one envisages between it and ancillary disciplines, are things that seem to me all but impossible to define in abstract terms. But they can be exemplified, and I had tried to do just that in a series of four articles on the Latin sacred music of William Byrd.* They formed the basis of a full-length study that was completed some time later.

One article reported findings on the authentic canon and chronology of the motets, based on a fresh survey of all the manuscripts and printed editions. Another analysed the way Byrd and his English predecessors handled a central technique of Renaissance composition, contrapuntal imitation. Another examined the verbal texts of Byrd's motets for evidence of their ideological context, which was that of the Elizabethan Catholic community at various stages of its turbulent history. Taken together, this amounted to at least a sketch of a comprehensive source study, a mini-study in historical style analysis, and a cautiously speculative essay – in Lowinsky's manner, as a matter of fact – on the 'relationship between music and society'.

And all this, I believe, is ground that any competent musicologist of the time would have covered if he or she had become interested in the 'problem' presented by this body of music. My other essay was a detailed study of a single short composition, the motet *Emendemus in melius* which Byrd put first in the book of motets he issued jointly with his teacher Thomas Tallis (the *Cantiones, quae ab argumento sacrae vocuntur* of 1575; it was their first publication). Here the effort was to draw on the results of all or as many as possible of the 'musicological' disciplines in order to clarify, or indeed discover, the aesthetic quality of the music itself. For this the model was, initially, the sort of 'close reading' developed by the New Critics.

Ends and means. The essay started out with musical analysis, line by line and sometimes note by note, in terms of texture, melody, harmony, dissonance treatment, and musical rhetoric aligned with the highly affective penitential text. (It was a loose and, to the minds of some, anachronistic sort of analysis in which certain standard concepts of tonal theory were modified for application to pre-tonal music.) *Emendemus in melius*, it turns out, is modelled very closely on an earlier composition by one Alfonso Ferrabosco. The musicologist's search for 'influences', often derided as reductionist or as determinist, need not be either; matched against Alfonso's routine work, the intensity and originality of Byrd's conception, his superb sense of shape, and his commitment to the sacred text stand out with especial clarity. The article also tried to show that in the historical context, which had to be reconstructed by a whole array of musicological techniques, *Emendemus in melius* could only be seen as a great novelty and a portent, a young composer's manifesto. And as is always true of such pieces, some of the excitement it must have caused in its own time can be recaptured by the imaginative exercise of historical criticism. For the historian of the arts, this is the analogue to the 're-enactment' of past events which Collingwood upheld as a prerequisite for historical understanding.

A moment ago, speaking of Iain Fenlon's projects, I fixed on criticism as the most glaring lacuna in Renaissance studies. A critical orientation for musicology is more, not less, important for music of the Renaissance than for the music of Romanticism. Conversely, the criticism of Renaissance music needs musicology more than does the criticism of later music. The *Emendemus* article ended on this very note:

With more modern music, we have stored up from childhood an unconscious fund of comparative material, which has coalesced for us into a working norm for criticism and comparative analysis. We have a sense of style. With Lassus or Byrd, we lack this. It has to be painfully recovered, piece by piece, detail by detail, influence by influence, till hopefully we attain some modest plateau of understanding. And if this is the goal, I do not see that we are in a position to refuse any proffered tools: whether analogical, theoretical, musicological, phenomenological, imaginative, speculative, historical, anachronistic, liturgical, statistical (p. 449).

In the model for musicology that I was advocating and still advocate, the movement is from the various branches and methodologies of music history towards actual music.

The most distinctive and, I believe, the most impressive of Lowinsky's own work as a musicologist has moved in just the opposite direction – from music to history. He has repeatedly drawn on music to enrich such broad categories as Renaissance humanism and mannerism, and less broadly to shed light on the particular cultural and intellectual scene in such localities as republican Florence and post-Reformation Antwerp.* More is at work here than the many-layered interpretation of texts set to music, or the tracing of associations between musicians, patrons, and intellectuals; Lowinsky – unlike Fenlon, for example – gets into the music itself and traces elaborate analogies between musical structures, both general and specific, and other forms of thought or culture. Heir to a tradition of *Geistesgeschichte* that went out of fashion in postwar Europe as well as America – another victim of neopositivism – Lowinsky is perhaps the most learned, tenacious, and brilliant exponent it has ever found from among the ranks of musicians.

He is also, unfortunately, a veritable magnet for controversies both fruitful and unfruitful, and a notorious controversialist. But that is another story. Lowinsky could have rightly complained that 'A Profile for American Musicology', drawn rigidly to the template of criticism, left no room for sweeping studies of music in its cultural context of the kind he has always championed. On the issue of criticism itself, he had less to complain of; in fact, the question for him seemed to be not so much whether criticism should be integrated with musicology as when. In many areas, he claimed, musicologists could not engage responsibly in critical interpretation because not enough facts had yet been gathered in. Unlike art and literary historians, musical ones were still pioneering in 'virgin territory', still tacking together the patchwork quilt.

This argument had been around for a long while. Curt Sachs, the doyen of the émigré scholars, had countered it with considerable gusto in 1949:

> Do not say: 'Wait! We are not yet ready; we have not yet dug up sufficient details to venture on such a daring generality.' There you are wrong. This argument is already worn out, although it will none the less be heard a hundred years from now, at a time when specialized research has filled and over-flooded our libraries so completely that the librarians will have to stack the books and journals on the sidewalks outside the buildings. Do not say: 'Wait!' The nothing-but-specialist now does not, and never will, deem the time ripe for the interpretation of his facts. For the refusal of cultural interpretation is a case of attitude, not of insight or maturity. The refusal is conditioned by the temperaments of individual men, not by the plentifulness or scarcity of materials.[14]

But there is another counterargument, philosophical rather than psychological in nature, which is more telling than this. The distinction between 'objective' fact-digging and 'subjective' interpretation cannot in fact be sharply maintained. This will come as no surprise to those who have done some reading in the philosophy of history, but it was not a point brought out in the various essays on the theory of musicology that were penned in those days. It was one of several important points urged on musicologists in the sustained critique of the discipline by Leo Treitler.

4

Treitler was a student of Strunk and Mendel at Princeton, where for a time Mendel's 'Evidence and Explanation' seems to have assumed almost scriptural status. No stranger to the rigours of 'low-level' explanation, Treitler started out his scholarly career with a critical edition of a Bach cantata for the New Bach Edition – the St John Passion problem in miniature. His main work is on plainchant, however, and like all medievalists he has a chip on his shoulder. For like all other aspects of medieval life, medieval music has had to wage an uphill battle for its understanding and appreciation. It has been systematically misconstrued by sweeping generalizations stemming from an evolutionary, deterministic ideology which was already well formed in the Renaissance. No doubt Treitler's pitiless analysis of the errors of evolutionary historiography owes much to Mendel's sharp analysis of the 'fictiveness' of 'high-level' explanation of this shifty sort. But neither in theory nor in practice has Treitler followed Mendel's lead, which was to back away from high-level explanation of *any* kind. Instead he has reformulated the problem of explanation according to a more modern, more flexible, and more comprehensive theory of music history.

Since deterministic historiography is the most immediate target of Treitler's polemic, he naturally parts company from Mendel on the issue of the methodological continuum, as I have called it: the assumption that causal explanation can and must be extended from low- to high-level phenomena. In one and only one of Haydn's hundred-odd symphonies, material from the slow introduction quite unexpectedly recurs at the end of the first allegro movement. What possible 'covering law' could explain this feature of the 'Drum-Roll' Symphony? Positivistic musicology cannot even begin to deal with questions on this level – the level that counts, if we care about the symphony as a unique event in history. The most valuable historical explanations, for Treitler, are not about the causes of events but about their quality:

... the explanations that satisfy historians are indeed explications, detailed unfoldings of the case under consideration, in the context of all that can be discovered about the attendant circumstances. These may be related through an interpretative transformation of facts, so that they manifest a recognizable pattern or theme. In this view explaining is a kind of ordering process, like explaining the functioning of a sentence. . . . [The historian] is credited, not with discovering that a particular phenomenon falls under a general law, but for finding that a number of elements may be brought together in such a way as to be made intelligible in terms of one another.[15]

This is a fair paraphrase of Isaiah Berlin's idea of 'thick' historical explanation, which Mendel had tried to deal with in his paper. And Treitler's use of the word 'explication' shows up the question-begging nature of Mendel's title 'Evidence and Explanation'. As J. H. Hexter observed around the same time, in an analogous critique of scientific methods proposed for history proper,

the questions historians are often most heavily engaged in answering are not why-questions at all but what-questions . . . a great deal of the activity of historians can be construed as having explanation as its aim only by so far extending the meanings of explanation current in analytical philosophy as to destroy even the appearance of synonymy and to impose well-nigh unbearable strains even on analogy.[16]

In his demand that musicologists turn their attention from why-questions to what-questions Treitler was reflecting the anti-positivist movement in the theory of history in the 1960s, a movement of which Hexter's *Doing History* was merely the tip of a single iceberg.

Treitler's attack on the deterministic presuppositions of so much music-historical writing also had its obvious parallels in thought about history in general. The attack had in fact been articulated for music in a rather remarkable book published in

1939, Warren Dwight Allen's *Philosophies of Music History*. By means of a dizzying survey of over three hundred music-historical writings from 1600 to 1937, Allen – who was not a musicologist but a historian who wrote this book and only one other – stressed the evolutionary current running through all important strains of them. Some idea of progress, it seems, was fixed immovably in the ideology of musicology, and this was true whether musicologists dealt on the broadest scale with the music of widely separated cultures or on a narrow scale with musical events of a single culture in close chronological proximity. At every level music was treated in terms of its antecedents and consequents, not as a thing in itself. Music passed through elementary stages to more advanced ones. What was more advanced was almost always seen as better.

Musicologists did not want to listen to Allen, who in any case took no part in musicology when it began to be widely practised in America, which was not until some time after his book was published. Treitler in the 1960s was able to extend Allen's analysis to representative current studies of all kinds. The targets of his polemic extended from textbooks and encyclopedia articles to monographs and broad semi-philosophical surveys of music history, which were still sometimes to be met with at that time. He also pointed out that in spite of their seemingly diverse ideological origins, there is an alliance between quasi-scientific musicological methodology, with its fetish of causal explanation, and deterministic history, with its fetish of 'inevitable' development. Underlying such history is the idea that categories as diverse as the symphony, sonata form, and 'the Baroque' are absolutes, absolutes whose evolution is in effect pre-ordained and can be traced through successive embodiments. Too often, Treitler charged, those embodiments are studied not in themselves – as works of art, historical phenomena, or formal principles – but as 'networks' of evidence for the presumed process to which they are subject.[17]

Thus the critique of musicology issuing from the theory of history, like that issuing from criticism, provides a discreet intramural echo of those familiar extramural complaints about musicology being 'unmusical'. Musicologists did not want to listen to Treitler any more than they had wanted to listen to Allen – even though his strictures were presented more pointedly, in a contemporary context, and very much from within the discipline. He probably received a more appeciative hearing from the readers of *Perspectives of New Music*, to whom he addressed a second attack on evolutionary history.* In this one, by analysing several musicologists' accounts of twentieth-century music, Treitler was able to provide a massive demonstration of the inadequacy and ineptitude of evolutionary history in dealing with the present or the recent past.

And for Treitler this is a very serious, indeed a fundamental failure. For what distinguishes the historian is not his subject matter – events of the past – but his method of dealing with any subject matter: by the treatment of it in its total context. Treitler did not spare the readers of *Perspectives* a lecture on their own ideological determinism, a determinism expressed in one way by Cage and in another by Babbitt. But his main concern, as always, was with the ideology of music history; and the breakdown of the evolutionary model for the treatment of twentieth-century music makes clear its poverty as a means of explanation for earlier centuries. What it makes only too clear is that in those earlier centuries, when the evidence is so much more 'thin', it can be distorted so much more easily to fit preconceived ideological patterns. Some years later, as the evidence rolls in on music of the 1960s and 1970s, the evolutionary approach to twentieth-century music seems even more hopeless than it did to Treitler in 1967.

The author whom Treitler deals with most extensively in 'The Present as History', incidentally, is Leonard Meyer, whose *Music, the Arts, and Ideas* 'is certainly not history in any ordinary sense' – as we have already seen – but whose 'main business is nevertheless the comparison between a present and a past'.[18] It is the old story of a quarrel growing sharper and sharper the closer the principals actually come to each other's position. For Meyer, too, trenchantly criticizes evolutionary history, and Treitler acknowledges the force of Meyer's analysis of the aesthetics of antiteleological music of the 1960s (an example of 'thick' history?). What he cannot condone is Meyer's continued reliance on ideas of evolution and teleology in his account of traditional music and modern traditionalism, and then his abandonment of these ideas in his account of today's 'fluctuating stasis'. This neatly divided picture of a then and a now could, if accepted, undermine Treitler's contention that the past, too, must be approached without deterministic presuppositions. It could indeed undermine the whole attempt of his long essay, which is to argue from the present about the right model for understanding the past.

What then is the appropriate model for the music historian? Treitler turns, as Mendel had, to Collingwood, Croce, and even earlier German philosophers of history such as Droysen and Dilthey who had insisted on the historian's empathy with his historical materials. If in 1961 Mendel had formally introduced musicologists to the neopositivistic ideal of history, in 1980 Treitler drew their attention to the notion of 'synchronic' as against 'diachronic' history, which had come to the fore in the 1960s and 1970s. Synchronic history, is 'thick' history which asks what, not why, and eschews chronological narrative with its seemingly inevitable presuppositions of causality and development. Phenomenological rather than evolutionary, it seeks to catch the individuality of its material and to stress its 'preventness'. History of music in these terms is, simply, criticism. And whereas (as we may remember) the context for Mendel's disquisition on music historiography was the whereabouts of a musical source document, the autograph manuscript of Bach's Brandenburg Concertos, the context for Treitler's was a short critical study of an actual piece of music, Beethoven's Ninth Symphony.*

By criticism Treitler seems to mean a comprehensive interpretation of what a work of art means in all its contexts — a process that is increasingly coming to be known, since Gadamer, even by musicians, as hermeneutics. Treitler says little about evaluation, a traditional aspect of criticism which remains distinctly under a cloud, and refuses to be drawn into the equally traditional argument about 'objective' versus 'subjective' judgments. But evaluation is obviously implicit in his choice of the Ninth Symphony as his example, and no terror of the subjective holds him back from placing high value on the historian's empathy with his material (which for Mendel constituted 'no evidence'). Treitler's rejection of the objective/subjective dichotomy is already implicit in his first theoretical essay, 'Music Analysis in a Historical Context' of 1966.* This hammers away at the theme of the complicity between observation and interpretation. Analysis depends on the selection of certain elements from among the many true elements existing in a work of art; it is not the correctness of the analysis that matters, but the grounds on which one set of facts rather than another has been chosen for emphasis. The argument in this early essay is somewhat inconclusive, the term 'analysis' being used so broadly that its reference becomes diffuse. What is clear, however, is Treitler's refusal to separate the observation of facts (which others might call the 'objective' side of musicology) from the uses to which those facts will be put for purposes of interpretation (the 'subjective' side).

(It follows, among other things, that the 'virgin territory' argument, which claims that musicology must first collect the many facts that are still out there waiting to be collected before attempting their interpretation, is based on a faulty premise. One can see this with particular clarity in Treitler's own field of speciality. If one conceives that the first, 'factual' stage of research into early plainchant consists of establishing the text of the oldest repertory in a critical edition, one is already operating under an interpretative assumption. Indeed, the hypothesis for which Treitler is best known states that in the early history of chant there never *was* a fixed repertory susceptible of having its text established in this fashion. Chant existed in an oral tradition like that described by Parry and Lord for the recitation of epic poetry. [The first of several important articles in which this hypothesis is developed and refined is called 'Homer and Gregory' – St Gregory of the so-called Gregorian chant.*] What happened to get written down, when music writing was reinvented in or before the ninth century, was merely one singer's improvisation or realization of shared, memorized rules for producing melodies in such a tradition. Therefore the collection of such written records or 'facts', with the idea of subjecting them to the scholarly process of textual criticism, would be thoroughly wrong-headed. This seemingly objective task would itself be tacitly influenced by prior interpretation.)

It remains to be seen how Treitler's kind of history will look at his first book-length study, now in progress, on music in the early Middle Ages. I have outlined his views at some length partly because he has come out to a position close to mine, partly because he has carried the critique of traditional musicology to a more radical extreme than any other writer in English. Much of what he says is hardly new, of course; Dilthey's theory of history was eagerly discussed in German musicological circles seventy-five years ago. Carl Dahlhaus (of whom more later) probed the whole nexus of music history and aesthetics in his *Grundlagen der Musikgeschichte* – which came out in an English translation in 1983 – and probed it very searchingly.[19] But it always seems necessary to repeat arguments in a new age, under new conditions, and in a new language.

How much influence either Treitler's arguments or my own have had on the changing course of musicology in the last twenty years is hard to say. Both are certainly best viewed as symptoms rather than as causes – Treitler would not like that – or even than as goads. However this may be, more has been happening than the increasing sophistication of positivistic methodologies at the hands of some of Dart's students in Britain and some of Mendel's in the United States. We have looked briefly at Bach research of the 1950s as a prime example of the older musicology. At the risk of seeming too symmetrical, and at the perhaps greater risk of seeming too worshipful, we can choose Beethoven research of the late 1960s and 1970s as an introduction to new trends in musicology today. This field, we shall see, has never lacked for philological rigour. Yet a critical orientation is built into its very source materials: an orientation towards a new musicology.

The new Beethoven research takes its point of departure from the documents, once again, from a new hard look at the original sources of Beethoven's compositions.[20] In this respect it is no different – no less traditional – than the work of Dart and his school on the one hand, or that of Dadelsen and Dürr at the Bach Institutes on the other. Where the great difference comes is in the nature of those sources. Two further differences stem from this: in the sort of questions the documents may be expected to answer, and in the sort of person who is likely to do the asking.

The documents that Spitta had studied in the nineteenth century, and that the new Bach scholars now restudied, were principally performance parts and scores – some of them in the composer's hand – of the Bach cantatas. This was music composed in haste, never intended for publication, and preserved for the most part in the practical form that had allowed for its original performances in the churches of Leipzig. Many of Beethoven's works, too, survive in autograph manuscripts. Initially these did not receive as much attention as Bach's autographs, since most of these works were published anyway, in editions we know Beethoven himself had supervised or at least tried to supervise. Not too surprisingly, he seems to have lost interest in (and lost track of) his autographs once the music was out in print.

He did not, however, lose track of another sort of document: his musical sketches. Beethoven's music, so far from being composed in haste, was sketched out ahead of time in truly amazing detail. What is also rather amazing is that he kept thousands of sheets of these sketches until his death, including some going back forty years to his youth in Bonn, before his real career had begun in Vienna.

The Spitta-figure in Beethoven research was Gustav Nottebohm, an eccentric Viennese pedagogue who was a student of Mendelssohn and Schumann and a good friend of Brahms. Nottebohm's comprehensive survey of Beethoven's sketches was hardly questioned or improved upon for the better part of a century, like Spitta's work on Bach. And like Spitta, Nottebohm came to these documents with a positivistic aim characteristic of the later nineteenth century. He was preparing a detailed chronological catalogue of all Beethoven's music, an analogue to the Köchel Catalogue for Mozart and many others that have since proliferated for other composers. Sketches for most of the individual compositions provided Nottebohm with information about their dating that he would never have been able to have obtained otherwise.

That over and above this the sketches also provide a fascinating record of the growth of Beethoven's compositions, from the earliest inchoate ideas to the final score, and even insight into the creative process itself, at least potentially – all this certainly did not escape Nottebohm's (and Brahms's) notice. Nottebohm was fascinated; and if ultimately he rejected this as a feasible area for research, it was not before publishing his famous monograph on a sketchbook of 1803 containing copious sketches and drafts for the 'Eroica' Symphony and other works.[21] Few products of musicology have attracted as much interest among musicians at large as this study of Nottebohm's. Among the most interested were Schenker and his influential disciple Oswald Jonas, both of whom wrote about Beethoven's sketches. The theorist Allen Forte, it will be recalled, included 'gaining information about compositional technique' as one of five points in his programme for post-Schenkerian study. In 1960 Forte published a whole book on the sketches for the Piano Sonata in E, opus 109, under the evocative title *The Compositional Matrix*.*

This interest in the sketches on the part of theorists is symptomatic; but there were a number of problems with *The Compositional Matrix*. One was that Forte came to the sketches with a firm *a priori* commitment to Schenker's system. Knowing what he wanted to find in the sketches, he tugged and hauled at them until he found it. Another problem was that he exhibited no 'control' over his documentary materials. He did not explain how he had transcribed the sketches (which is no job for an amateur: they are notoriously hard to decipher), how he knew which came first, how many others exist which he had not transcribed, and other such important matters.

For this Forte was not exactly to blame, since in 1960 there was no edition of the sketches for opus 109 (there still isn't) nor even a simple inventory that could have led him to all the various sketchbooks and sketchleaves held by various libraries. Musicologists were spending endless hours on the life and works of obscure composers, he might well have complained, while dragging their feet in making available material of prime interest pertaining to one of the greatest. (If Forte was disinclined to enter this complaint, I entered it for him in 'A Profile for American Musicology'.) A rough-and-ready checklist of the Beethoven sketches was issued only in 1969, a satisfactory guide to them only in 1985. This takes the form of a meticulous chronological description and analysis of all Beethoven's fifty-odd sketchbooks, complete and incomplete, the ink-written desk ones and the pencil-scrawled pocket ones, by an Anglo-American team of musicologists, Douglas Johnson, Alan Tyson (the senior British member), and Robert Winter.* This *catalogue bien raisonné* is complemented for the period before Beethoven began using actual sketchbooks – before 1798, before the first string quartets and the First Symphony – by Johnson's even more detailed study of his sparser sketches made on a be-wildering multitude of loose papers.*

The point about 'completeness' is that most of the sketchbooks were mutilated. Some were completely dismembered into separate pages to be given away as souvenirs. It is only by the application of much paleographical and musicological expertise that they can be reconstructed, as it were, in concept. Thus, for example, loose sketchleaves in libraries at Berkeley, Bonn, Leningrad, and New York are shown to belong with a mutilated sketchbook at Berlin – and it is shown just where they belong, between which pages. At last musicians interested in any particular work or period can know where all the sketches are, which have probably been lost, and in what order the survivors were originally bound in books (often – not always – the same as the order in which they were written).

Tyson's use of paper studies for this reconstruction process was even more sophisticated than that of the Bach scholars some years earlier. To repeat a point made in the first part of this chapter, in connection with Renaissance studies: it is not that Tyson's techniques were new in themselves, but that what is known in other areas of humanistic scholarship is not always known or applied to musicology. (One sometimes wonders if anything is discussed in faculty clubs and senior common rooms besides political and meteorological trivia.) In any case, the job was done. This rationalization of the inchoate mass of sketch materials by the new Beethoven scholars counts as the major achievement since Nottebohm, comparable to the famous revision of Spitta's cantata chronology by the new Bach scholars.

But there is a great difference between the two groups of musicologists — a difference stemming initially, as I have said, though only initially, from the nature of the documents they study. The Beethoven scholars are much less likely to rest on these essentially positivistic laurels. (English and American scholars; I need not tell the story here of the almost comical positivistic impasse in German Beethoven studies of the 1950s, centred at the Bonn Beethovenhaus and Beethoven-Archiv.[22]) Indeed, although the lesson of *The Compositional Matrix* has not been lost on later Beethovenians, they have not waited for airtight bibliographical control before plunging in and interpreting the sketches. The material is certainly difficult; but as has already been said, the sketchbooks can provide incontrovertible evidence about the *Entstehungsgeschichte* of Beethoven compositions — their various stages of evolution from simple to complex (or occasionally from complex to simple), complete with false detours, sudden inspirations, laborious spells of work on details, backing and filling, and all the rest. To give one or two examples: for the 'Pastoral' Symphony, eight very different-sounding one-line drafts can be found for the development section (which is thirty-seven bars long) of the Andante, the 'Scene by the Brook'.[23] And for the Quartet in C-sharp minor, opus 131, Robert Winter identified five fascinating shorthand 'overviews' showing, in schematic form, how the highly problematic sequence and balance of the various movements was originally posited, modified, and finally resolved.*

This evidence can be turned in two directions – each of them less incontrovertible. It can be turned towards an understanding of Beethoven's creative process in general, or it can be turned towards an understanding of the particular work in question, in its final form. It is this second direction that has proved to be the most attractive. The kind of musicologist who has been attracted to this kind of work is one who is also interested in criticism and analysis. (And more analysts would be attracted to it, too, if there were as many analysts interested in musicology as there are musicologists interested in analysis.)

It is a matter of taste and tact, perhaps, how deeply one wishes or feels able to plunge into 'the compositional matrix'. To some it may seem like a compositional vortex. Tyson himself began as a textual critic and a bibliographer – he prepared the first trustworthy edition of Beethoven's Violin Concerto, and issued a 'Köchel' for Beethoven's older contemporary, Muzio Clementi – and he does not involve himself with analytical minutiae, though even his most technical articles seldom fail to include shrewd and sensitive remarks on the music itself. The field may be said to be spread out between Tyson on the right wing and Forte on the left. Still a relatively new field, and save for the Johnson-Tyson-Winter *The Beethoven Sketchbooks* still lacking in major monuments, something of its potential may be suggested by two articles by quite young scholars, dealing in each case with Beethoven's piano variations. In each case analytical techniques are used along with conventional musicological ones.

Christopher Reynolds's study of sketches for the so-called 'Eroica' Variations, opus 35 (the model for the 'Eroica' Symphony finale) originated in a complex case-history of the composer's movements back and forth between two different sketchbooks.* Determining the correct order of sketches is a highly sensitive task over which researchers lose much sleep. But Reynolds also shows, among other things, how Beethoven would make subtle changes to the beginnings and ends of variations when he changed their order during the sketching process, so as to smooth over the newly formed continuity. Such a discovery sensitizes the critic to factors of continuity between the seemingly discrete members of the work in its final, definitive version.

More comprehensive yet are the findings of William Kinderman concerning the Thirty-Three Variations on a Waltz by Diabelli, opus 120.* This great work was nearly finished in 1819 – how nearly, we now see more clearly as a result of source studies by Winter and Kinderman – when the composer dropped it for a surprisingly long period. Then in 1821 he intercalated several new variations within the basic sequence that was already established, as well as expanding the conclusion. Kinderman analyses the special characteristics of the added variations, and on the hypothesis that they were added in order to clarify the structure of the work as a whole, arrives at the most persuasive account of that structure that has yet been offered. Transcending the sketches, as I would say, and indeed also transcending the conventional bounds of analysis, Kinderman then goes on to develop a concept of parody in certain of the variations which significantly enriches the critical texture of his discussion.

Beethoven's autographs – his original copies of completed compositions – have also yielded up information of great interest to criticism. Such documents are the stock in trade of the editors of critical editions, of course. But when (as in Beethoven's case) the autographs are not fair copies but include second thoughts and corrections, they can be looked at in another way: not for direct evidence as to the work's correct text, but for a gloss upon that text – a gloss of the same kind, basically, as that provided by sketches. Nearly all the surviving Beethoven autographs are, in fact, so profusely corrected and overwritten that it seems almost unbelievable that the copyists were able to thread their way through them in order to prepare printers' copy. A generous amount of composition took place while Beethoven was writing the autographs themselves. In short, these 'working autographs' must be seen as records of the last (and in some ways, perhaps, the most interesting) stages of the compositional process started in the sketchbooks.

This point has been stressed by Lewis Lockwood.* In the autograph of the opening allegro of the Sonata for Cello and Piano in A major, opus 69, the entire development section was recast: Beethoven systematically reversed the roles of the two dialoguing instruments, crossing out old readings and superimposing new ones right on the page. He created a graphic chaos as he involved himself in endless changes of balance, figuration, pitch, and — as Lockwood shows especially well — register. Lockwood's lengthy study can be read on many levels: it is an exemplification of methodology, a virtuoso exercise in decipherment and transcription, and indeed even (most traditionally) a prolegomenon to a critical edition of the sonata. It can also be read as an analytical study which offers both to explicate each of Beethoven's countless changes, and also to illuminate the detailed structure of the final version of the work arrived at as a result of them. This was surely the real heart of Lockwood's essay, and the reason it could be printed in *The Music Forum*, a serial devoted not at all to musicology as conventionally conceived, but to theory and analysis (Schenkerian analysis; I have mentioned the interest in Beethoven sketches shown by Schenker and various Schenkerians).

For all his professed admiration for Schenker, though, Lockwood's analysis is not very Schenkerian. The student dealing with a composer's sketches and 'working autographs' has a control — dare one say, a higher control — that is not available to speculative theory, even when theory appeals to the authority of great music (as it usually does, or claims to do). What he has before him to work with are the composer's second, third, fourth, and fifth thoughts about one particular musical point after another. Such work can be characterized as musicology oriented towards criticism in two senses, then: towards the musicologist's concept of and response to the work of art as art, and towards the composer's own self-criticism. The idea is of course to get the two senses to collapse into one.

6

A good deal of work has also been done in recent years on the sketches and autographs of other composers.[24] Beethoven scholarship serves as a model for this only in the most general way, for no composer has ever been such a copious sketcher as Beethoven or so compulsive a hoarder of sketches. (Some have been compulsive throwers-away of sketches.) But even if no more than one or two late drafts for some composition are available, or for that matter only a corrected autograph, there may still be something significant to be learned about the music.

One of the earliest examples of this work, a 1968 dissertation published in a sumptuous edition a few years later, was by a Bach specialist whose later work was discussed in Chapter 2, Robert Marshall.[25] Marshall surveyed the by no means copious sketches and corrections made by Bach over the entire corpus of manuscripts of his cantatas and other choral music. But of course most of the material available for this kind of investigation dates from later than Bach's time – from the nineteenth and twentieth centuries, when composers have been seen as supreme artists rather than as craftsmen, and when in consequence all of their writings and scribblings have been piously preserved. Schumann, Mendelssohn, Chopin, Berlioz, Brahms, Verdi, Liszt, Wagner, Mahler, Debussy – musicologists have unearthed evidence from sketches and autographs for what is now usually called the 'compositional process' of all these masters. The net effect, let me stress again, has been to shed new and often unexpected light on one work after another belonging to the traditional canon of music. *Fingal's Cave, Dichterliebe*, the 'Fantastic' Symphony, the *Ring, Pelléas et Mélisande* are just a few of the works which – along with a whole clutch of Beethoven compositions – have come under the sketch scholars' scrutiny.[26] Sketch scholarship almost inevitably merges into criticism.

And partly or perhaps largely as a result of this type of research, American scholars have found themselves occupied more and more with more recent music. Palisca in 1962 had recorded that the nineteenth and even the late eighteenth centuries were 'comparatively neglected' as areas of musicological research. One of the most widely noted phenomena in musicology of the 1970s was its firm step into the nineteenth century.

Only slowly – slowly, but I should like to think surely – have musicologists taken the further step into the twentieth. Even more sumptuous than Marshall's Bach study was a 1969 facsimile edition of a long-lost sketchbook that turned up for Stravinsky's *Le Sacre du printemps*. The first to discuss this extraordinary document, the composer's long-term associate Robert Craft, was a conductor and a critic. The second person to do so was a theorist – Allen Forte, once again, in *The Harmonic Organization of 'The Rite of Spring'* (1978). The third person was a young musicologist, Richard Taruskin, who wrote about 'Russian Folk Melodies in *The Rite of Spring*' in 1980.[27] Schoenberg, Berg, Webern, Tippett, and Britten are some other twentieth-century composers whose sketches have been investigated. Now that the fascination with modernism seems to be waning among composers and theorists, perhaps phobias about it are also being overcome by musicologists.

The step into the nineteenth century was acknowledged by the foundation of the journal *19th-Century Music* in 1977, at the University of California. The step into the twentieth was prefigured by the first article in the first issue. Written by the composer Richard Swift, this made its intentions plain by its title '1-XII-99: The Structure of Schoenberg's *Verklärte Nacht*' and was manifestly analytical rather than musicological in orientation. The founding editors – Swift has since joined them – were indeed musicologists, and it is indicative that they all had interested themselves in composers' sketches, the composers in question being Berlioz (D. Kern Holoman) and Beethoven (Robert Winter and myself). But they had other equally strong interests, too – in criticism and in performance – and the thrust of the journal has deliberately been eclectic. Its submissions have included no great glut of sketch articles; studies in analysis, bibliography, biography, criticism, and performing practice have made up as prominent a proportion of the contents. A vigorous journal called *Early Music* had been started in London five years earlier, and there was some thought that one called *19th-Century Music* might balance the ledger and even match its appeal (here we were overoptimistic). One did not foresee that a polarization along these lines would develop in the British musicological community, at least to the extent that 'Early Music' and 'Nineteenth-Century Music' alternate as topics for annual summer conferences which have now become a fixture.

The nineteenth-century summers are the less crowded; yet one feels there is a significance in the turn towards nineteenth-century musicology that goes beyond a head-count of its practitioners. A number of reasons have been proposed to account for the phenomenon. It has been said, not too persuasively, that the sources of earlier music have inevitably been used up, driving musicologists like ravenous herds from the well-cropped meadows of the Renaissance to the rich dank marshlands of Romanticism. I myself have just drawn attention to the minor stampede set off by sketch studies. With the passage of time, the great healer, music of the nineteenth century and even that of the early twentieth retreats to the more distant and sedative past. Another factor which might be thought to have contributed to the growth of nineteenth-century studies in Britain and America, but which evidently did not, was their prior growth in Germany.

Carl Dahlhaus of the Free University of Berlin, the leading figure in German musicology today, is another who made the trek from the Renaissance to Romanticism. Beginning with a dissertation on Josquin Desprez, he turned in the 1960s to problems of the nineteenth and twentieth centuries in general, and Wagner in particular. A prominent contributor to the enormous series *Studien zur Musikgeschichte des neunzehnten Jahrhunderts* (fifty-nine volumes to date, since 1965), Dahlhaus brought one phase of his work to a consummation in a magisterial book on *Die Musik des neunzehnten Jahrhunderts* of 1980.[28] But the wider range of his thought is indicated by his

steady interest in systematic musicology, aesthetics, historiography, melodic, harmonic, and rhythmic theory, analysis and
criticism, and contemporary music – he has written (or at least
coauthored) books on all these topics and more. Dahlhaus is a
metahistorian, and the philosophical and sociological dimensions
of metahistory, even when not expressed in Dahlhaus's relent-
lessly dialectical and frequently gnomic style, are not easy for
British and American musicologists to absorb. The lack of
impact of this scholar's work in the late 1960s and 1970s is less
remarkable, perhaps, than the great interest it seems to have been
exciting just recently. Six of his books have appeared in translation (and Dahlhaus is not easy to translate) in a six-year period:
an unprecedented density of publication for a serious writer on
music, let alone a foreign one.[29]

The significance of the turn towards nineteenth-century
studies lies, I think, in two simple facts which are related in a
simple enough way. The first is that for better or for worse, the
largest body of music that gains an immediate response from
musicians at large is music of the nineteenth century. (Qualification is required here, of course; it will be provided in just a
moment.) By working with nineteenth-century music, musicologists work directly with compositions that move and attract
them. They are very unlikely to devalue or demean them in ways
that Treitler and I have deplored – as moments in a hypothesized
evolutionary process, as elements in an arbitrary 'explanation',
as fodder for philology, or as art 'objects' susceptible to objective
manipulation.

The other fact is that when musicians come to this music and
try to understand it as aesthetic experience, they find powerful
critical methodologies already in existence. They are the
methodologies encompassed under the term analysis. That
analysis is a formalistic construct with serious limitations for
criticism is something I have emphasized above. But I have also
emphasized that it came into being in order to validate a
treasured repertory, and I think that it is in this spirit that
musicologists engage with analysis today. By confronting the
whole paradoxical situation anew, in the field of nineteenth-

century music, where it developed in the first place, they have the opportunity to make a start towards new modes of understanding.

The most interesting of recent musicologists working with nineteenth-century music have not taken over standard analytical systems complete but have inched their way towards more comprehensive analytical methodologies of their own, which is to say towards critical methodologies. Among others, the work of Richard Kramer on Beethoven, Anthony Newcomb on Schumann, Robert Bailey and Newcomb again on Wagner, Walter Frisch on Brahms, and Roger Parker on Verdi may be mentioned.[30] Not so incidentally, some of these men – Newcomb and Frisch – have learned something from the writings of Dahlhaus.

But the reader will object that nothing that has been said above applies or should apply solely to the music of the nineteenth century. Do not Bach and Handel, Berg and Stravinsky exert an appeal comparable to that of Schumann and Wagner, and do there not exist for these composers' scores, too, analytical methodologies of a power comparable to those available for nineteenth-century ones? The point is willingly, even eagerly conceded (and apart from the question of analysis, be it said that pre-Bach as well as post-Stravinsky music can also generate the same passions). The nineteenth century is simply the richest – no, let us say only the largest, the best-known – repository of such music. As a purely strategic matter, to press for a critical orientation to musicology is more important in Renaissance circles, as I said earlier, than in Romantic ones. Twenty years from now, the surge of scholarly interest in nineteenth-century music will probably be seen as no more than the cutting-edge of musicology's new thrust towards criticism.

In any case, it is patently arbitrary to separate off Beethoven from Mozart and Haydn when making generalizations – even heavily qualified generalizations – about nineteenth-century music and musicology. The more so since it may very well be that Charles Rosen's *The Classical Style: Haydn, Mozart, Beethoven* of 1971 provided the most influential model for the kind of work I have been describing in the 1970s and 1980s. We shall have more to say about *The Classical Style* in a moment. Among the many other tributes it received, it was chosen as the subject of a panel discussion at one of the annual meetings of the American Musicological Society: not a very insightful occasion, by all accounts, but one with symbolic importance – for this book, which from the traditional musicological standpoint could scarcely be more heterodox, and cheeky to boot, is apparently the only one to be distinguished in this way in all the fifty-odd years of the society's meetings.

Had something begun stirring within the depths of the discipline? Some years later, in 1981, another of the meetings featured a series of seemingly anodyne panels on musicology – 'Current Methodology: Opportunities and Limitations', 'The Musicologist Today and in the Future', and the like, contributions to which were printed in a book entitled *Musicology in the 1980s*.[31] The panelists, some of whom were in their thirties as they entered that decade, others in their fifties, vented a surprising amount of disgruntlement with positivistic musicology on the one hand, and sympathy for criticism on the other. Richard Taruskin read a manifesto opposing positivism as a basis for the historical performance of music.[32] Another of the younger scholars, Rose Rosengard Subotnik, the premiere analyst and expositor of Adorno's thought to the English-speaking community, spoke on 'Musicology and Criticism'.* Her carefully reasoned and eminently reasonable exposition of the necessity of criticism for the musicological endeavour could hardly be bettered.

Agreeable as it was to hear the message of 'A Profile for American Musicology' echoing down the decades, reinforced by new arguments and developed by an important new critical sensibility, it was disappointing to hear Subotnik's pessimistic appraisal of the progress of criticism over that time.

Outside of journalistic criticism, which is not my concern here, American music criticism is an elusive and fragmentary phenomenon. For the most part it consists in scattered, highly

> divergent essays by individual scholars who seldom identify
> their enterprise as criticism, and who work in relative
> isolation, since there is rarely more than one such figure in any
> American music department, since few of their students can
> afford to remain in criticism, and since few, if any, have
> generated even a small, identifiable school of critical methods
> or thought. . . . Collectively they have had relatively little
> impact on the character and direction of American musicology
> as an institutional whole (pp. 145–6).

Collectively we have done rather better than that, I think, as the
discussion over the last few pages has tried to indicate. Subotnik's view of criticism is radical, abstract, and dialectical;
between criticism and its antithesis, positivistic musicology, she
sees an impasse. My own view is more pragmatic and eclectic.
What I see is infiltration. If this has not already been made clear
enough at a number of points in this book, a final example from
another field of nineteenth-century studies should make it even
clearer.

Verdi research over the last twenty years or so makes quite a
remarkable story. All sorts of people seem to get involved with
it, doing work of all kinds and on all levels. They flourish in all
opera-conscious countries, from Hungary to Mexico, but particularly in Italy, of course, Britain, and the United States.
Musicological editors in Chicago and Milan have started a
magnificent critical edition. Other musicologists have studied
Verdi's settings of Italian verse forms, his borrowings from or
echoes of Donizetti, the changes in his melodic style over the
years, the significant alterations he made to the autograph of
Falstaff before and after the premiere, and many other problems.
(They have not been able to do much with his sketches because,
mysteriously, these are kept under lock and key by his heirs.) A
BBC producer has written a monumental three-volume study of
the operas, a historical-critical study notable *inter alia* for the
virtuosity with which Verdi's work is situated in the context of
otherwise forgotten operatic traditions. A retired opera director
is producing massive collections of letters, libretto drafts, and all

other conceivable documents relating to individual operas. Theorists have analysed the tonal structure of the operas as wholes, and the inner coherence of arias such as 'Ernani, Ernani, involami' – music that analysts of Tovey or Schenker's type would have placed beneath the salt, to put it less saltily than they might well have done themselves. A psychologist has examined obsessive themes that recur in Verdi's oeuvre in relation to his own life history, itself the subject of much new research and demythification. A musicologist-turned-semiologist has analysed the operas to yield up death figures and ritual structures. A critic-temporarily-turned-musicologist uncovered pages of *Don Carlos* that were cut from the score – actually, and very fortunately, they were sewn together – just before the premiere, and showed how important they were to the dramatic shape of certain scenes. The Metropolitan Opera restored some of these pages and videocast them to the millions. Another critic has transcribed from early recordings several hundred improvised cadenzas and *puntature* for Verdi arias, sung by artists whom the composer knew or could still have known. A stage director has written about the official *disposizioni sceniche* for individual operas that were issued by Verdi's publisher under his sanction; in these stage guides, matters such as decor, costumes, blocking, gesture, and so on are specified in detail. Using such a stage guide, a conductor, director, costumier, designer, lighting man, and *Dramaturg* collaborated at a conference of the Verdi Institute (there are indeed two Verdi Institutes, one at Parma and the other at New York) to produce *La Forza del destino* in 1980 in a way approximating the first performance of 1862.

It would be pointless to try to determine which of this work should be classified as musicology, theory, analysis, criticism, or praxis. Much of it could only be characterized in terms of mixed genres. Among the great composers, Verdi is one of those who have in recent decades risen most sharply in critical estimation; he is also one of those who have been most intensely studied. The activities that have just been sketched add up to a confused, variable, exciting, beneficial sum which contributes to the understanding and appreciation of Verdi's operas as scores, as sound, as spectacle, as drama, as social commentary, and as personal testament. Whatever we call this work, it is work that is headed in the right direction.

7

One of the most brilliant and important books on music to appear in recent years, Charles Rosen's *The Classical Style*, also falls into no ordinary genre.* Heterodox from the standpoint of traditional musicology, it is equally or perhaps even more so from the standpoint of traditional theory.

The reader may be inclined to laugh at this statement as a peculiar sort of negative Procrusteanism: for while Rosen is also an academic – he has a PhD in French literature, and teaches music courses at a university – he is first and foremost a concert pianist, who from his student days on could not have cared less about historical and theoretical orthodoxies. But Rosen does not disclaim these orthodoxies; he acknowledges them, by means of sharp, explicit attacks on both in the Introduction to *The Classical Style*. Then he methodically builds up his own heterodoxies. In doing so, he draws abundantly from both traditions – and from other, non-musical intellectual traditions as well.

'Methodically' may also seem like a peculiar word, in view of the book's loose structure and the impression it initially gives of a certain self-indulgent sprawl in the exposition. On closer acquaintance, one comes to see how this serves Rosen's purpose in allowing him to make a truly comprehensive survey of his material, without setting up expectations – which he has no intention of fulfilling – that everything will be 'covered' equally, let alone completely. He can move around easily within the huge repertory of classical music, he can vary his approach to it by exploring analytical and critical ideas of very many kinds, and he can also comfortably slip in numerous germane digressions. Polemics about various musicological *bêtes noires* are dotted through the book – the use of a continuo in Mozart's piano concertos, for example, and the whole issue of historical performance. There are cameos about classical music as a mirror of the intellectual history of the Enlightenment – on Haydn's art as an example of the pastoral genre; on *Don Giovanni*, with its unruly combination of liberalism and eroticism, as 'an attack, at once frontal and oblique, upon aesthetic and moral values'.[33]

This book is unusually rich and multifarious, then – even, at first, bewilderingly so: like the subject itself. The book's structure recognizes the richness of classical music without becoming overwhelmed by it. The master principle that keeps everything on the track is Rosen's commitment to musical analysis. A theme that recurs again and again is that of the composers' manipulation of 'the musical language'; 'coherence', 'balance', and 'symmetry' are structural values that earn this critic's highest praise. We also hear about grace and charm, however, and about elegance and wit, even despair, passion, and glory. This throwback to Tovey has been widely noted (though Tovey, by comparison, always seems on the point of pressing his affective language into a dangerous semi-poetic analogue of the music itself, whereas Rosen seems to slip in affective words almost reluctantly, wary lest they reach past a decorous minimum level of specificity). In Britain, where Tovey epigones are still to be found, the throwback may not have proved as unsettling as it did, I think, in America.

For Rosen, the classical style is that in which all elements of music are in the most perfect (hence 'classical') equipoise – motif, line, tonality, harmony, rhythm, phrasing, texture, figuration, dynamics, and more. Drawing on this central insight, his analyses repeatedly point to the relationship between material and structure, between the single musical gesture and large-scale formal articulations and proportions. In detail, his method of analysis is eclectic, drawing on thematicism more than on Schenkerism, but always notably alert to the quality of music's movement in time (recalling Tovey, once again). We have the sense, says Rosen in a striking sentence, that in classical music 'the movement, the development and the dramatic course of a work can be found latent in the material, that the material can be made to release its charged force so that the music . . . is literally impelled from within' (p. 120). This is the organicists' creed of an entelechy generating a work of art from within (though 'organic' is a word Rosen stays away from): a familiar burden of analysts. And in the broadest sense, Rosen's synoptic effort to bring elements of rhythm, phrasing, and so forth on to a par with pitch elements corresponds to that of such recent theorists as Epstein and Lerdahl and Jackendoff.

But if Epstein has bothered systematic analysts by his informal *modus operandi* in *Beyond Orpheus*, Rosen has scandalized them by his hit-and-run tactics.[34] Perhaps he has analysed all the pieces fitted into *The Classical Style*'s loose structure with all the rigour the analysts expect (this must certainly be true with the piano pieces, at any rate). But he writes only as much as he wishes – or, rather, needs – about each one. So he can write thirty pages on Beethoven's 'Hammerklavier' Sonata and no more than a single paragraph on Mozart's G-minor Symphony, a work whose dissection seems to be enjoined by some music-theoretical College of Surgeons as earnest of initiation among the orthodox. Criticizing Schenkerian orthodoxy in his Introduction, Rosen observes that among other shortcomings, this routinely minimizes salient features in the music at hand ('a failure of critical decorum'[35]). His own analysis maximizes salient features; indeed, it deals with nothing else. From the standpoint of traditional theory, this is very heterodox indeed.

So also is Rosen's preoccupation with the classical *style*. 'In my business "stylistic" and "style" are dirty words,' an un-embarrassed analyst, Peter Westergaard, announced to a sub-dued gathering of musicologists in 1972. 'Of course we use them, but rarely with serious intent.'[36] Rosen does not speak about the universals of music, or of tonal music; he hammers away at the unique distinction of a style that flourished for no more than about fifty years and its differences from earlier and later styles of tonal music. (He does, however, overstress the 'universality' of this style within its own short lifespan.) Also heterodox is Rosen's clear if heavily qualified – indeed, polemically qualified – commitment to normative form types such as sonata form, rondo, sonata-rondo, and the like. In his *Sonata Forms* of 1980 he makes elaborate taxonomies of such types, taxonomies of a kind that have been out of fashion since the days of Tovey, at least outside of music-appreciation textbooks. All this sounds, to a theorist, very much like musicology.

But *of course* Rosen has a profound interest in music history. This obvious fact – which has become more and more obvious in Rosen's work since *The Classical Style*, his first book and, amazingly, his first piece of extended writing – lay hidden only from traditional musicologists, stung by those antimusicological polemics and appalled by Rosen's approach to the concept of musical style. In brief, Rosen conceives of style in ideal rather than normative terms.

> Even in respect to historical importance and influence, but above all as regards the significance of the musical development of the eighteenth century, the work of Haydn and Mozart cannot be understood against the background of their contemporaries; it is rather the lesser man who must be seen in the framework of the principles inherent in Haydn's and Mozart's music – or, at times, as standing outside these principles in an interesting or original way. Clementi, for example, stands somewhat apart . . . (p. 22).

The last line or two of this citation could only have been written by someone with an appetite for history. Rosen repeatedly makes historical judgments, some of them, again, being heterodox. He hangs tough, for example, on the issue of precisely when the classical style should be said to emerge – with Haydn's six String Quartets, opus 33, of 1781, rather than with the opus 20 Quartets of 1772. Mozart's Piano Concerto in E flat, K. 271, of 1775 is 'perhaps the first unequivocal masterpiece in a classical style purified of all mannerist traces'.[37] Again, instead of the familiar trisection of Beethoven's output into formative, mature, and transcendent periods (a concept only slightly softened in the latest edition of *Grove's Dictionary*) he proposes a startling new bisection into a classicizing proto-Romantic period, up to around

1804–6, followed by a classical one – including a genuinely pre-Romantic little blip in 1815–16.

What is more, the looseness of the book's structure scarcely hides the intention to encompass not all, certainly, of the music of the classical style, but all the music that Rosen judges to be the best. Haydn's quartets, symphonies, and piano trios after the mid-1770s, and his late sacred music; Mozart's operas, piano concertos – treated in unusual detail – and string quintets; Beethoven's piano concertos, sonatas, and variations (the author is, after all, a pianist especially known for his Beethoven) – this is Rosen's canon, and he goes methodically through it all. He even goes through it more or less chronologically. If this is not to be called music-historical writing, it is hard to know what is.

Yet if this *is* historical writing, it is history of a kind which (as I have urged) 'provides a platform of insight into individual works of art'. If this is analytical writing, it is the 'true analysis' of David Lewin's dichotomy which 'must always reflect a *critical* attitude toward a piece'. To improve upon Edward Cone's formulation in his response to Lewin, it is writing that calls upon 'all modes of knowledge, including the theoretical, the analytical, *the historical*, and the intuitive, to help us achieve a proper critical response to a piece of music'.[38] To many pieces of music.

I think this central point has been understood, with varying degrees of clarity, by all readers of *The Classical Style*: and that is why I have guessed that it was Rosen who provided the most influential model for the gradual and still cautious shift of American musicology in the 1970s and 1980s towards criticism. The word 'model' should be dropped, though, and something like 'encouragement' put in its place. It is pretty unthinkable that Rosen's unique, brilliant synthesis of history and theory could ever be emulated directly, even by someone who might conceivably have as cultivated an ear as his (for prose, as well as for music). Nor is his enviable stance vis-à-vis the academy – both in it and against it – widely available. Nonetheless, for those who are fogged in by the more orthodox academic constraints, *The Classical Style* is the sort of work that extends horizons, encourages the taking of risks, dispels some of the fog, and raises ambitions.

5. Ethnomusicology and 'Cultural Musicology'

Charles Louis Seeger was born in 1886 in Mexico City.[1] His parents, New Englanders of good family – his father was an importer – indulged his childhood passion for music without fostering it seriously. They sent him to Harvard, where he associated happily with other artistically inclined young men and appears to have studied nothing but music: though this with minimal reference to the professors there, conservatives out of sympathy for the music of Strauss, Skriabin, Mahler, and Debussy which fascinated Seeger. After winning a college prize for composition nonetheless, he took the step that was usual in those days and went to study in Germany. He spent some time as assistant conductor of the Cologne Opera. On his return he published some songs and gave concerts with his new wife, a violinist from New York society.

In 1912 he travelled west again, to join the new music department at the University of California – and at his first lecture, as he reported later, ran out of things to say halfway through the hour. After this experience he got busy cultivating his intellectual talents, which were possibly even more remarkable than his musical ones. Folk music and the then unknown topic musicology were included in his curriculum, as well as the music of Schoenberg and Stravinsky. One of his first students, a lifelong friend and influence, was the already radical composer Henry Cowell.

Berkeley contributed to the first phase of Seeger's radicalization, after he was taken into the Sacramento Valley and shocked by the condition of the agricultural workers there. A conscientious objector in 1917, ostracized by his academic colleagues, he lectured on Bertrand Russell's 'The Philosophy of Pacifism' to the International Workers of the World in San

Francisco. Increasingly Seeger found it difficult to reconcile his career as a composer and promulgator of 'elite' music with his moral outrage at the deprivation of the masses of his fellow-men. He gave up composing and for many years searched vainly for some sense of purpose. The search included a bizarre episode in which he took his family in a homemade automobile house-trailer to rural North Carolina, so that he could play free sonata recitals in churches and Grange halls with his wife.

After their separation Seeger settled in New York. He taught at the Institute of Musical Art, forerunner of the Juilliard School of Music, was active (though not as a composer) in con-temporary-music circles, became a close friend of Carl Ruggles, and took as his second wife the avant-garde composer Ruth Crawford, one of his students at the Institute. To some it has been a cause of regret that after her marriage Crawford plunged herself with such enthusiasm into Seeger's projects instead of writing more music.

The second stage of Seeger's radicalization took place in the 1930s, when Cowell introduced him to the communist-inspired Composers' Collective. He came to feel that composers should be producing music 'from below' – that is, music in a folk or popular style that the people would understand, enjoy, and respond to – rather than 'from above'. Hans Eisler, the refugee Marxist composer, and Aunt Molly Jackson, a Kentucky union organizer and folksinger, were major revelations. Then a new, climactic, twenty-year-long phase of his career began in 1935 when he moved on and up to Washington, as an administrator in two of Roosevelt's programmes to combat the Depression, the Resettlement Administration and the Works Progress Administration, then later in the Pan-American Union and the International Music Council of UNESCO. On the national, inter-American, and finally international spheres, Seeger always worked to promote music that comes from 'below', rather than music imposed from 'above'.

The active and contemplative sides of his personality reached fruition around the same time. Ever since childhood, evidently, Seeger had a furiously racing speculative mind, but his real writing career began only now, in his fifties. It was not only that in this period he learned about Anglo-American folk music and South American music of all kinds, making use of his government positions to foster important programmes of folksong collecting and recording. He also began to produce more or less formal work in philosophy – though he himself would have rejected this term (as would no doubt professional philosophers also) on the grounds that he was no more than an amateur in that discipline. But Seeger was in fact a brilliant autodidact in all the many fields he touched upon – philosophy, musicology, ethnomusicology, folklore, and the technology required to design his various melographs, which are electronic mechanisms for the precise visual graphing of melody. Only the field he abandoned, traditional Western music, was an exception: and for his teachers in that field he held nothing but amused contempt.

Seeger published the last, though still preliminary version of his grandest work under the title 'Tractatus Esthetico-Semioticus', a comprehensive synoptic theory of human communication in which music plays one part among many.* It was mooted as early as 1915. In scope, this essay can be compared with, say, Susanne Langer's well-known *Philosophy in a New Key* of 1942 – a comprehensive study of symbolism with chapters on language, myth, ritual, and art, the art chosen for exemplification being music. A related, secondary part of Seeger's work was a new taxonomy for music study, a new all-embracing scheme of the ways in which music can be encompassed in verbal terms. This was the framework for musicology in the old sense, or systematic musicology, as has been mentioned early in the present book. The universal schemes of Adler and Riemann, which encompassed 'comparative musicology' (as ethnomusicology was called before Jaap Kunst introduced the term in 1950) along with the history of Western music and much else, were not so old when Seeger was studying in Germany. Presumably he encountered them there. From his first years at Berkeley, systematic musicology remained the obsession of the contemplative side of this very active musician's life.

Two themes running through all of Seeger's writings seem to me particularly noteworthy. The one which is usually remarked he called 'the linguocentric predicament' or 'the musicological juncture'. This is the incommensurability of verbal and musical communication, the insuperable problem – seldom appreciated by musicians, according to Seeger – that results when words are used to convey anything other than scientific fact. Speech-knowledge of music, he stressed again and again, is very different from music-knowledge of it. Another obsessive theme, less frequently remarked upon, is a concern for value and valuation. Given to dialectical formulations, which however he insisted should not be interpreted in Hegelian terms, Seeger pitted valuation and criticism against science and description as the two basic modes of human inquiry. He slighted neither, at least in theory, and tried to draw on general value theory to develop equally detailed schemes for musical valuation and musical description.

There has never, apparently, been a thorough, fully considered review or appraisal of Seeger's thought. Reviewers must have either thrown up their hands at it or been scared away (poor Seeger was reduced to writing a sort of self-review in an amusing made-up conversation with a friend and a student, published in 1970, which is as illuminating as it is entertaining[2]). No one has read him, I imagine, without being impressed by his penetrating sharpness and clarity of mind, and without being frustrated by his maddening penchant for abstraction. Like most autodidacts, he was temperamentally disinclined to build on others' work, and so his own suffers from inadequate confrontation with various thinkers to whom he was successively introduced: Bloomfield, Saussure, the logical positivists, Wittgenstein – to say nothing of others (such as Langer and Meyer) whom he missed entirely or ignored. To borrow a phrase from the 1960s – a decade that the septuagenarian Seeger found highly congenial – it would seem that in his philosophy, Seeger never really got it together. And as he acknowledged just as frankly, he never really got it together in his career, either, despite the variety and distinction of his many accomplishments. It was his son, the radical folksinger of the 1940s and 1950s Pete Seeger, who was able to reach out to the masses in a way that was impossible for the reluctant natural aristocrat who had sent that son (and his folksinging sister Peggy) to Harvard, just as he had been sent before them. 'By the inability of his father to do anything else, Peter began to look at things from below up,' Seeger reminisced, near the end of his life. 'He did what I ought to have done. I didn't see it until later.'[3]

I have told the Seeger story at some length because Seeger is very much to my purpose in writing this chapter, or so I feel: and this for a number of reasons. First, he exemplifies vividly one typical factor in the ideological makeup of ethnomusicology, middle-class antagonism towards conventional middle-class culture (middle-class antagonism: for while music may come from below or be imposed from above, musicology always comes from above). This ideological orientation is reflected openly or less openly in their work by many ethnomusicologists: openly by John Blacking, for example, when he writes bitterly in his widely read Ganz Lectures *How Musical is Man?* of the constrained musical education he received in England as a boy. Blacking is of the generation of the angry young men of the late 1950s, and he shows it. Interest in folksong and folk culture, of course, has been associated with anti-establishment attitudes ever since its earliest days at the dawn of Romanticism. From John Lomax to Joan Baez in America, and from Cecil Sharp to Peggy Seeger and her husband Ewan McColl in Britain, folk-music enthusiasts have tended to align themselves either vaguely or explicitly with various parties of the left. And this tendency finds its global echo in ethnomusicology. Discussing the purposes of (actually, the drives behind) postwar ethnomusicology, Alan P. Merriam singled out among others the 'White Knight Concept' and the 'Dutiful Preserver Concept': concepts that presumably do not require further elucidation.[4]

Second, Seeger testifies just as vividly to the attraction, the magnetic force that ethnomusicology exerts upon Americanists. One of his most striking essays pictures the Americas as an ethnomusicologist's dream laboratory for the study of musical acculturization.* The conquerors and colonizers brought their own art and popular music with them, bringing both into confrontation with the folk music of native Indians and imported African slaves. At first European art music decayed in the New World; then later colonists cultivated it anew in order to emulate the home country; then, after the various independence movements, attempts were made to render it national and finally international. In a breathtaking inter-American historical survey, Seeger distinguished the attitudes of five generations of 'republican' composers. Carlos Gomes and Louis Moreau Gottschalk discovered (and demonstrated) that Americans could write respectable European music; Alberto Nepomuceno and Edward MacDowell introduced some folk and popular national elements to their music in a cautious and uncertain way; Heitor Villa-Lobos and Charles Ives did the same much more emphatically and with greater technical proficiency and individuality; Carlos Chavez and Aaron Copland were exponents of a neo-European style showing 'a degree of integration that practically obliterates distinction of nationality, even though this is still a selling point'; and Alberto Ginastera and Milton Babbitt – still in their thirties when Seeger wrote – worked with a stylistic homogeneity and confidence born of a sense of 'America's taking its place in the large world of Occidental music'. The problem for an American composer of art music of Seeger's generation, as he saw it, was how to involve himself with the vernacular tradition. This is also the problem for the American musicologist who seeks to study his own music from before around 1900 and also, Americanists will insist, after.

It is almost irresistible, with all this in view, to compare Seeger with the Northern American composer he named as the representative of his own generation. Seeger and Ives (twelve years his senior) both came from solid New England families who sent them not to conservatories but to the right colleges, where the traditional, European-based music instruction was to the taste of neither. They resisted furiously the academic 'rules' of composition, Ives refusing to resolve a certain dissonant ninth that Horatio Parker had blue-pencilled, Seeger characteristically working out his own complete system of purely dissonant counterpoint. More profoundly, they reacted against the elite art music of their time, which in one way or another they felt to be un-American. Ives fumed about Rollo and the old pussy-cats; Seeger, as was his way, wryly but repeatedly protested against 'the genteel tradition' and 'the make-America-musical movement'. Both men found ways to deal with the American musical dilemma – what to do about the vernacular tradition – in musical terms, Ives before he gave up traditional composition (if the adjective may be allowed in his case) by citing Stephen Foster songs and gospel hymns in his sonatas and symphonies, Seeger after giving up composition by his contributions to *The Workers' Songbook*, John and Alan Lomax's *Folksong U.S.A.*, and later *The Army Songbook*.

But over and above this, it was clearly necessary for both men to deal with the problem also in ideological terms. Ives became a mystic populist, Seeger a sort of utopian communist and a metaphysician of human communication on the broadest possible scale. These concerns, given his universalist inclinations, led him inevitably to ethnomusicology.

Seeger's involvement with ethnomusicology was long-standing, intimate, and highly official, yet also paradoxical. In the 1920s he sent or at least urged Cowell to study with the leading figure in comparative musicology, Erich von Hornbostel, at Berlin; in the 1930s, he and Cowell taught the first American courses in that subject. He was one of the founders of the American Society for Comparative Musicology (as well as of the New York and the American Musicological Societies), helped to bring Hornbostel out of Nazi Germany, and initiated the publication of Helen Roberts's pioneering comparative study of American Indian music (but abandoned it when he went to Washington). In the 1950s he was again a dominant – indeed, a domineering – force in the new Society for Ethnomusicology. Yet he does not appear to have been very interested in Indian or any other non-Western musics. As an Americanist, Seeger directed the few *bona fide* research papers in his long bibliography towards Anglo-American topics: nineteenth-century square-note hymnody, the Appalachian dulcimer, and the American dissemination of the 'Barbara Allen' tune. It was the idea of studying all musics that appealed to Seeger, not those musics themselves as subjects for actual study.

This is another reason why Seeger is very much to my purpose: for as I confessed at the outset of this book, I too am not very interested in non-Western musics. My interest in ethnomusicology amounts largely to an interest in what it can bring to the study of Western art music. What concerns me is the ethnomusicologists' critique of musicology. There are separatists among scholars of both camps who feel that as a practical matter they work with such disparate materials, with such incommensurable methods, and with such divergent ends in view that it is a waste of time to try to talk, let alone relate what they are doing. But Seeger, as a systematic musicologist second and foremost (*first*, I think, he aspired to become a philosopher), was the universalist *par excellence*. To the end of his long life he resisted any partitioning of musical scholarship. 'Continuation of the custom of regarding musicology and ethnomusicology as two separate disciplines, pursued by two distinct types of students with two widely different – even mutually antipathetic – aims is no longer to be tolerated as worthy of Occidental scholarship,' he wrote in an article of 1961, a sort of ethnomusicological epitome of his metatheory.[5] Earlier he had found many occasions to chide musicologists for their ethnocentric and class-centric attitudes. Later he was more inclined to chide ethnomusicologists for their neglect of cultural change (that is, history) and musical analysis.

He deplored equally the notorious polarization within ethnomusicology itself, and warned that this could lead to its actual fragmentation. He watched this polarization grow during the 1960s, as the field itself grew rapidly in America, and as he himself grew more and more closely involved with it as an elder statesman at Mantle Hood's Institute for Ethnomusicology at the University of California at Los Angeles. His position there was listed as 'Research Musicologist', incidentally, not 'Ethnomusicologist'. He collected his main writings in a book called simply *Studies in Musicology, 1935–1975*.*

'Ethnomusicology today is an area of study caught up in a fascination with itself,' wrote Alan P. Merriam in 1964, as the topic sentence for his influential book *The Anthropology of Music*.* One of his reviewers, Harold S. Powers, agreed: 'Sometimes it seems as though American ethnomusicologists spend almost as much time defining their field as working in it.'[6] Every student becomes fluent in the theory and philosophy of the field to an extent that can bewilder musicologists; perhaps in the last analysis Seeger can be thanked for this. And since not everybody has a head for theory, a lot of fuzzy material of this kind is written by ethnomusicologists long past their student days. Seeger cannot be blamed for the fuzziness.

Yet the contrast with the profoundly unreflective situation in musicology, which I have commented on before, is unquestionably damaging to the latter field. Within a dozen years of the big expansion of musical studies after the Second World War, two strong and distinct leaders had emerged in American ethnomusicology, taking fairly clear positions which were subject to debate, rebuttal, reformulation, and counter-rebuttal, and which provided sources of emphatic intellectual influence. With the possible exception of Leo Treitler, such leaders as emerged in the much larger field of musicology were notably deficient in thinking (and writing) about the philosophy or merely the unspoken assumptions underlying activity in their field.

Merriam and Hood moved naturally to define the polarization that has always been evident in Western studies of non-Western music, and that sparked many exchanges in the pages of *Ethnomusicology*, the journal of the American Society for Ethnomusicology. There are still some for whom it persists as the basis for alignments in the field today.[7] The difference between the poles has been expressed in various ways: as between a primarily socio-cultural approach to the subject matter and an internalist one; between an anthropological orientation and a musicological one (where the term now refers to the study not just of Western art music but of any music *qua* music); or between 'context musicology' and 'product musicology' (potentially a less confusing, if a more grating usage; we shall stay with what Seeger called the 'ordinary, cant use' of the term musicology, meaning the study of Western art music).

Merriam, as a cultural anthropologist and a thoroughly committed one, enjoyed a special position in the vaguely deployed field of postwar ethnomusicology. Most earlier ethnomusicologists had entered it by way of folklore or musicology. Merriam brought to the field not only a dour diligence in polemics, but also the prestige enjoyed at that time by anything smacking of science, or even social science. His own field work was done among American Indian and African tribes; his last two books are anthropological studies of the Basongye of Zaire which draw only marginally on music. Merriam's famous definition of ethnomusicology as 'the study of music in culture' carries with it a corollary saying what ethnomusicology is not. It is not the study of music or musics as autonomous systems or structures.

The definition has the advantage of crispness but the disadvantage of always requiring qualifications and explanations which instantly grow fuzzy. Implicit in the definition, according to Merriam, is

> that music sound is the result of human behavioral processes that are shaped by the values, attitudes, and beliefs of the people who comprise a particular culture. Music sound cannot be produced except by people for other people, and although we can separate the two aspects [the sound aspect and the cultural aspect] conceptually, one is not really complete without the other. Human behavior produces music, but the process is one of continuity; the behavior is shaped to produce music sound, and thus the study of one flows into the other.[8]

The trouble is that this slightly mystical 'flow' scarcely survives the minutiae of Merriam's anthropological methodology. He may have succeeded to his own satisfaction in incorporating the 'sound' aspect of music into his own work, but to others the flow looks to be largely in one direction – from sound to society. John Blacking, who was mentioned in passing above, is a leading British anthropologist-ethnomusicologist who also insists programmatically (indeed passionately) on the cultural orientation of his work. But one gets a much richer sense of the actual music of an African tribe from Blacking's books and records than from Merriam's, or from those of his students.

As for Mantle Hood, his predilections can perhaps be read in the circumstance that when he came to write *his* influential book, in 1971, he named it not after an ideal discipline, as Merriam had done, but after a real-life person, *The Ethnomusicologist*.* It is an unabashedly personal book. Ethnomusicology, as Hood defines it, 'is directed toward an understanding of music studied in terms of itself and also toward the understanding of music in society'.[9] ('No relatively independent academic discipline', Seeger had written, 'can be expected to confine itself to the view of a thing *in a context* to the exclusion of the view of the thing *in itself*.'[10]) Hood in this definition pointedly puts music *qua* music in the first position, insists on the qualification 'studied in itself' – a qualification which troubles anthropologists, apparently – and evokes spectres of lengthy fights within anthropology itself by substituting the word 'society' for Merriam's 'culture'. Hood's own research area is the art music of Java, music which has a history and a notation. His main scholarly work, indeed, is best described as music theory – a study of the mode systems (patet) in Javanese gamelan music.

It is also significant that Hood's proudest innovation at the UCLA Institute was having everyone actually perform non-Western musics. Naturally Seeger was more attracted to this than to Merriam's kind of ethnomusicology; by being introduced to music 'from the inside', or 'from below', students were gaining not only speech-knowledge but also music-knowledge of it. It is also understandable that Hood, unlike Merriam, has always been interested in engaging in dialogues with musicologists. He shares with them an interest in music 'in its own terms'.

Merriam's kind of ethnomusicology we do not need to consider here. As Powers pointed out, Merriam's patiently structured system of definitions, models, techniques, methods, and frameworks for field research contains one obvious flaw — obvious, at least, to someone who has worked with a non-Western music that has a history and a notation. In cultures such as those of Java and India, 'where musicians are professional, where musical activity can be discussed to a significant extent in terms of itself, apart from ritual, social, linguistic, or other cultural determinants, and where forms are manipulated and musical entities reified', a view of that music through the eyes of its own makers and listeners can only be obtained by considering 'the music in itself'. Powers also observes that

> useful contrasts have been set up between the 'critical' establishment and evaluation of the material [of ethnomusicology] as though from within the culture and 'objective' sampling and analysis of the material as though from outside the culture. If a scholar is able to write of the music of a particular culture, at whatever level, from somewhat the same sort of practical experience that one has a right to expect from a Western musicologist on Western music of the not too distant past, his work is or can become 'critical'. If he writes, by choice or necessity, as an observer from outside the culture, be it Bushman or Byzantine, his work is or must be 'objective'.[11]

This is as much as to say that the 'objective' approach of cultural anthropology is a last resort for music we do not understand from the inside.

As for that pregnant phrase 'by choice or necessity', what has just been pointed out about Hood holds also for Powers. In the music these men choose to study, the necessity of objectivity is something they strive to obviate by participating in its performance. I am inclined to echo Merriam's grumble that playing non-Western music — like playing Western music — by no means necessarily leads to understanding it (in either of Seeger's modes), especially when the playing is done in Westwood, California, rather than in the field.[12] Yet participation gives ethnomusicologists at least a measure of that practical experience which allows them – requires them, I should say – to do work that can be called critical.

Hood's kind of ethnomusicology we do need to consider, if only because he and other like-minded colleagues can often be found holding forth to musicologists about it (usually, be it said, at the musicologists' express invitation). Hood and Frank Harrison did this in concert back in 1963 in the *Musicology* volume of the 'Humanistic Scholarship in America' series, the one strictly musicological contribution to which (by Palisca) we discussed in Chapter 2. Harrison is an Irish medievalist, now retired, author of a magnificent study of *Music in Medieval Britain* (1958), who taught for extended periods in the United States, England, and Holland, and who in middle life made a dramatic shift to ethnomusicology.

A number of messages seem to come through in these more or less friendly harangues. The most general exhortation, that musicologists give up their ethnocentric bias, can be quickly dismissed, coming as it does with little grace from scholars whose aim of an objective study covering the whole range of world music is egregiously culture-bound to Western social-scientific ideology. Ethnomusicologists do not tell native theorists of Indian music, Ewe drummers or inner-city blues singers to stop concentrating on or loving their own music. We need also waste little time with Blacking's rather portentous claim that only after understanding Venda music of the Transvaal has he been able to understand Western music properly.[13] One is glad for Blacking; but he has not done anything to help *us* with Western music, however much he may have helped us with the repertory of Venda children's songs.

Much more serious is the advice that musicologists devote a great deal more attention to the *context* of the music they are studying. To quote Seeger, once again:

Thanks to anthropology, contextual documentation has reached a high level of technical proficiency with respect to tribal musics. It is somewhat less strong in the realm of Western folk musics. It is still very weak in dealing with the idiom of 'high', 'professional', 'fine' arts of music. (Strange, that we still lack a name for this idiom!) It is deplorably weak in dealing with the context of the 'popular' idiom – another, with no proper name.[14]

This message is a multiphased one. To change the metaphor, it contains a number of different strands which it is worth spending a little time untangling.

3

Let me first – in the present context – quickly tie up one loose end from an earlier chapter in this book. Those musical scholars who treat music as a series of autonomous objects or organisms, apart from the context of other pieces, repertories, and so on, are typically not historians but analysts. Strictly speaking, then, the ethnomusicologists' lectures should be beamed more directly to them than to musicologists. Musicologists themselves, indeed, are often ready to lecture analysts about myopia and insensitivity to the context of the works they are analysing. This we have seen in Chapter 3.

But of course the ethnomusicologists' point goes much further than what might be called the musical context of music (though it is more usually – and most imprecisely – called the 'historical' context). In question is the entire matrix of extra-musical social and cultural factors which to some extent form music and to some extent are formed by it. In a much-quoted passage from the *Musicology* volume, Harrison spoke for the social context, stressing

the need to consider the relation between all the circumstances of music making and the styles and forms of musical composition, rather than to regard musical forms as autonomous growths that come and go according to the inclinations of composers and the tastes of audiences. It becomes no less essential to re-create as far as possible the function, social meaning, and manner of performance of every type of musical work than to establish the notes of the musical texts that make the re-creation possible. With the further emphasis on the history of music as an aspect of the history of man in society, the traditional enterprises of musicology can no longer be pursued in vacuo (p. 79).

In Palisca's essay, it will be recalled, the typical musicological enterprise turned out to be 'the establishment of the notes', the preparation of critical editions. 'Re-creation in any full sense cannot be divorced from the original function of the music,' Harrison continued, 'any more than a musical work from another society can be fully understood apart from its social context.'

Sounding a variation of his own on this theme, the Americanist Gilbert Chase has hopefully proposed adoption of the term 'cultural musicology', by analogy with cultural anthropology. 'I favor the *idea* of an "ethnomusicology" of Western music; but I do not favor the terminology,' Chase announced in a forceful paper on 'American Musicology and the Social Sciences'.*

What we need is a term of larger scope that will contain the same idea – namely, the sociocultural approach to musicology.... Paraphrasing the previously quoted description of the task of cultural anthropology [by David G. Mandelbaum in the *International Encyclopedia of the Social Sciences*], we might describe the task of cultural musicology as being 'to study the similarities and differences in musical behavior among human groups, to depict the character of the various musical cultures of the world and the processes of stability, change, and development that are characteristic to them' (p. 220).

In another, similar paper Chase remarked on the 'historico-centric' bias of musicology and urged acceptance of Lévi-Strauss's notion of the basic equivalence of history and anthropology as studies of cultures that are removed, either by time or space, from our own.[15]

All this rattling of social-scientific sabres was calculated to make musicologists nervous, and it probably was successful in this. Actually what Chase was trying to do was point out to them that history itself in the last fifty years has absorbed much from sociology, economics, and anthropology. But even fifty years ago historians – and musicologists with them – were well acquainted with what they called social history and intellectual history, the history of ideas. Chase's paper 'American Musicology and the Social Sciences' was presented as a seminar, and the discussion following it has been printed. Pressed to enlarge upon 'cultural musicology' as applied to Western art music, Chase gave what I am tempted to call a highly ethnomusicologico-centric response:

> Very few of us really know what to do with art music in a sociocultural context. . . . Charles Seeger has stated that he would like to see the techniques of ethnomusicology extended to include the art music as well as the folk and popular music of the West. I agree with this in principle, but thus far – at least in the domain of art music – no one has shown us how this is to be done in actual practice (p. 224).

It is not that Chase and Harrison are wrong to point out that most musicologists pay too little attention to anything outside the strictly musical context of the music they are studying. The point is readily granted. Musicologists, especially those holding on to the old positivistic ways, have much to answer for. But on the other hand, there have also been repeated attempts, some of them very well publicized within and even outside the discipline, to deal with Western art music in terms of social and cultural history. To say that no one has shown ways of doing this is certainly hard on – in fact, screamingly callous towards – Curt

Sachs, Paul Henry Lang, Friedrich Smend, Edward Lowinsky, and Theodor Adorno, to name only a few older scholars who have worked along those lines, and who have already been mentioned in this book. Leonard Meyer, from a later generation, is another.

Their influence, either in detail or in general principle, is also evident on musicologists from later generations still. Iain Fenlon is only one of many British and American students of Renaissance music who have recently been concentrating hard on the close workings of church and court patronage. In a striking essay on 'Music and the Myth of Venice', Ellen Rosand has related the emphatic support of music for which the Serene Republic was famous to its political ideology and cultural self-image. Rose Subotnik has interpreted the inner principles of classical and Romantic music in terms of the Kantian and post-Kantian world views. Fenlon's work could be classified as musical social history, perhaps, Rosand's as cultural history, and Subotnik's as a contribution to the history of ideas.[16]

Not everyone will admire all of this work; I have expressed reservations about Fenlon's, for example, on account of its over-emphasis on social considerations at the expense of what I consider responsible treatment of the music as music. But for the purpose of the present argument, the point is that music's relation to the socio-cultural matrix is a major concern for many musicologists of the present, as it was for many of the past. It is hard to think of any serious musicologist, furthermore, for whom it is not at least a minor concern.

The contextual approach to musicology has also found a spokesman from a still younger generation. Gary Tomlinson, whose first book is on Monteverdi's response to the tension between late sixteenth-century humanism and neo-scholasticism, especially in the matter of musico-poetic rhetoric, has urged musicologists to consider the fluid model of culture due to Clifford Geertz. Culture is not an agent, a force, or a *Geist*, and still less a fixed structure to be objectively determined, as some anthropologists of Merriam's generation seem to have thought. Rather it is to be viewed as a construction of the historian, taking shape and gaining coherence from the reciprocal (and rich and haphazard) inter-action of his evolving assumptions with his increasingly meaningful data, the events he selects for inclusion in the context. In this the cultural anthropologist and historian are exactly alike: just as there is no culture of Bali except for the anthropologists' construal – his thick description – of it, so there is no culture of sixteenth-century Mantua apart from our interpretation. . . . [A]s Collingwood put it, speaking only of history: 'There *is* no past, except for a person involved in the historical mode of experience; and for him the past is what he carefully and critically thinks it to be.' It is clear as well that the artifacts of culture exist for us only insofar as we perceive meaning in them in a cultural web. And this holds alike for Balinese shadow-plays, the puppets used in them, the poem that Monteverdi set to music, and Mozart's G-minor Symphony.[17]

Presumably this would be entirely acceptable to Chase – or for Treitler, whom Tomlinson invokes along with Geertz and Collingwood.

But possibly what Chase meant to convey was a somewhat different message: not simply that musicologists should work along the same broad general lines as ethnomusicologists, but that they should adopt actual ethnomusicological methods, tech-niques, and findings. If so, he is of a mind with those movers and shakers of musicology and ethnomusicology who plan inter-national congresses. For such occasions topics have to be con-jured up that will stimulate contributions from scholars of widely different ideological and professional inclinations. A case in point was the 1977 congress of the International Musicological Society, especially since its location at Berkeley, California, reasonably called for the lofty general theme 'Inter-disciplinary Horizons in the Study of Musical Traditions, East and West'. Many sessions brought together musicological and ethnomusicological participants: 'East European Folk and Art Music', 'Islamic Influences', 'Music in Urban Centres Past and

Present', 'Court Dance East and West', 'Transmission and Form in Oral Transmission', 'Eastern and Western Concepts of Mode', and others.[18]

To speak only (and briefly) of the latter two topics, the oral transmission of music is a central issue in folklore and ethnomusicology that holds a special interest for musicologists who study early plainchant – the earliest music of the Western tradition, music which was originally not notated but passed down from generation to generation of unlettered clergy. I have already mentioned (in Chapter 4) Leo Treitler's 'Homer and Gregory', which treats Gregorian chant according to the Parry–Lord model for the recitation of epic verse. This approach provided Treitler with a new angle of attack on a problem that is inextricably bound up with early chant transmission, the highly intricate problem of interpreting chant notation over the course of its first few centuries. As for the concept of mode, that has had a particularly rocky history in Western music from Plato to Palestrina. Harold Powers is a rare example of a scholar who has studied Western and non-Western music with equal care, in particular the classical Indian and the Western concepts of mode in theory and practice. Powers, to my apprehension, has shed more light on the meaning of mode in sixteenth-century music than any of the other musicologists who have worked on this stubborn problem: and there have been many.

But the medievalists in general are dubious about Treitler's work, the ethnomusicologists are suspicious of Powers's, and the consensus seems to be that the application of ethnomusicological methods to historical studies of Western music is in a state of doldrums. This is the view, for example, of one uniquely well-placed observer, Claude Palisca – who was closely involved with that 1977 congress, and more distantly with a similar one at Strasbourg five years later. In between, he was the co-chairman of an informal symposium on American musicology, papers from which were published under the title *Musicology in the 1980s: Methods, Goals, Opportunities.* (Some of these papers were mentioned above, in Chapter 4. Another which deserves mention here is 'Applications of the History of Ideas' by the

Canadian Renaissance scholar Rika Maniates, a student of Lang.)

Since Palisca's essay in the *Musicology* volume of 1963 has been picked on more than once in this book, it seems only fair to allow him the last word, especially since Palisca is such a good sport about it. 'I have been doing penance every ten years since my essay in that publication,' he recalls in his Introduction to *Musicology in the 1980s*:

> Ten years ago UNESCO asked me to prepare the section on music in the mammoth study, *Main Trends of Research in the Social and Human Sciences*, part 2, published finally in English and French in 1978. I mention this because anyone reading my two essays will easily conclude that the forward-looking trends I identified have mostly evaporated. I have utterly failed at divination. . . . Some of the trends I thought promising in 1970 were: the application of ethnomusicological method to historical studies of Western music, that is, looking at how music functions in all levels of a culture [new theories of musical structure, computer applications, and the broader public diffusion of musicological findings]. None of these appear on the present agenda. Musicology advances (if Leo Treitler will permit me that verb) in unpredictable ways (pp. 11–12).

If ethnomusicological methods have not taken, then, it is not for lack of trying. The reason for the relative failure seems clear enough to me. There are really only a limited number of areas – such as oral transmission and concepts of mode – where ethnomusicological research itself can impinge directly on the study of Western music. Western music is just too different from other musics, and its cultural contexts too different from other cultural contexts. The traditional alliance of musicology has been with the humanistic disciplines, such as history, criticism, and philology, not with the social sciences (as Chase complains). This alliance is still the best basis for developing a contextual framework for Western music: and all the better in that humanistic scholars today are learning so much from social scientists (as Chase, perhaps not unnecessarily, reminds us).

It is one thing, though, to draw on modern historiography, with its ample provision for insights from anthropology and sociology, and quite another to draw on those disciplines directly for the understanding of Western music. The latter process has not had uniformly brilliant results in reference to non-Western musics, as the lingering polarization within the field of ethnomusicology testifies. Musicologists need to maintain a sharply sceptical attitude, I think, to the message they are receiving about the virtues of trying to adopt ethnomusicological methods to their own work.

4

Another – perhaps the last – strand of the ethnomusicologists' critique concerns the matter of folk and popular music. Musicologists spend much too much time on music 'from above', and not enough on music 'from below' which coexists with art music. Now it happens that in a field I know well, Elizabethan music, there is someone whose work stands out for its combination of the modes of historical musicology and folklore. In this enviable ambidexterity John Ward can be compared to Powers, though their styles and interests are very different. Ward has discovered more than his coworkers would in their fondest dreams have thought possible about Elizabethan popular music. His articles and lengthy reviews are miracles, treasure troves, cornucopias; I have devoured each of them greedily as they have appeared, down to the last line of the last of their plentiful footnotes. But what Ward says about 'Greensleeves' and 'Fortune my Foe' touches me less deeply than what Oliver Neighbour, in *The Consort and Keyboard Music of William Byrd*, says about the ways in which a composer of art music uses these and other popular tunes in his variations for virginals and his fantasias for viols.

It also happens that the richest contextual study I know of any music deals with nineteenth-century American music in the vernacular tradition: William W. Austin's *'Susanna', 'Jeanie', and 'The Old Folks at Home': the Songs of Stephen C. Foster from His Time to Ours* (1975).* The self-conscious leisurely spread of this title sets the tone for a rich consideration of 'the ramification of Foster's meaning' viewed in a great variety of contexts. One context is the biographical (and the fact that Foster was himself such a shadowy figure may have cast a spell over the whole of Austin's discourse, in which the line between the allusive and the elusive is admittedly often crossed). Another is the social context or, rather, the plural social contexts of singing in mid-century America: singing at home, in church, and on the stage. Another is the commercial or economic context. Complicity was already well established between popular singers, music publishers, theatrical concerns such as the Christy Minstrels, and the entire 'world of publicity' to which songwriters were a mere appendage.

Still another context is an ideological one. In question here is a small but centrally important group of songs which Austin, unlike some other students of Foster, distinguishes from the two usual main categories of the composer's work, minstrel songs ('Oh! Susanna') and sentimental ballads ('Jeanie with the Light Brown Hair'). 'Pathetic plantation songs' were from the start associated with the abolitionist movement, one of whose propagandists was a close friend of Foster in his youth. 'Massa's in de Cold Ground' originally included a reference to Uncle Tom in its lyrics. 'The Old Folks at Home' ('Swanee River') was regularly sung in the wildly popular plays derived from the Harriet Beecher Stowe novel.

What fascinates and disturbs Austin – and now we come to historical and authorial, personal, or autobiographical contexts – is that these particularly famous plantation songs, with their patronizing, entirely false image of slave life, came to be regarded by the end of the century as Negro folksongs – and this by Blacks as well as by Whites. Even another half-century later, in the time of Black awareness and militancy during which Austin brooded over his book, they seemed to occasion as much affectionate acceptance as angry rejection. What does this tell us

Ethnomusicology and 'Cultural Musicology' 177

about Foster's manifold meanings? What can the songs have meant to some of the many musicians who have sung, arranged, or quoted them: Charles Ives, *passim*; Aaron Copland, in *A Lincoln Portrait*; Thea Musgrave, who cites Foster in reference and in tribute to Ives; Ray Charles, in his extraordinary 'Swanee River Rock'; Ornette Coleman; and finally Pete Seeger, who of all these musicians takes the most sharply critical – yet still ambivalent – position towards items in the plantation song category?

The book itself is one American musician's extended inquiry into the meaning of his vernacular tradition, which is an inter-racial tradition. One thing the author shows is that neither his own White liberal values nor radical Black values provide any easy answers. To the point of mannerism – self-conscious mannerism, surely, once again – the text is dotted with questions, mostly questions about meaning. Meaning for Austin is not a set of hard-edged facts and judgments focused on the matter at hand, but a network of possibilities, probabilities, and ambiguities drawing one further and further into the infinite reaches of historical subject matter. Some of the questions are rhetorical; only a few of the others are answered or answerable; some are Unanswered Questions in an Ivesian sense. In both form and tone, this study is as shifting and open-ended as is the *Rezeption* of Foster's fragile but undying art itself.

There is a chapter, incidentally, on 'Foster the Craftsman, 1849–51'; but there is no extended treatment of the strictly musical context of the Foster songs – no positivistic style-analysis of their place in the evolution of some ideal song-type, let us say, on the way from Thomas Moore's *Irish Melodies* to George F. Root's 'people's songs'. Austin has published plenty of technical musical analysis in his time – of Debussy, Bartók, Webern, Ellington – but in *'Susanna', 'Jeanie', and 'The Old Folks at Home'* he was prepared actually to forgo music examples. Like so much else about this surprising book, this lacuna seems to make a quiet statement about method.

More broadly, in the matter of method, Austin might almost have set out to exemplify the sort of enterprise that the historian

William J. Bouwsma has recently identified as 'the history of meaning'. Writing in a symposium on 'Intellectual History in the 1980s', Bouwsma observes that the history of ideas used to be but no longer is regarded as the highest type of work in his dangerously fragmented discipline.[19] After Darwin, Marx, and Freud, man's intellectual attributes can no longer be seen as 'higher' or more important than other human attributes. Hence those historians who are less interested in battles, laws, administration, and diplomacy have tended to move away from the study of 'ideas' – in effect, the ideas of thinkers drawn from the ranks of the elite – to such areas as popular religion, the status of women and the family, attitudes towards death, punishment, and so on. But the history of ideas has taken on new life, says Bouwsma, in a new, somewhat polymorphous mutation. A concern for explicit or implicit meanings permeates some of the most seminal of recent historical writing, writing which is unclassifiable according to standard academic categories (as Austin's book is unclassifiable) because it brings together political, social, economic, intellectual, and even artistic insights in the service of a history that turns away from 'raw historical experience (i.e., what happens to people) to what human beings have made of that experience'.[20]

Artistic insights: for whereas traditional intellectual history, drawing on philosophy, tended to ignore the arts as unintellectual, or at least unverbalizable, the new history of meaning approaches them with fresh respect. And while such history obviously deals with the experience of people of all ranks and classes, it also 'does not exclude attention to the creation of meaning by elites; it leaves open the considerable possibility that this may be of the greatest interest'. Finally, the historian's interest in art as expressive and integrative behaviour points to cultural anthropology, which is 'centrally concerned with the construction and symbolic expression of meaning in every dimension of human activity'.[21] Bouwsma does not say that historians should adopt the method and techniques of anthropology (or of musicology, art history, or literary criticism). He does express the hope that anthropology itself will take on more of a historical dimension. The same hope, we have seen, has been voiced about ethnomusicology.

Two widely noticed books by historians that make use of music are adduced by Bouwsma: Lawrence W. Levine's *Black Culture and Black Consciousness: Afro-American Folk Thought from Slavery to Freedom* (1977), and Carl E. Schorske's *Fin-de-Siècle Vienna: Politics and Culture* (1980).* Dealing with Afro-American folksong and dance, Levine analyses words and meanings with even less reference to strictly musical considerations than Austin devotes to the popular music of Foster. Dealing with Viennese elite culture, on the other hand, Schorske in his final chapter 'Explosion in the Garden: Kokoschka and Schoenberg' discusses Schoenberg's music in some detail, in particular the first number of the Stefan George song cycle *Das Buch der haïgenden Gärten*. The music of 'Unterm Schutz von dichten Blättergründen' is included in his book – the musical text of the entire song – next to reproductions of a dozen paintings and graphics by Kokoschka (and one by Schoenberg).

The absence of printed music from Austin's book, I have suggested, hints at an intention to probe non-musical rather than musical contexts. Just as programmatically, the presence of music in Schorske's announces the author's determination to probe musical ones. Schoenberg has long been a private preserve for the royal hunters of the Princeton School, and it was a foregone conclusion that the music-theory establishment would wrinkle up its nose when Schorske put in for a provisional licence (just as it had done when Austin turned in his). But it would ill befit the 'cultural musicologist' of Chase's fantasy to seem in any way to patronize Schorske's work. In a rather wonderful way his discussion of Schoenberg – and of Kokoschka, Klimt, Schnitzler, Hofmannsthal, and the 'Ringstrasse' architects – distributes its energy equally between the socio-political context which is the nominal theme of Schorske's study, and the works of art themselves. It is quite impossible to say which side of the equation mainly moves or animates the author, or which mainly informs the reader. The study of behaviour and the study of 'music sound', in Merriam's formulation, flow into one another with exemplary smoothness.

'No relatively independent academic discipline can be expected to confine itself to the view of a thing *in a context* to the exclusion of the view of the thing *in itself*,' wrote Seeger.[22] But almost in his next breath he explicitly acknowledged that almost all individual scholars strongly favour one of these views over the other. Seeger himself never achieved an approximately even balance, and the same is true of most ethnomusicologists today and most musicologists. My own hesitation before contextual studies, expressed a number of times in this book, is founded on the impression that they are usually tilted much too far towards the consideration of contexts. They usually deal too little with the music as music. Schorske's reading of the Schoenberg song is neither complete nor ultra-sophisticated in a technical sense (and I seem to be coming close to patronizing him after all). But either by design or – as one rather suspects – inclination, he has achieved a rare balance of richness between consideration of art in its context and in itself. In this his work provides a significant model for musicologists, as for students of the other arts.

Finally, musicologists can read another message in Schorske's *Fin-de-Siècle Vienna* and in a few other books like it – another message to mull over, along with the multistranded one they are being sent by the ethnomusicologists. This is that if they, the musicologists, do not write the contextual history of Western art music, someone else will write it for them. That someone is less likely to be an ethnomusicologist than a historian.

Years ago, musicologists had a stock complaint about the history of ideas: that its practitioners of whatever persuasion and on whatever level, from Spengler and Lovejoy to M. H. Abrams and Wylie Sypher, would treat of philosophy, science, literature, the visual arts, fashion, sexual mores, and everything else but never of music. There was something both querulous and smug, but perhaps especially something safe, about this complaint. How long could such a situation be expected to survive the determined educational efforts of the musicologists, from the music-appreciation courses they have now taken charge of to their interdisciplinary graduate seminars – not to speak of the barrage of music of all eras, kinds, and climes on radio and records? How long, in particular, could it be expected to survive the changing complexion – Bouwsma's 'mutation' – of the history of ideas itself?

In the famous 'Overture' to *The Raw and the Cooked*, as Gilbert Chase reminds us, Lévi-Strauss singled out music and myth as the two most promising areas for the structural analysis of cultures. Having so pronounced, Lévi-Strauss wrote his wrong-headed account of Ravel's *Bolero*. Otherwise he has all but completely ignored music – actual music, as distinct from ideas about it – and one can sympathize with the frustration of ethnomusicologists as they struggle to make themselves heard in the seemingly tone-deaf conclaves and enclaves of anthropology. Historians, I believe, will be more receptive to overtures by musicologists. There are new opportunities today for initiatives in 'cultural musicology', though these may take a course different from that which Chase anticipated.

6. The Historical Performance Movement

A musicologist and veteran director of ensembles specializing in music of the sixteenth and seventeenth centuries, Denis Stevens, has distilled the experience of his career in a book called *Musicology: a Practical Guide* (1980).[1] The bulk and heart of the book consists of a large section on 'Applied Musicology'; introduced by a chapter on 'The Presence of Early Music' – its emphatic presence in today's concert life, which Stevens simply accepts as a donnée – this section goes on to several 'how-to' chapters on ornamentation in early music, instrumentation, vocal tone colour, and the like. There is practically no other matter in the book.

This thoroughly blinkered view of the topic would have made even Thurston Dart blush. One would never learn from Stevens – who has also written numerous articles and books on medieval English polyphony, Monteverdi, and other subjects – that musicology is seriously implicated with the history of music, that history has merit in itself, or that history has anything to do with criticism. Yet there is something seductive, too, about this vision of the applicability of scholarship to the non-scholarly world. Probably more than a few musicologists have greeted this self-announced 'practical guide' to their discipline with a twinge of instinctive sympathy. As for people outside the discipline, the only reason most of them pay musicology any heed at all is because it unearths music they can hear in concerts and on records.

It is worth considering for a moment – the question is not entirely whimsical – whether Stevens could have written anything analogous about 'applied theory' or 'applied ethnomusicology'. In previous chapters we have tried to see how musical intellectuals construe music: music they have heard and played and grown up with, or reconstructed from historical documents, or travelled to distant lands to observe, or – when they are composer-theorists – actually willed into existence. What have they offered in return to the 'practical' world of music, the world of music performed, heard, and recorded?

The clearest answer, of course, comes from avant-garde theory. Its contribution to the repertory is avant-garde music, and from the Second World War at least until the 1970s, avant-garde music stood out as the most prestigious link between the not-so-ivory tower and the marketplace. The contribution of tonal theory to the repertory is zero; as was remarked above, the analysts' gaze is riveted on the canon of accepted masterpieces, masterpieces that have long been and still are played regularly (too regularly, in some cases). Surprisingly or not, tonal theorists are almost totally silent on the subject of musical performance; having no coherent theory in this area, they do not even offer an explicit performance model for music already in the repertory. One can discern, however, an implicit one. While this is commonly regarded as diametrically opposed to the model upheld by the musicologists, we shall see that common ground can be found for both.

Ethnomusicology stands programmatically aloof from the various repertories of Western art music, even when it does not harbour a positive animus against them. While many Western composers have been struck by non-Western musical ideas and have incorporated them in their work, the impact of non-Western music on concert life here has not been significant, Mantle Hood's confident assertions about the bimusicality of Western man to the contrary notwithstanding. Indeed, such energies as ethnomusicologists expend on repertories tend to be expended abroad, where some strong efforts have been made to preserve native traditions in the face of Western acculturation. Students of popular music, whom I have associated with ethnomusicologists, are more ambivalent about interfering with musical traditions as these are buffeted by the forces of social change. The jazz specialists who issued record anthologies such as *The Smithsonian Collection of Early Jazz* and the Rutgers University Institute of Jazz Studies *Archive Collection* cannot have done so without some qualms, qualms that by freezing this repertory they were falsifying a tradition whose essence is not history but contemporaneity, not stability but flux.

Musicology, on the other hand, has a whole long catalogue of music to contribute to the repertory and a definite theory as to how it should be performed. The catalogue consists mostly of 'early music' – early by comparison with that of the so-called standard repertory – but also includes later works (such as Rossini's *Semiramide* and Berlioz's *Béatrice et Bénédict*) which never got into the repertory or else dropped out. All this music, according to musicological doctrine, should be presented – as far as this is possible – according to the reconstructed performing traditions and conditions of its own time and place.

And in the postwar period the performance of early music, like that of avant-garde music, has been a vital and innovative thing. By comparison, the situation in 'traditional' music has been relatively stagnant, except for an occasional figure such as Glenn Gould or Pierre Boulez or Maria Callas (who was in any case a sort of historical performer, in her own way). This is another unhappy but unsurprising result of the impasse caused by modernism. It is easy to say that each new generation will bring something new to a closed repertory of great works whose meaning can never be exhausted. In fact, the dwindling number of really interesting new pianists, violinists, conductors, and singers for these works has now become a familiar subject of lament. Some of the irritation that historical performance often seems to excite can doubtless be laid to the frustrations inherent in this situation.

In any case, historical performance has served and still serves as a lightning-rod for discharges of high tension between musicologists and other musicians. It is when actual pieces of music are taken off the shelf and played or sung that voltage begins to shoot up and conflicting currents can be most clearly measured. Musicologists sometimes like to take credit for the amount of old music that is to be heard nowadays. They regularly take the rap for the alleged low quality of much of that music. They are blamed especially for the alleged low standard and style of its execution.

Neither the blame nor the credit are fully deserved, I think. For though it may seem paradoxical, the relationship between musicology and the historical performance movement is somewhat tenuous and sometimes thorny. Arnold Dolmetsch, the great turn-of-the-century pioneer, set the tone when he distanced himself from the musicologists of his own day and grumbled incessantly about the way *they* distanced themselves from actual music. Such complaints are still common in 'early music' circles today. There are some typical masochistic barbs in Stevens's *Musicology*.

Musicologists may protest that they are deeply committed to performance, and of course in a way they are. Any scholarly edition of music is an invitation to a performer, and musicologists have been known to press such invitations quite hard, lobbying, consulting, and masterminding early-music concerts when they are given a chance. Stevens was a producer for the BBC Third Programme of the early 1950s. But getting music performed according to reconstructed historical traditions is a different, more specialized matter: it presupposes research into the instruments and performing practice of past eras. And research of this kind has traditionally occupied only one small corner of the field. While many musicologists dabble in historical performance, only a few concentrate on it as a field of study, and of those that do, one cannot point to many in recent years whose work has projected them into the front ranks of the discipline. Figures such as Thurston Dart in Britain and Howard Mayer Brown in the United States are exceptional.

Thus while musicologists may claim with some justice that it is their ideology that sustains the historical performance movement, they cannot enter the same claim as far as its actual development is concerned. The key figures in the movement are historically minded performers. All of them dabble in musicology (just as many musicologists dabble in historical performance) and some of them do a good deal better than that.

But while harpsichordists and conductors can sometimes write important research studies they cannot, obviously, sustain such activity if they are to maintain their careers in front of the footlights and the record-studio microphones. The extraordinary example of Dart, who methodically divided his life into five-year periods devoted alternately to playing and researching, has not found imitators. Historically minded instrument-makers are also important – though today only a few of them aspire to virtuosity on the instruments they build, as Dolmetsch did. They work closely with expert players, and indeed there are cases of collaborations of another kind, that between a musicologist and a performer or performing group, in which the former assumes a role something like that of the *Dramaturg* in German theatrical and operatic productions.

Craftsmen, artists, scholars, and various hybrids of the three, all closely dependent on each other despite frequent crises of mutual distrust, make up the restless world of 'early music' – a world with more than its fair share, one is sometimes given to feel, of enthusiasts and ideologues, gurus and groupies, dilettantes and cranks. Despite this, it is impossible to escape the conviction that the strength of the historical performance movement stems directly from the rich, varied, and sometimes spiky compost that is produced when all these types are thrown together and left to warm in music's glow. And there seems to be no doubt that the movement is going from strength to strength.

2

The history of the historical performance movement in music has not yet been written: which seems strange, incidentally, for the field offers an attractive topic for anyone interested in contemporary arts and ideas. This is not the place to write that history or even to sketch it.[2] I shall try only to suggest how the movement has evolved since the 1950s in relation to the changing course of musicology.

Musicologists seek to reconstruct and understand the music of the past. We have already heard at some length about the reluctance of postwar scholars to move past the reconstruction stage, their inclination to stay with limited positivistic tasks and to shirk interpretation. It is perhaps worth spelling out, then, how the investigation of performing practice of the past fits into a theoretical model for positivistic musicology.

The editing of critical texts, we remember, was one of the main accomplishments credited to American musicology of the 1950s. Like the philologist, the musicologist labours to establish the texts of old music. But unlike literature, music consists of much more than texts – or to put it another way, a text is a much less complete record of a work of art in music than it is in literature. After arriving at a critical text, therefore, a second step is logically necessary in the reconstruction process. The musicologist must establish or try to establish all those features of the music that conventional musical notation leaves out.

Among these are absolute pitch level and the tuning of scales, tempo and various aspects of rhythm, local ornaments such as trills and mordents, the large-scale embellishment of long melodies, cadenzas, and the like. In medieval and Renaissance music there is the problem of supplying *musica ficta* – sharps and flats that are not notated, but left for musicians to provide on the spot according to somewhat obscure rules of thumb. In Baroque music, where that problem is largely though not entirely obsolete, there is the one of filling out the unnotated background part for the harpsichord, organ, or other continuo instrument.

A third step, also logically necessary, consists of research into the instruments by means of which all this notated and unnotated music was transformed into sound. Some of these instruments do not survive outside of museums – examples are the crwth, the pommer, and the viola bastarda – while others survive in forms that are very different from what they once were, as the result of radical technical evolutions. Such are the violin and the piano. One has to determine which instruments are to be used and in what combinations for particular works or repertories (for this is by no means always specified) and investigate their actual physical constitution – the material and the manufacture – in order to estimate how this influenced their tone quality. Then one has to approximate the techniques by which they were bowed, blown, or fingered. The hope is to go beyond tone quality itself, and to gain some insight into the means of articulation and nuance that were both natural to particular historical instruments and were also in use at a particular historical time.

Several observations come to mind in connection with this three-step programme. The first addresses its feasibility. As the verbs in the above paragraph suggest, the success with which the chain of investigations can be carried out varies from stage to stage and, just as importantly, from era to era. Even the certainty of establishing a critical text dwindles alarmingly as we go back in time, and in fields of research such as improvisatory practice and the playing of long-obsolete instruments, the results are obviously more uncertain yet. The most intrepid of researchers might be baffled by the problem of how to reconstruct medieval singing (though some ingenious ones have come up with some suggestive ideas on the basis of field work among singers of non-Western music). It is not my wish to minimize the amount that can be found out about historical performing practice; rather the reverse. But it is well to get clear that knowledge of any one aspect of it can seldom be secure, and that there will always be gaps in the total picture.

We shall return to the obvious implications of this later. For now it may be worth mentioning that it also helps explain the mild paradox touched on above, the paradox that although historical performance is central to the ideology of musicology, musicologists have been slow to turn their research activities in this direction. Let us not speak of reasons of personal predilection or capability – predilections for criticism or cultural history over performance as areas of inquiry, for example, or capabilities below the really expert level of practical musicianship required for almost any research in performing practice. A more general reason is that musicologists traditionally prefer to work in areas where the results seem less speculative. Given the choice between preparing an edition of Josquin's Masses and determining how they were sung, a musicologist will opt instinctively for the former undertaking. The three-step programme outlined above, then, is a theoretical model rather than a picture of the discipline as it is actually practised. Furthermore, so long as musicology was constricted by the positivistic viewpoint, it distorted the study of performing practice in two ways. On the one hand, when positivistic musicologists did work in this field, they shied away from the less certain areas of research within it, even when their importance was patent. On the other hand, they tended to behave much too dogmatically about such results as they were able to obtain in more certain areas.

A second observation is by way of response to what is probably the commonest objection to the whole idea of historical performance. This addresses not the feasibility of the idea but its value. What is the good of all this attempted reconstruction? Why is it worth reconstructing historical conditions when old music is heard by modern listeners with ears attuned to the sonorities of the nineteenth century, and with minds locked into the sensibilities of the twentieth?

The thing to grasp about this objection is that its terms apply equally well to the scores of old music as to its manner of execution. For the strict 'modernist', Beethoven should presumably be heard (if at all) only as rewritten by Stockhausen or George Rochberg. Even Adorno, who in his famous article 'Bach Defended against his Devotees'[3] recommended the Bach transcriptions of Schoenberg and Webern, did not go that far — though he might have, who knows, if his ideological orbit had extended to *Pulcinella* and *Le Baiser de la fée*. But *pace* Stravinsky, the 'modernist' sensibility evidently favours hearing just the notes the original composer wrote, no more no less, just as it prefers seeing the painting without layers of yellow varnish, reading the poet's unbowdlerized text, and so on.

If musicologists are asked to reconstruct the scores of old music, it is hard to see why they should stop at that stage and not proceed to the other two outlined above. If there are putative contemporary values in hearing Handel's Concerto Grosso in B flat with Handel's notes rather than with the extra ones added in Schoenberg's transcription, there should also be putative values in hearing the piece played with Handel's ornaments and embellishments on Baroque string instruments and harpsichord. To think otherwise is to place mistaken emphasis on the bare score itself at the expense of the total experience of music. Theorists and analysts often do make this very mistake, to be sure. We shall come back to their problems with historical performance a little later.

Once we have started talking about values we find ourselves in deepish waters, which musicologists in particular find difficult to navigate. A third observation about their three-step programme may help us keep our bearings. This is that strictly speaking, the entire programme can exist on a level prior to that of interpretation. Establishing a critical text can be done with a minimum of historical or critical interpretation, and likewise research into historical performing practice can go forward with little if any attention to musical interpretation – to what is really meant by 'interpretation', I think, when musicians talk about the way they perform pieces in the standard repertory. When we speak of a certain conductor's interpretation of a Mahler symphony, it is not the right instruments and balances of instruments that we mean, nor the correct notes and the treatment of acciaccaturas. Musicians deal with such matters in ways which are certainly not identical but which fall within a broadly accepted, reasonably narrow range of variation. What we mean by a conductor's interpretation is something less easily analysed: it is the way he brings his own musical personality to bear on the symphony in order to bring out its substance, content, or meaning. Better, it is what he makes – interprets – of the symphony's meaning. It has often been observed that musical interpretation in this sense can be regarded as a form of criticism.[4] Some observers regard it as, in music, the highest form of criticism.

The stereotype of the 'intellectually disreputable' interpreter who exploits music as a vehicle to express his own personality – the sobriquet is Charles Rosen's – should not be used to discredit interpretation: though we may as well admit that he or she is not always easy to distinguish from more reputable colleagues. We may also admit that both musical 'personality' and also that other category of which musicians are so tender, intuition, are always heavily constrained by the norms of a performing tradition (not to speak of the brainwashing applied by some particular teacher). Nevertheless, they do exist, and within a tradition they are the precious qualities that distinguish one performance from another, in a way that Walter Benjamin's 'mechanical reproduction' of a work of art – or that a recording – does not. There is always at least some personal element in interpretation; interpretation is an individual, even an idiosyncratic matter. Historical performing practice, on the other hand, is by its very nature normative.

3

I do not think that I am forcing the meaning of 'interpretation' as applied to musical performance, but I am attempting to limit it, for it seems to me that the appropriation of this term by the historical performance movement – an appropriation of long standing, to be sure – has caused much confusion. Thurston Dart's harpsichord playing was idiosyncratic, too, as much so as anyone's conducting of Mahler. But the mischievous implication of his influential book *The Interpretation of Music* of 1954 (so called even though it was all about *early* music) was that interpretation is a normative matter, not an individual one. The only advice Dart offered to musicians was that their work be 'idiomatic' – that is, well suited to their instrument – and 'stylish', by which he meant not 'smart' or 'polished' but simply 'in style', in historical style.

This mischief seems to have been deliberate. Dart's famous predecessor as a writer of tracts about historical performance (and as an appropriator of the term 'interpretation') was Arnold Dolmetsch, and Dolmetsch in his *The Interpretation of Music of the 17th and 18th Centuries* of 1915 had laid out his priorities differently.* His first chapter was on 'Expression', and here Dolmetsch said straight away that 'The student should try and prepare his mind by thoroughly understanding what the Old Masters *felt* about their own music, what impressions they wished to convey, what was the *Spirit of their Art*' (p. xiii). Feeling, impression, spirit – these were categories which (like substance, content, and meaning) would not do at all in the positivistic 1950s. Dolmetsch had tried to support his discussion of expression with citations from several old texts, among them an unusually revealing preface written by Girolamo Frescobaldi in 1615 to an edition of his keyboard music. Dart cited this same preface, but he cited it simply in order to make some technical points about musical notation.

What Dart called 'stylish' everybody else at the time called 'authentic', a baleful term which has caused endless acrimony – understandably enough, for the word resonates with unearned good vibrations forced by moralists such as Benjamin and Sartre, as well as by those art connoisseurs who evoke it to confound forgery. 'Contextual' would have been a value-free substitute. But 'authentic' has now acquired the same cult value when applied to music as 'natural' or 'organic' when applied to food. Whatever we call it – historical, stylish, authentic, contextual – such playing can obviously be good, bad or indifferent: good or bad in at least two senses, technically and interpretatively. The criteria of authenticity and virtue were bound to become confused when conductors, players, and singers began to see that appeals to authenticity (rather than personal intuition, as in the old Romantic days) might be used to defend bad performances; and when musicologists claimed or at least implied that authenticity would guarantee good ones. For Dart was not the only musicologist in the 1950s to slight interpretation, though he may have done more than any other individual to confuse this whole issue.

Authenticity is no guarantee of a good performance, certainly. But does the reverse hold: can there be such a thing as a good one under conditions of, say, gross inauthenticity? Such conditions were met with much more frequently in the 1950s than they are today – a measure of the gathering strength of the historical performance movement. Those deathly slow caricatures of the Mass in B minor sung by massed church choirs, bosomy contraltos and bumbling basses accompanied by the town orchestra without continuo – one does not have to be much of a purist to rule them out of consideration. But one would indeed have to be a purist, and a rather stiff one, to dismiss Janet Baker's singing of *Dido and Aeneas* or Horowitz's playing of Scarlatti sonatas as, if not unidiomatic, unstylish. This goes to show how limiting Dart's terms were and, once again, how wrong he was to slight interpretation – the process by which a unique musical personality works on music in order to bring out its substance, content, or meaning. Performance, as has been remarked above, can be regarded as a form of criticism. One can admire an artist's interpretation, as one can admire a critic's, for such qualities as its brilliance, integrity, distinction, and coherence, even when one is convinced it is rather far wide of the mark.

Better to be brilliant and coherent and less wide of the mark. Authenticity should not be valued in itself, only in the service of the ever-better interpretation of music. This rather simple principle has always animated serious historical performers, even those of the 1950s, whose efforts seem to be remembered today with so surprisingly little affection. 'Barbaric gropings', they are called by one modern critic, who is a historical performer himself:

This was a period of the 'sewing machine' style, sometimes called the 'Vivaldi revival', when German chamber orchestras enthusiastically took up 'terraced dynamics', when historically-minded conductors urged players to stop 'phrasing' and when repeat signs in the music occasioned a blaze of preposterous embellishments. 'Motoric rhythms', it seemed, revealed a new species of musical gratification – the freedom from feeling.[5]

That such playing existed is a matter of record (long-playing record) and no doubt it was fostered by positivistic musicology.

But the influence of musicology in the historical performance movement has been exaggerated; its *de facto* leaders were not musicologists, as we have seen, but performers, who were doing their best by the music that moved them. There were many fine players of the 1950s (including Dart) on whose surviving records one can hear ample evidence of rhythmic flexibility, dynamic variety, unobtrusive ornamentation, freedom, and feeling.

Also exaggerated is the contrast between the supposed scholarly reserve of historical performers and the self-indulgent Romantic licence of traditional ones. We shall return to this point later. There are warm and cool personalities in both categories. One would scarcely call Alfred Deller a less emotional artist than Kirsten Flagstad.

4

A parenthesis: when speaking above about the contributions of musicology to today's repertories of performed music, I remarked that these included a whole catalogue of music – mostly early music – as well as a definite theory as to how it should be performed. It often seems as though the first of these donations is forgotten in the heat of arguments about the second. Those who remember the 'early music' scene of the 1950s remember it as gratefully, I think, for the unknown music it introduced as for the revelations it provided of new-old ways of performing by which known and unknown music could take on unexpected meaning. The catalogue included some extraordinary (as well as much ordinary) goods. Even for the hostile, authenticity would seem a small price to pay for a first chance to hear works such as, for example, Monteverdi's *L'Incoronazione di Poppea*. No version of this opera, I expect, will ever move me as much as Walter Goehr's original 1953 recording, though Raymond Leppard's later version was both more authentic and more beautiful, Nikolaus von Harnoncourt's more so than Leppard's, and Alan Curtis's more than Harnoncourt's.[6]

It is a mistake, in any case, to imagine that historical perform-ance in the 1950s was paralysed by the spectre of authenticity. Noah Greenberg could never have called the original New York Pro Musica Antiqua production of *The Play of Daniel* authentic, when the music was interspersed with a running commentary in English alliterative verse written and spoken by W. H. Auden clad, if memory serves, in a cassock. Musically and visually, as well as textually, *Daniel* was a characteristically ambivalent product of the twentieth-century sensibility playing upon the past. A few years earlier, in *The Rake's Progress*, Auden had engaged with a different, greater collaborator in a not altogether different sort of exercise.

5

Continuity in the Western tradition of art music can be traced back to around 1800: to a time when, as we have seen, the works of Haydn, Mozart, and Beethoven were perceived as masterpieces in a new way, and as masterpieces that had to be preserved in the permanent repertory. This repertory was added to, generation by generation; whole generations of works were not taken out. Presumably there has been some kind of corresponding continuity in the performing tradition of all this music, though we will be well advised not to overestimate its extent. Nineteenth-century musicians also reached back to the Baroque period and appropriated the music of Bach and Handel. They did not make the attempt to reconstruct its performing traditions. As in our century that attempt has been made, it has naturally required or stimulated much research, the writing of books and papers, declarations of doctrine, and polemics of which no end can as yet be glimpsed.

It is therefore not surprising that so much more seems to be written about musical performance from a historical standpoint than from any other. Musicians who work within the 'living' tradition do not need to write – or talk – about music; they are the doers, not the talkers, and so one has to say they have every right to view musicology, theory, or any other kind of intellection about music with a certain detachment. (That detachment may range anywhere from mild dilettantish curiosity to outright derision.) A musical tradition does not maintain its 'life' or continuity by means of books and book-learning. It is transmitted at private lessons not so much by words as by body language, and not so much by precept as by example. Only exceptionally is this process broadcast into a semi-public arena, usually in a not very satisfactory form, at master classes where voyeurs and auditeurs strain to catch something of the intercourse between master and pupil. The arcane sign-gesture-and-grunt system by which professionals communicate about interpretation at rehearsals is even less reducible to words or writing. It is not that there is any lack of thought about performance on the part of musicians in the central tradition, then. There is a great deal, but it is not thought of a kind that is readily articulated in words.

Though not for lack of trying. Books written (or dictated) by performers are a very mixed bag, ranging from the anecdotal to the metaphysical; all, however, include some material, on some level, about real issues of performance. This material is seldom very illuminating – though one sometimes feels that illumination is just around the corner, just as far as the gramophone. Reading books by the great artists is not the best way to gain understanding of their artistic secrets.

Reading the best of these books, written by some who are among the most distinguished in their fields and also among the most thoughtful, one finds the authors returning again and again to the problem of interpretation, as I have tried to formulate it: the way in which the musician's individuality is to be brought to bear on the individuality of works of art. Therefore discussion of performance tends to fuse with discussion of music itself in the most thoughtful of these books, such as those of Alfred Brendel and Erich Leinsdorf in recent years (years which have not yielded up much in this genre), and of Schnabel, Szigeti, Walter, and Scherchen in earlier times. What are the respective roles in the musical experience of the creative and executive faculties? Does the musician have some 'responsibility' to the composer or to the score? What is the ethical status of that responsibility, and what is the ontological status of the score? How does the performer's own individuality enter in? One reads with admiration, sympathy, and sometimes even anguish of the efforts of musicians to reconcile in their minds these seeming irreconcilables. And one turns to their recordings to grasp how the resolutions are actually made.

Musical theory is almost silent on the subject of musical performance. Is this despite, or because of, the sense of solidarity so many theorists and analysts profess and clearly feel with the performer's position? Routinely chided for their private aversion to that position, at least the musicologists have a public theory that gives performance a central place. In the absence of anything analogous on the part of the theorists, one may be forgiven for wondering whether for some of them the actual sound of a piece is simply a surface nuisance, a sort of *Vor-vordergrund* to be got past as soon as possible in the search for deep backgrounds and rich middles. The whole thrust of the ideology of theory and analysis is to focus the attention of its practitioners on the single score that happens to be in front of them, as though the notes in that score existed outside of any wider context. For Jeffrey Kresky, as was remarked in Chapter 3, this anticontextualism is so ingrained that he can write about a Wagner opera excerpt without so much as mentioning the words (composed, like the music, by Wagner). There is nothing in Kresky's book about performance, either.

Almost the only modern theorist who keeps performance firmly in mind whenever he writes is Edward Cone, and the reason for this welcome anomaly is that he is an anomalous theorist: on an admittedly shifting scale of categorization (which anyhow he himself would not accept), Cone is less a theorist than an analyst and less an analyst than a critic. In any case, in his influential and notably humane little book *Musical Form and Musical Performance* (1968)* Cone took it on himself to expound what one suspects to be the tacit position of most analysts, namely that the principal function of performance is to articulate relationships that are brought out by analysis. He did this, it is true, with considerable circumspection, adding to the publication of his three lectures on this topic an 'optional post-lude' which presents a much wider view of musical aesthetics (but does not focus it very sharply in terms of actual musical performance). I wish Cone had made it clearer that the analysts' position represents a drastic simplification of the problem of interpretation as performers themselves see it. Their role is to bring out the 'content' of the music before them, but for the analysts that content is limited to the music's structure; therefore interpretation comes down to the articulation of musical struc-ture. And the mechanism by which this takes place is usually not considered to be within the sphere of the theorist's speculation.

In one of his major essays, 'Analysis Today', Cone wrote that the analyst's insights 'reveal how a piece should be heard, which in turn implies how it should be played. An analysis is a direction for performance.'[7] In *Musical Form and Musical Performance*, he proposes, to begin with, that since a central element of musical form is the weighting of cadences, the pianist playing Mozart and Chopin should emphasize distinctions in the weight of cadences (over and above, that is, their inherent distinctions as written in by the composers). He also says something about the technical means by which this is to be accomplished, though as compared to his careful discussion of analytical subtleties, his remarks about performance nuance seem hasty and uncharac-teristically vague. One reason for this may be his reluctance to seem to 'freeze' interpretation; for while Cone sees analysis as a direction for a performance, he is at pains to stress that there can be no single, ideal analysis and hence no single, ideal interpre-tation. And another reason may be that in addition to all the other things listed above, Cone is a pianist, and his deepest instincts as a performer warn him away from prose as a medium for communicating thought about interpretation.

Schenker, incidentally, whose views on so many matters were so much more extreme than anyone else's, also took an extremist line about musical performance. For him, the performance of a masterwork – and he dealt only with masterworks – was an objective and inevitable result of its structure. Indeed performance directions are fundamentally superfluous, since the composition itself expresses everything that is necessary. . . . Performance must come from within the work; the work must breathe from its own lungs – from the linear progressions, neighbouring tones, chromatic tones, modulations. . . . About these, naturally, there cannot exist different interpretations [*Auffassungen*].[8]

Schenker, then, would have rewritten Cone's 'an analysis is a direction for a performance' as 'my analysis is the direction for the only possible performance'. 'Keine "*Auffassungen*"!' he cries in his unpublished *Entwurf einer Lehre von Vortrag*. Yet elsewhere he spelled out in detail (though he did not publish) his ideas as to how the performer must realize those nuances which the work's structure uniquely, though obscurely, specifies. This is not the only contradiction to be found in Schenker's views and speculations about performance: the views, once again, of a deeply committed performer.

6

It may seem unfair to criticize Dart and other musicologists' treatment of the problem of interpretation when no one – no performer, no theorist – has been able to proceed with it very far. But the problem is a central one for all who attempt to deal with musical performance, and musicologists among this company err not in failing to solve it but in trying to give the impression it does not exist. To slight questions which are not, by their very nature, open to positive answers – that is the typical positivist ploy. Musicologists are traditionally distrustful of the personal, intuitive aspect of interpretation, the legendary abuses of which by no means died out with the generation of de Pachmann. The idea that the performer should use music as a vehicle to express his own personality may indeed be 'intellectually disreputable' today, as Rosen said; but Rosen's refusal to 'beat a dead horse, even one whose ghost still walks' made his walloping of historical performers in the same article seem cruel and unusual.[9] The trouble with musicologists, on the other hand, is that they are, or were, too ready to extrapolate their antipathy towards this cantering ghost into a basic distrust of the musician's intuition in general.

Not all musicologists, however. In 1980 a musicologist of the younger generation who is active as a historical performer came out with a ringing defence of 'imaginative response, empathetic identification, artistic insight – all euphemisms, of course, for intuition'.* Indeed intuition is essential for the re-creation of a historical performance style, Richard Taruskin claimed, for musicological research cannot provide this by itself. If, as we have said, objective knowledge of any one element of historical performing practice can seldom be very secure, and there will always be gaps in the total picture, something must fill in the gaps if the performance is to carry any conviction. Significantly, Taruskin spoke of 're-creation' rather than 'reconstruction'. Whatever we say about a historical edition of music – and it is far from clear *what* we should say – a historical performance style cannot be an objectively antiquarian construct. It is a unique, difficult blend of old and new, a play of the contemporary creative sensibility upon the past.

An understanding of this, and an acceptance of the contingency it implies, is a new note which has been sounding for some time in musicological and 'applied musicological' circles. And while Taruskin's framework for his polemic was the time-honoured conflict between 'The Musicologist and the Performer', which disarmingly or not he projected as an interior dialogue in his own mind, the conflict evaporates when one sees his position as consonant with musicology according to the less positivistic, more comprehensive and humane definition which I have tried to develop above.

The problem of the performer's intuition is not one that worries the analysts (except perhaps for the posthumous Schenker). Where they err is in failing to see that even on their own terms, interpretative strategies are a function of a historical style or tradition. They fail to see this because their attention is riveted on a single repertory and the single performing tradition that goes with it (single though, of course, multilayered). The 'intuition' a performer brings to music can, I believe, be de-mystified at least to the extent of identifying two areas of its application. Although it may be hard to imagine musicians thinking of them separately, one area is their insight into the music they are addressing – a matter of criticism pure and simple, as I see it – and the other is their own personal amalgam of choices from the stock of interpretative techniques available to them in their own performing tradition.

Here is what you want to do, here is how you do it. To take the simplest possible example: for the purpose of stressing a particular note or chord (which would be part of the complex of actions required to weight one of Cone's structural downbeats) various technical means are at hand. The musician can employ more vibrato, less vibrato, more volume, less volume, delay the attack, anticipate it, separate the note off from its surroundings with a minuscule rest, and so on. All these means belong to a particular musical tradition – our own, so we are inclined to recognize no other. It is transmitted securely enough from generation to generation by example and imitation, so we see no pressing need to try to do the impossible and codify it in words. Nor is there much talk about the intuitive process of judgment by which musicians choose among these interpretative means, choose how much to use them, and how to combine them with others.

These techniques belong to today's performing tradition, today's current history. For music of the past – lost traditions – historical performers seek (among other things) analogous ways to articulate the structure of past music. The intuitive process of judgment remains – and must not be allowed to drain off into one of the many pools left by the ebbing tide of positivistic ideology, as Taruskin quite properly insists.[10] For the purpose of stressing a chord in Baroque music, more volume or less volume were not options open to harpsichordists. On the other hand, they had other means at their disposal, such as ornamentation, which have atrophied since. Some common ground might be found for the musicological and analytical positions if it could be

acknowledged, first, that structural articulation is a salient feature in the interpretation of all music, and second, that for this
purpose every age and even every instrument has its own combination of means.

It would certainly be a mistake, however, to suggest that the
activity of historical or any other performers should be limited
to the single area of structural articulation (even though this is
an important area, in my view, and one that has not been
enough stressed in the performing-practice literature). That
would be to take the analysts too much on their own terms.
Dolmetsch wrote of the feeling, impression, and spirit of music,
and he was right to do so. The intuition of the performer – the
performer as critic – is needed to play upon all this, not only
upon the music's structure. And the intuition of the performer
as technician is needed not only to project structure but also
sonority, mood, expression, display, conviction – the fact that
the terms get more and more nebulous does not mean that the
qualities they are attempting to approximate are less important
to the musical experience. Many people who strongly favour
'analytical' playing would walk out on a pianist who tried to
do nothing more than articulate structure in a Chopin or a
Debussy recital.

This is perhaps the place to make the obvious if delicate point
that not all musicians are good critics or interpreters. It may be
salutary from time to time to urge more reliance on personal
intuition, but it is also a little cruel, for intuition can let you
down, and not infrequently does (usually does, the truly
calloused concert-goer may be heard to mutter). It is also
obvious that the relative demands of, say, sonority and structure
on interpretation can differ from any particular body of music or
any individual piece to the next. And it is conflicting views or,
rather, convictions about such matters – differences about what
counts in music – that lead to differences about what counts in
performance. These, at any rate, are the only non-trivial
differences. The real issue is not historical performance at all,
but the nature of music.

This is why it is right, however tedious, that discussions of historical performance should always keep circling back to Bach. Musicians in general care as deeply about Bach's music as any other; they *know* they are attuned to its 'spirit' and consequently have strong feelings about its interpretation. Only specialists entertain such feelings about Dufay and Marenzio, Scarlatti and Rameau.

With this issue we finally touch bottom in the matter of differences about historical performance, differences animating polemics which are seldom conducted in such basic terms. Issues of this kind can only be resolved by criticism. They will be resolved well only by critics – writers or performers – who are alert to both historical and analytical considerations.

7

Taruskin's manifesto on 'The Musicologist and the Performer' perpetuates old-fashioned stereotypes of these two categories, as I have already suggested, but apart from that it can be taken as indicative of a new undogmatic spirit among historical performers of the 1970s and 1980s. Not all of them, I expect, will go along with everything he says; but at the very least, proclamations – and implications – about 'authenticity' are much rarer today than in the 1950s. Aims and claims are more modest and realistic, as appears from two representative statements of the 1970s from the pages of the influential journal *Early Music*.

In the first of these statements, the Baroque violinist Marie Leonhardt announces no more ambitious a hope than that of playing pieces 'in such a way that the composer, or a contemporary, would recognize them; at worst, without bewilderment, and at best, with pleasure'.[11] In the second statement Michael Morrow, then leader of one of the more robust ensembles for Renaissance and medieval music, Musica Reservata, observes that

Where there is no surviving tradition – and performing style is something that can only be learned by imitation, not from books – any piece of music, medieval, renaissance, baroque, what you will, offers the modern performer the potentiality of countless possibilities of interpretation. . . . [S]upposing a medieval or renaissance listener could hear a modern performance of a chanson by Binchois or a Dowland lute song solo, for instance, would he say (I use modern English of course) 'How can anyone ruin such fine music in this way?'; or would he exclaim 'What the hell is that? Some Moorish barbarity no doubt.'[12]

The positions taken are basically alike, despite the rather amusing differences of tone and emphasis in the way they are expressed. In the time-travel fantasies of these two musicians, one gathers, Morrow would be only too glad to settle for recognition, however derisive, while Leonhardt feels there is some chance she might be met with understanding and even pleasure. The difference stems, of course, from their different fields of activity – vocal music of the Middle Ages and Renaissance, and instrumental music of the eighteenth century, respectively. As far as the former repertory is concerned, research over several decades has revealed much but also made it clear how much can never be known. Research has produced a much more confident picture of music in the eighteenth century.

In eighteenth-century performance the most striking ideas have come out of the Netherlands. There the historical performance movement has been presided over since the 1950s by Gustav Leonhardt, Marie's husband. 'Austere' is the usual word for Leonhardt's keyboard playing, but what has made him such a remarkable force is his austere insistence on subtlety of interpretative detail. Under his general influence Dutch and Belgian string players, chief among them Wieland and Sigiswald Kuijken, have developed a distinctive style of playing by, in effect, taking the findings of musicologists seriously. A set of precepts laid out in eighteenth-century manuals had been known since the turn of the century, but until fairly recently players (and audiences) found them too radical to follow. Long and moderately long notes are begun quietly, increased in volume and then decreased again (*messa di voce*); passages of even notes in the score are played in a delicately irregular rhythm (*notes inégales*); vibrato is applied selectively, largely for purposes of emphasis; and the omnipresent ornaments are played lightly but at the same time with heightened expressive intent.

Most significant is the fact that this arsenal of interpretative techniques is employed in the service of a new – or, rather, an old – aesthetic of Baroque music. According to the frequently loquacious theorists of the time, music like oratory moves the passions by the application of stylized devices comparable to the figures of speech and topics of classical rhetoric. Historical performers have been trying to feel their way into the scale figures, arpeggios, appoggiaturas, dissonances, and other elements that were codified by those writers.

> There are now a number of musicians who . . . wish, as it were, to 'speak' in tones, to express passions, to move the audience. They know the principles behind the various styles. Their whole art diverges from what we used to hear: the type of utterance is quite different (fiery and uneven, rather than *sostenuto*); they no longer play a 'big line', the broader style being subordinated to rhetoric and affect.[13]

With its mercurial rhythms, affective dynamics, mannered phrasing, and exaggerated 'rhetorical' treatment of caesuras, such playing is not easy on the ears of traditional string players brought up to cultivate silky legato and singing tone. And it is no easier on the minds of analysts trained to conceive of a musical composition as a serene hierarchical structure, not a passionate network of small music-rhetorical figures.

Thurston Dart was as powerful a force for historical performance in Britain as Leonhardt was and is in Holland, though in a very different way. What he conveyed was not an ideal of a certain type of playing but simply the idea of 'applied musicology' – and this infectiously, to young musicians inter-

ested in all kinds of early music, as well as in that which Dart
made his own. Whereas Dart himself specialized in the English
virginalists, the French *clavecinistes*, and the orchestral music of
Bach, the most distinctive British work in historical performance
has probably been done in medieval and Renaissance music. It
seems fair to say this, even though in the early 1980s perhaps the
most impressive of all historical performance projects, the
Oiseau Lyre recording of all sixty-five Mozart symphonies on
old instruments, was mainly British in impetus and personnel
(with a musicological assist from an American, Neal Zaslaw).
The real distinction of the project was due to the remarkable
Belgian violinist Jaap Schröder, who as leader or concertmaster
'directed' – he did not conduct – the orchestra, Christopher
Hogwood's Academy of Ancient Music.

As is so often the case in Britain, ideology counts for less than
tradition, and historical performance stands in a somewhat
ambivalent relation to the strong native tradition of choral
singing. The choral foundations of Oxford and Cambridge, for
example, have supplied many early-music singers and even some
entire ensembles. Yet no doubt on account of the very strength
of that tradition, all the British a-cappella choirs that I have
heard have sounded conservative; this is true even when they
cultivate distinctive performance ideals, such as the unusually
high pitch upheld by the maverick musicologist David Wulstan,
director of The Clerkes of Oxenford (a choir which incidentally
grew directly out of Magdalen College, Oxford). Madrigal
groups – madrigal singing is out of fashion nowadays, in any
case – have offered nothing seriously new in the way of either
sonority or interpretation.

So the journal *Early Music*, which was founded after Dart's
death at least partly, it seems, in order to stake the claim for
Britain as against the Netherlands in historical performance, was
half right to lay such stress on instrument-making, instrumental
music, and the playing of antique instruments. Among English
ensembles of the 1970s, those combining voices and instruments
were the most interesting and adventurous. (Also, no doubt, the
most readily marketable in concerts and on records.) Both

Morrow's Musica Reservata and the Early Music Consort of London, in its brief career under David Munrow, provided a welcome note of vigour – even roughness – where daintiness, blandness, faintness, and wan melancholy had long held sway. Much is speculated about singing without vibrato, or with vibrato of a very different kind than is heard in the modern opera house (or, for that matter, the modern Oxbridge chapel). Such singing can be heard in non-Western musical traditions, but in the performance of Western music only Morrow's lead singer Jantina Noorman – Dutch by birth, American by training – seemed able to carry it off in a convincing fashion.

Her inspired screeching, one suspects, is the way the performance of older music has to go – not the way of such expert but suspiciously mellifluous groups as Pro Cantione Antiqua, made up exclusively of men's voices from bass to countertenor. (Since the time of Deller, countertenors have been a British speciality, though some impressive ones have also emerged in the United States – and Belgium. Just as Lecce in the heel of Italy once exported castrati to the opera houses of all Europe, so London now jets countertenors to her recording studios.) Emma Kirkby, whose subtle work with Anthony Rooley's Consort of Musicke *inter alia* dates from the late 1970s, cultivates a less radically aberrant yet still highly distinctive vocal sonority, one that seems to simulate aspects of countertenor quality. We have yet to hear, however, choruses of Kirkbys.

A word, only, about historical performance in the United States, where the situation must be granted to be at best disorganized. Since the 1950s, no individual musician or ensemble has made anything like the impact Noah Greenberg did with the New York Pro Musica Antiqua at that time. (Greenberg's most important predecessor, Arthur Mendel and his Cantata Singers, we have mentioned in passing in an earlier chapter.) The United States lacks that strong radio and recording support which it is not too much to say has kept historical performance alive in Holland, Britain, and of course especially Germany. Hence Americans have made their careers abroad – as is true of many 'traditional' performers also. A medieval-music group that many would rank above Morrow's or Munrow's was settled by Thomas Binkley at Munich; the Early Music Quartet became the Studio der frühen Musik. Alan Curtis and Shirley Wynne produce operas and ballets by Monteverdi, Cesti, Rameau, and Jommelli at festivals and opera houses in Europe. On the other hand, every other college in the country has its resident historical performance group or 'collegium musicum' (to flaunt one of the last and silliest of Latinisms still left in American academic jargon). They do a lot of good; both Noorman and Binkley came out of George Hunter's Collegium at the University of Illinois. But they do more good in disseminating early music than in establishing high standards of execution, as a rule, since the directors are necessarily committed to student musicians, with their inherent limitations.

It has been clear for some time that in tolerating relaxed standards – of instrumental and vocal technique, but more particularly of interpretation – the historical performance movement has been its own worst enemy. This is an international problem, not necessarily more severe in the United States than anywhere else. For the general raising of standards, extra-academic music institutions are a necessity. Therefore the establishment of the Aston Magna Academy and annual summer festivals in 1972 was a welcome development, even though a dozen years later it is still too early to gauge their impact on the musical life of the country beyond Great Barrington, Mass. Their activities are confined, in any case, to music of the seventeenth and eighteenth centuries.

8

Unbewildered recognition: this criterion of Gustav and Marie Leonhardt's would seem to have much to recommend it over *authenticity* for use in discussions of historical performance. Unlike 'authenticity', 'recognition' would be less likely to be confused with virtue, since we can envisage bad performances being 'recognized', in this sense, as readily as good ones. ('*La conosco pur troppo*,' says Leporello.) And as for those good ones, it now seems to be accepted frankly and gladly that they depend on largely intuitive factors such as taste – that *bon goût* which is constantly invoked by old writers – imagination, and sensitivity of interpretation. Beyond this, however, the musicologist will not be prepared to go. The solipsistic modernist who asks 'Why play or sing it *now* in a way that would have been recognized *then*?' may or may not be forcing an issue of some philosophical moment, but it is not one that can reasonably be expected to get much of a hearing from people who spend their lives trying to understand music of the past.

Those who try to understand music of the not-so-distant past, too, have something to learn from its performing traditions. Such is the conviction underlying the extension of the historical performance movement to cover music of the late eighteenth and nineteenth centuries. This is a relatively new development whose significance, perhaps, has still not been sufficiently appreciated.

If the harpsichord can stand as an apt symbol for historical performance in the 1950s, focused as it was on music of the Baroque period, the corresponding symbol for the 1980s is the 'Mozart piano' or fortepiano, with its wooden frame, relatively light stringing, shallow touch, simple action, and thin, clear, varied tone. Paul Badura-Skoda is one who has lived through this development. In 1957, when the thirty-year-old pianist and his musicologist wife Eva wrote an admirable book on Mozart interpretation, centred on the playing of Mozart's piano concertos, they came out squarely against playing these works on contemporaneous instruments.* Instead they did their best to suggest how the modern piano could be made to simulate the sound of the old. But over the next twenty years they changed their minds. Today Badura-Skoda is one of the leading players of Mozart, Beethoven, and Schubert on the Walter, Schantz, Broadwood, and Graf fortepianos known to those composers.

The parallel between the extension of historical performance into the nineteenth century and the similar extension of musicology will not have escaped the reader. While the latter extension did not lead directly to the former, both, I believe, can be regarded as symptoms of the same general broadening of horizons. As early as the mid-1960s Treitler was insisting that musicology is not characterized by a limited subject matter, music of the distant past, but by the attitude it assumes towards all music. Simply put, the musicologist sees music as fully as possible in its total context. The extension of musicology into the nineteenth century was not a direct answer to this call, once again, but another symptom of the same underlying change in the face of the discipline.

Historical performance, as we now see more clearly than before, is essentially an attitude of mind rather than a set of techniques applied to an arbitrarily delimited body of early music. The real issue is not a special repertory which has somehow acquired charm or prestige on account of its earliness, and which is to be played in a special, aberrant fashion, but a comprehensive theory of performance covering music from the earliest times we care about up to the present. It is perhaps worth stating the truism that those who accept this theory advocate that contemporary music be played 'historically', too – that is, in contemporary style and on contemporary instruments. They would not wish to hear the Carter Double Concerto for Harpsichord and Piano played by a Baroque harpsichordist and a Romantic pianist.

From the standpoint that has been developed above it must seem ironic that *Early Music* began publication when it did, in 1973. For by that time it was already an intellectual anachronism – as was pointed up by the editor's reference to an article about fortepianos in his first issue, which showed, he said, 'that from time to time we shall move outside the strict definition of early music as "pre-classical"'. In the daily (or, rather, quarterly) life of the journal over the last dozen years, 'from time to time' has meant 'very infrequently'. It is not too much to hope that by moving into the nineteenth century with or without official blessing, the historical performance movement will finally move away from the old-world ambience it inherited from William Morris by way of Arnold Dolmetsch. There is something of Kelmscott and Haslemere still living on in *Early Music*.

Other things about the historical performance movement have been clarified, or will ultimately be clarified, by its extension into the nineteenth century. One is the image of its votaries expending so much of their energies on music of less than the highest rank. While some attention has been paid to the likes of Anton Reicha and Fanny Hensel, Mercadante and early Meyerbeer, most of the activity has focused on Mozart, Beethoven and Schubert, Rossini and Verdi. The nineteenth century had a fixation about great composers, and this is reflected by historical performers of nineteenth-century music.

Another thing is the widespread and stubborn conviction that historical performance is inimical to 'expression' in music, that indeed it seeks to repress emotion, and that it owes its basic impetus to a reaction against Romanticism. To be 'authentic' in nineteenth-century performance is to *be* Romantic. One lesson taught by history – though not, it seems, easily learned – is that all music is expressive but that music is not all expressive in the same way. Deller sang Dowland expressively in one way, Callas sang Rossini expressively in another. It is possible to play expressively, even emotionally, without playing in a 'Romantic' style – by which is meant the relic of a mid-twentieth-century style fossilized from the late nineteenth century, itself some way removed from Romanticism proper. If Malcolm Bilson plays Mozart on the fortepiano with more emotion than Clifford Curzon or Lili Kraus did on the modern piano, the reason, I think, is not to be sought in the repressive mechanisms of any of these artists, but rather in their tools. It is almost impossible to play Mozart emotionally on a modern piano without sounding vulgar.

As was remarked above, a fine book by the Badura-Skodas on the historical performance of Mozart's piano music came out in the 1950s. What has happened subsequently is that they and others have begun to use original instruments restored, or new instruments constructed according to original models. Reading *Early Music* with its regular articles on the construction and technique of nakers, shawms, gitterns, clavicymbellums and the like, its analyses of fine points of distinction between different styles of Louis XV harpsichords, and its lovingly illustrated quarterly London Salerooms Reports – reading all this can persuade an outside observer that the historical performance movement is beset by an epidemic of instrumental fetishism. In some cases, indeed, the malady is well advanced. Yet it is also important to understand that the importance of instruments goes beyond that of producing an 'authentic' or 'recognizable' sound. 'The Mozart Sound' was something the Badura-Skodas felt obliged to write about in their book – this is the title of their opening chapter – but the actuality of that sound cannot have come clear to them before they started practising seriously on the fortepiano itself. It is only as one gains technique and experience on an instrument that it yields up its more subtle sonorous secrets. Moreover what I have called interpretative mechanisms – aspects of playing that are not strictly sonorous, such as the control of dynamics, ornamentation, articulation, and phrasing – are all understood by the fingers, as it were. On the level of nuance, an instrument dictates its own performing practice – independent, to some extent, even of the performing style of any particular time and place.

It takes time to perfect technique and refine interpretation on any instrument. It takes much more time with a historical instrument, whose physical condition is always a bit of a mystery, and of which there is no great constellation of masters to listen to and learn from. Even in cases where performing traditions have been in existence for several generations – as with the harpsichord from the time of Landowksa to Kirkpatrick and Leonhardt, and the Baroque organ from the time of Schweitzer and Straube to Weinrich and Walcha – this means less than might at first appear. For the historical makers and restorers have not been idle, and each generation is challenged by a newly refined group of instruments. Players of other instruments are challenged similarly, with less of a tradition to go on. Lute and flute players cannot look back much farther than to the 1950s, to figures such as Julian Bream and Frans Brueggen. With the Baroque violin, despite numerous and valiant previous efforts, a secure tradition does not really go back of the 'Netherlands school' of the 1970s, which has been characterized briefly above.

This goes to explain why the advance in standards of execution of Baroque music between the 1950s and the 1980s has been rather slow, though steady. It also makes it seem less surprising that not many fortepianists have yet emerged of the calibre of the best contemporary harpsichordists. The same is true of chamber-music groups and orchestras devoted to the historical performance of late eighteenth- and early nineteenth-century music. It is still too early for them to have made the impact we can expect of them, or their followers, not far in the future. Yet some very good things have already been done: performances by the Esterhazy Quartet, for example, of quartets by Haydn and Mozart, and some of the Academy of Ancient Music Mozart symphonies.

9

No one who has heard Beethoven's 'Moonlight' Sonata or the Sonata in D minor, opus 31 no. 2, well played on the fortepiano will ever be entirely happy with them again on the modern piano. In a natural way, true to its own capabilities, the old instrument provides this music with clarities and sensitivities which the new instrument can, at best, simulate only in a way that holds it back from realizing *its* capabilities. Certain notorious problematic Beethoven markings in the scores make immediate sense in the sonorous world of the actual instrument he played when he wrote them. On a modern instrument they simply cannot be realized, or can be realized only most awkwardly (that is why they are notorious).

We can feel sure that Beethoven would have been unhappy with his sonatas on the modern piano, too. But I think we can also feel sure he would have recognized them – without too much bewilderment. To approach the matter from the other end (our end), what Badura-Skoda and Bilson do with classical and Romantic music is from a modern standpoint less radical than what the Kuijkens do with Baroque music, let alone what Morrow and Binkley do with music of the Middle Ages and the Renaissance. An 1810 Broadwood fortepiano does not differ from a 1980 Bösendorfer as much as a harpsichord differs from a 'Mozart piano', or a viol from a violin, or a recorder from a flute. Likewise in the matter of 'idiomatic' playing, as Dart would have put it, there is less difference between playing a Broadwood and a Bösendorfer than there is between playing an un-remodelled Stradivarius (if you can find one) with an old bow and a modern violin with a modern bow. And over the last two hundred years or so, the piano is the only major instrument to have undergone this much (or even this much) mutation. Technological advances in the nineteenth century appreciably altered the majority of wind instruments, but they were not altered as much as the piano was.

All this is by way of making the obvious point that the whole issue of historical performance tends to evaporate as we approach the turn of the twentieth century. Historical performance becomes, simply, performance, and once we have sound recordings, we no longer have to ask what the composer and his contemporaries would have recognized (though we may have to deal with our own bewilderment). The questions become questions of interpretation. Musicology evaporates into criticism. And a whole new area of musicological research has opened up, the analysis of early sound recordings for evidence of nineteenth-century practice. It is something of a scandal to see how slow, once again, musicologists have been to take this up.

It might be said, in any case, that the history of the self-destruction of the historical performance movement begins or at least takes a sharp turn at precisely the point under discussion, the point at which the movement extended to classical and Romantic music. Since around the beginning of the nineteenth century, and only since that time, our musical repertory has been continuous and accumulative, and there has also been some continuity in the performing tradition. Admittedly, this is not as strong as is often believed. Even so, the historical task with music after 1800 is one of revising a tradition that is already there, rather than of reconstructing one that has been forgotten. To put it even more strongly, whereas historical performers dealing with Josquin and Monteverdi have to re-create a tradition, those dealing with Mozart and Schumann have to work within one. They may sometimes feel they are working against a tradition, but they are still working from within.

Bach – we keep circling back to Bach – is a slightly more complex case. For while it is true that his music was taken into the nineteenth-century canon, his performing tradition was not. The 'traditional' Bach playing of the nineteenth century was an *Ersatz*, and so what the historical performance pioneers of the early twentieth century were doing was really reconstruction, not revision. As a matter of fact, what they did also involved destruction of the *Ersatz*, and that is why it met with so much controversy and opposition.

Revision is less radical than reconstruction – less exciting, perhaps, but also less controversial. At least it ought to be less controversial, for with Mozart and Schumann there ought not to be any basic ideological gulf between historical and 'traditional' artists as far as insight into the music itself is concerned. This entirely apart from the instruments or ornaments they employ. Such a gulf does exist with Bach, one often feels, and if it does not exist with Josquin and Monteverdi, that is only because the traditional musician has no interest or stake in their work whatsoever. I spoke above about a common ground for the analytical and historical positions on the matter of musical performance; such ground is most solid in respect to classical and Romantic music, which is the analysts' real domain. It is not clear why, in principle, Paul Badura-Skoda and Alfred Brendel should disagree about the structure of the 'Moonlight' Sonata, though they project that structure in different ways on their different instruments (strictly speaking, different forms of the same instrument). Badura-Skoda's instrument gives him those interpretative mechanisms to project structure (and sonority, and whatever) that Beethoven and his contemporaries happened to know about, that is all.

Charles Rosen is an artist who has strongly opposed the historical position, on grounds that are essentially those of the analysts.

> The act of composing is the act of fixing those limits within which the performer may move freely. But the performer's freedom is – or should be – bound in another way. The limits the composer sets belong to a system which in many respects is like a language: it has an order, a syntax and a meaning. The performer brings out that meaning, makes its significance not only clear but almost palpable. And there is no reason to assume that the composer and his contemporaries always knew with certainty how best to make the listener aware of that significance.[14]

We know better today, Rosen seems to be saying, with our modern techniques of analysis into musical order, syntax, and structure. Maybe so, maybe not. But in any case, what reason is there to believe that one modern musician using the wrong instrument will always know better than another modern musician using the right one?

When in 1980 Malcolm Bilson wrote an article in *Early Music* on 'The Viennese Fortepiano of the Late 18th Century', it was one of the few articles that journal had carried on music of so unearly a period.* It was one of even fewer in which specific passages in particular pieces of music are actually cited and their interpretation discussed in sensitive detail. In conclusion, Bilson in effect enunciated a credo for historical performers:

> I have often heard it stated by scholars and others interested in performance on early instruments that they would rather hear a great artist on the wrong instrument than a mediocre player on the right one. I am no longer willing to accept that statement. . . . (p. 161)

He should indeed be unwilling to accept that statement (which is indeed heard often, only too often) because it forces an invidious choice, obviously, as Bilson went on to point out. The reasonable choice to consider is whether one would rather hear a good player on a historically plausible instrument or a good player on an implausible one. The statement also conveys an innuendo which has, in this area, little to support it; for to the historical performer of classical and Romantic music no latitude is granted for the kind of amateurish playing and singing which has sustained half of the 'early music' world ever since the time of Dolmetsch, and driven the other half to despair and occasional bouts of self-loathing. Serious discussion of standards in this area cannot be furthered by appeals to greatness or mediocrity. Bilson, Badura-Skoda, Brendel, and Rosen are all very good players, all interpreters of unquestioned distinction.

> For a mediocre performance it does not matter what kind of instrument is used. This is not merely a platitude; the choice of instrument only becomes meaningful when the artist has something very specific to express. . . . Musicians who do not are in no way better served by authentic instruments than standard modern ones. . . . I would like to hope that it is not the sound of the instrument that pushes the [historical performance] movement forward, but rather the searching for an ever-better interpretation of the music . . . (pp. 161–2).

It seems to me hard to shake this position. 'An ever-better interpretation of the music': this is what critics work for, as well as performers, and what musicologists ought to work for. As a goal, it surely animates all performers equally: the majority who concentrate on the music of the standard repertory, the cadre of contemporary-music specialists, and historical performers specializing in the Baroque, medieval, and Renaissance periods as well as in the Classical and Romantic.

7. Coda

Britain and America, it has been said, are two countries separated by a common language. One feels there may be some substance behind the quip. May there also be some merit to the proposition that a universal language (which music has been said to be) separates British and American musicology? Some characteristics of the pursuit as understood on one or the other side of the Atlantic were commented on in the Introduction to this book, and have been returned to sporadically in the main exposition and its development. As a coda, I should like to try to assemble and solidify some of these observations. How separate, really, are British and American musicology?

As a matter of fact, invidious comparisons between the two formed the subject of an unlikely but drawn-out series of letters to the editor of *The Times Literary Supplement* in 1973. Few will remember this shrill altercation with pleasure, if at all; but in view of a theme that has come to the surface more than once in these pages, I cannot resist recalling it and recalling that what started the whole thing going was a critical edition – to be exact, a review by an anonymous if readily identifiable Englishman of a volume of Renaissance motets and madrigals edited by an American.

How hard it is to get beyond *editions* in discussions and controversies about musicology! At issue was not a point of music history or aesthetics, not a composer or an actual piece of music, but a detail of editorial procedure: the editor's policy for supplying the unspecified sharps and flats (*musica ficta*) in this music. People who make editions, as I remarked in Chapter 2, never tire of arguing about the policies and procedures involved – at times acrimoniously, and at times also tendentiously. It remained for Frank Harrison, in one of the more sensible of the *TLS* letters, to point out the contingency of edition-making, and its irrelevance to what he sees as the musical essentials of living performing traditions. He was speaking as one who knew – as an ethnomusicologist who had first been a medievalist, wearing which hat he had prepared critical editions and even edited a whole series of them. (He has since edited another.) Never one to forget a social context, as we have seen, Harrison also remarked that obviously musicology was bound to be understood differently in Britain and America, since its status, training methods, and career structures in the two countries differed so greatly.

Harrison was wrong about this last point, I think, or rather he was out of date. What he was remembering was the situation he had surveyed for the Harrison–Hood–Palisca *Musicology* volume, around 1960; and it has been mainly since that time that British musicology (if not ethnomusicology) has grown steadily more institutionalized on the academic level, hence closer and closer to the American model. We had something to say about this in Chapter 1. It is often pointed out, for example, how much British musicology has owed to outstanding scholars whose training and activity were essentially outside the academic orbit. But in the 1970s there were few of these giants still around, however large they may have loomed in the past, and by now any that come to mind are distinctly senior. Students of Westrup and Dart, holding music degrees, occupy professorships and other positions of importance in musicology. And those (not Harrison) who in 1973 contrasted the 'amateurism' and 'musicality' of British musicology with the 'computerized efficiency' of American must now be viewing with mixed feelings the fashions for highly professional paleographic source studies in Britain, and for nineteenth-century studies with their orientation towards criticism in America.

Of recent trends in musical scholarship, these are the two that have seemed to me to stand out the most in our respective countries: these together with increased British activity in theory and analysis. I am far from wishing, however, to draw some new facile contrast between national schools or scholarly temperaments. Some qualifications that were noted in Chapter 4 should be recalled here. First of all, the neopositivistic movement in Renaissance and medieval studies is Anglo-American in scope, with Iain Fenlon and his like-minded compatriots joined and no doubt outnumbered by Americans. If in Britain its intellectual lineage can be traced to Dart, in America it can be traced to Mendel, Reese, and others. Second, work in nineteenth-century music – also carried out by many from both countries – is often oriented no more than potentially towards criticism, and then to formalistic criticism of the kind I have complained about so much, traditional musical analysis. The two trends are most striking when seen as new departures or at least new emphases in the history of musicology in the two countries. They are less persuasive as indicators of difference, let alone separation, between British and American musicology today.

One is struck, rather, by the extent to which over the last generation British and American musicology have come together. Not the least important reason for this is the simple social one – the frequency of personal exchanges. Scholars have gone from one country to the other as university students, researchers, visiting professors or lecturers, and (especially from Britain to America) as permanent appointees. They have been unconcerned about the pitfalls of their common language; they have even adopted each other's jargon. Alerted by Harrison, furthermore, we can pinpoint another social factor – indeed, a specific socio-economic one – that has contributed significantly to the levelling of British and American musicology. This was *The New Grove Dictionary of Music and Musicians*, a commercial venture of some power and of several phases, the first of which peaked in 1980 after more than ten years of preparation.*

Over the course of that ten-year period, *Grove* imprinted itself more and more deeply on British and American musicology. It may seem bizarre to assert that a dictionary project, even a very elaborately conducted dictionary project, should have had a major effect on an entire discipline in two countries; yet such was the case. Besides recruiting a very large number of staff musicologists and advisers from both countries, it deflected the work patterns of most others. There were few figures of any stature or promise, old or young, who were not called on to make contributions to it. After the twenty-volume dictionary itself came out in 1980, the publisher Macmillan went on to a second phase, a long series of spin-offs: *The New Grove Mozart*, *The New Grove High Renaissance Masters*, *The New Grove Dictionary of Music in the United States* ('Amerigrove'), *The New Grove Dictionary of Musical Instruments*, and so on. It seems safe to say that there will be a major *Grove* presence in musicology for at least the next ten-year period – the period during which this book has been written, and during which it will be read.

2

In the generous wave of promotion associated with *The New Grove*, much nostalgic attention was paid to Sir George Grove himself and his original dictionary, begun almost exactly a hundred years earlier. A fishmonger's son, untrained in music, Grove was first a highly successful engineer, then secretary of the Crystal Palace, site of the Great Exhibition of 1851, then an amateur biblical scholar, editor of *Macmillan's Magazine*, indefatigable writer of articles on a variety of subjects, and a chief organizer and first director of the Royal College of Music. He was, so we read in *The New Grove*, 'in nearly every way a typical "great Victorian", with a zest for self-education, a conviction that the achievements of the nineteenth century could hardly be surpassed, [and] a belief that most objectives were attainable through hard work'. For the Crystal Palace concerts he wrote hundreds of 'analytical programme notes', some of which are preserved in his famous *Beethoven and His Nine Symphonies* of 1896; he subedited a biblical dictionary before forming the idea of founding a musical one. The persistent idea that English musicology is, in the best sense, amateur goes back to *Grove's Dictionary*. For before that time there really was no musicology in Britain, only musical antiquarianism.

And perhaps the persistence of the idea owes something to subsequent inept editions of the dictionary, those of 1904–10, 1927, 1940, and 1954. However this may be, the planners of the next edition, around 1970, turned their backs decisively on amateurism and its dreary perennial hanger-on, parochialism. They took as one of their models the great German musicological encyclopedia *Die Musik in Geschichte und Gegenwart*, the last of whose bulky fourteen volumes had just been issued at the end of a twenty-year-long sequence. They deemed it necessary to match the depth and authority of coverage of *MGG* if *Grove* was to supplant it as essential fodder for graduate students and their seniors. On the other hand, Sir George's humane sweep and breadth of coverage – extended even further than ever before, of course – would also be necessary if *Grove* was to lay claim to universal appeal. This claim was central to its marketing, and America was central to its market.

Hence from the start *The New Grove* was a resolutely international but particularly an Anglo-American enterprise. Its capacious editorial and advisory structures were nearly half American in composition, as was also its squad of fifty-odd fledgling musicologists enlisted by the editor-in-chief to check, correct, revise, coordinate, and in general usefully to tug and haul at the contributions of the more than 2500 far-flung authors. (The editor, Stanley Sadie, is a Cambridge PhD in music, a specialist in Mozart and music of the classic era. Sadie is also editor of the *Musical Times*, a busy, diversely packed, and very important monthly, and for many years was a music critic for the London *Times*.) I shall say a word about the nature and quality of *Grove*'s contents in a moment; for now I wish to stress only how much it accelerated those personal and intellectual exchanges that have brought musicologists closer together. In the words of one of the inner circle, the Anglo-American interchange that took place on every editorial level was 'the stuff of a Henry James novella'.[1] None of the British and American musicologists who were swept up in the *Grove* epic, he meant to say, was ever quite the same kind of scholar afterwards.

The most vivid testimony to this, probably, is to be discerned from a *Grove* article that was greeted with admiration, indeed awe, in all serious reviews of the dictionary. (An account of the reviews of *Grove* – ranging from a magisterial reckoning by Carl Dahlhaus to a self-indulgent causerie by Anthony Burgess, and from an extended invective by one of the dictionary's heaviest contributors, in *Inter-American Music Review*, to a diffuse panegyric by a decad of miscellaneous specialists, covering two volumes apiece in four monthly issues of the *Musical Times* – would make a mock-epic of its own.[2]) The article in question was a highly original forty-page treatment of 'analysis' by Ian D. Bent. To say that it is remarkable the job was done so well would be to patronize the author, a young medievalist who became a senior consulting editor at *Grove*. But it *is* remarkable that so ambitious and serious an article should have been essayed at all in Britain, given the lack of a strong local tradition of theory and analysis. 'The British are at their most anti-Teutonic in their suspicion of far-reaching theories of music,' Arnold Whittall has said; indeed, they do not often take kindly to the sort of far-wrenching German prose that Bent mastered. It does not detract from Bent's accomplishment to observe that such an article would not have been written had *The New Grove* been laid out along the same insular lines as the old. Bent as author and editor was responding to the central importance of analysis on the American music-intellectual scene.

I would not go so far as to say that the lack of interest in criticism in America was responsible for the fact that no such article was written on that topic; I would not go so far because I believe that British indifference was equally responsible. Instead an item from the 1954 *Grove* was reprinted – one of very few such cases – with small additions: a classic but Tory essay by an English scholar of the old school, the opera specialist and foremost Handelian of our time, Winton Dean. Dahlhaus has remarked on the insularity of *Grove*'s coverage of aesthetics and, he might have added, criticism or hermeneutics.

Ethnomusicology, on the other hand, was extremely well represented. Sadie singles out this fact as 'the biggest departure' from earlier *Grove*s, and I would quibble with him only to the extent of regarding the dramatic increase of material on non-Western and folk music as itself only one aspect of a more basic departure, the dictionary's new scholarly professionalism. Over a million words, it is said, are devoted to such material. The article on 'India, subcontinent of' is over twice as long as 'analysis', and a humbling 'Appendix of Terms Used in Articles on Non-Western and Folk Music' runs to eighty-six double-column pages in six-point type. Mantle Hood, as we have seen in Chapter 5, has been as important an advocate for ethnomusicology as he has been a scholar and a teacher; Hood was the supervising editor in this area. If ethnomusicology is still waiting in British universities for its turn at bat, thanks to Hood it has had its substantial innings in *The New Grove*.

As was mentioned above, a group of young British and American musicologists – many of them still graduate students at the time – worked together, and rubbed up against one another, as the dictionary's subeditors. Their names are listed on the Acknowledgment pages of Volume 1, and it will be interesting to see how many of them become intellectual leaders of the coming generation. David Fallows, Iain Fenlon, Paul Griffiths, and perhaps others can already be seen to fall into that category. Also appearing on those pages is the maiden name of the former music editor of the Cambridge University Press, which from the mid-1970s on has seemed more and more to dominate scholarly book publication on music in English. Among many major ventures embarked upon by Cambridge, one seems calculated to formalize this situation: a series of large anthologies of theoretical, aesthetic, and critical writings on music, in translation, from the whole range of the history of Western music.[3] This will not replace, but will vastly expand upon Oliver Strunk's one-volume *Source Readings in Music History* (1950), a central ornament of the famous W. W. Norton music line of the postwar era. Most significant yet – because it militates, once again, against parochialism – is the ambitious programme at Cambridge of translations of books by such German authors as Ernst Bloch, Thrasybulos Georgiades, and

Carl Dahlhaus.[4] British interest in Dahlhaus's work would have been awakened by his contribution of several key articles to *The New Grove*.

What was heartening about *The New Grove* itself was how much was actually new, not merely the reshuffling of matter to be found in *MGG* and a mass of specialized locations. Fresh research was conducted for many articles; and especially for American musicologists, it was a very good thing to be made to step back from detailed concerns and draw together facts which, while not always strictly 'new', were often very little known and never before placed in their appropriate context. It was a great cross-Atlantic accomplishment. It revolutionized music information retrieval. It triumphantly registered state of the art as of the 1970s. This present book would have been a much poorer thing – could scarcely have been written at all – without it.

3

And yet: a dictionary, even the best dictionary, is essentially just another trophy of positivism. It is a static rather than a dynamic thing, an immovable object rather than an irresistible force. Synoptic, celebratory, retrospective, and sterile, it stores but does not generate, transform, light up, or blossom. And as a storehouse, it accommodates the stalks of positivism more naturally than the petals of interpretation. If anyone is inclined to see the 1970s as notable chiefly, in musicology, for a great Anglo-American dictionary of music, this should not be a cause for undue self-congratulation in either country. (It is not clear, I must say, that anyone *is* so inclined.) *The New Grove* may have brought us closer together: but only, so far, in aid of circumscribed goals.

Are there contradictions inherent in the last two paragraphs? Besides achieving prodigies of assembly and organization (and reorganization) of knowledge, *Grove* occasioned new research and has led to new understanding. Yet this was really a fringe benefit. It is in the nature of a dictionary to record knowledge, not develop it; and yesterday's state of the art becomes today's received opinion. Furthermore, it is in the nature of a dictionary to accentuate the positive. Those who consult dictionaries – scholars, students, journalists, amateurs – are looking for information that is authoritative, straightforward (they hope), and uncontroversial; they are not looking for individual interpretation, speculation, dialectic, or intellectual yeast of any kind. A responsible author writes dictionary articles with this in mind (and the *Grove* subeditors were there to nudge the less responsible). It is no accident that *Grove*'s composer articles are especially prized for their work-lists, the most reliable and complete to be found anywhere; or that its longest article (163 pages) is on 'sources' (there is no article on 'history of music', nothing analogous to Friedrich Blume's famous essays in *MGG*); or that the next longest article is the truly invaluable 'periodicals'.[5] The best dictionary in the world can be no more than a springboard for an evolving discipline. It cannot be an end in itself.

While attempting to clarify contradictions, incidentally, I should perhaps add a word about my attitude towards that other great quintessential positivistic activity, the making of critical editions. Of course no reasonable being can be opposed in principle to editions, any more than to dictionaries; of course it is important to make music available. All or very nearly all musicologists, me included, do this kind of work. To mention only one example of many that flood to mind, Harrison's three-volume edition of the music of the Eton Choirbook brought an entire chapter of English musical history to light – that grand and wonderfully florid ritual polyphony of the late fifteenth century, Magnificats and votive antiphons by John Browne, Richard Davy, Robert Fayrfax, and others, which he has aptly compared to contemporary Perpendicular architecture. This music can now occasionally be heard, on select occasions, in Oxbridge chapels and elsewhere. What appalls me, as I have already said in Chapter 2, is that musicologists as a corps spend so much more time in establishing texts than in thinking about the texts so established. Editions are published; they are reviewed acrimoniously or, more often, not at all; then they gather dust on the library shelves from which they are retrieved more often by the lone choirmaster or harpsichordist in search of new repertory, it seems, than by the scholar in search of new understanding.

Once again, an edition is not an end in itself. It is a means towards musical performance and historical criticism. And there is a real question whether at this point in the history of musicology editions are as helpful as recordings: or to put it more precisely, as the occasional inspired recording. Half a dozen books of early madrigals by the *cinquecento* master Luca Marenzio were published by Alfred Einstein in 1929–31, in an edition that fell victim to the Nazi regime; some late ones had been anthologized around the turn of the century by Luigi Torchi. In the mid-1970s not one but *three* complete editions were begun; but by that time the world was in less dire need of middle-period Marenzio than of a convincing public model of how *any* Marenzio should sound. This was provided for the first time, I believe, by a record put out in 1982 by the Concerto Vocale, a collaboration of the countertenor René Jacobs and the musicologist Thomas Walker.

If the 1970s was a decade of consolidation, consolidation not without its creative component, the opportunity exists for the 1980s and 1990s to be decades of progress: and I am thinking particularly of progress in interpretation, both musical and critical. The second phase of the *Grove* operation consists of spin-offs which entail a new round of dictionary-making. What makes sense from Macmillan's point of view is ominous for the discipline of musicology as a whole. It will be a sad day for musicology if dictionary fetishism becomes established along with edition fetishism.

'Progress' in historiography is a sufficiently suspect concept (as Leo Treitler and others warn us); if progress in scholarship is also suspect, we can speak simply of 'motion'. No centrifugal motion is possible within positivistic scholarship. At best it is like an inward spiralling or drilling, at worst it is like treading water. It will continue as long as there are new parchment manuscript strips to extract from book bindings and stemmas to refine, unaccountably neglected Chopin nocturnes to analyse by Schenkerian or set-theoretical methods, and musics to describe of still undiscovered jungle peoples. One hardly needs a crystal ball to predict that a dreadful lot of this work will be done; it slots easily into present systems of education, publication, and so on, and it suits the temperaments of many workers. The thing about treading water is that you don't have to look where you are going.

One cannot predict motion, only hope for it: hope for it and try to detect it in signs of perturbation, disturbance, aberrance or outright turmoil within the orthodoxies that are established so heavily by academic custom. Some such signs have been examined in the various chapters of this book. Only in ethnomusicology is the author too poorly equipped to have a sense of trends that may be worth watching. Chapter 3 took off from a rousing recent essay proclaiming the breakdown of orthodoxies that have been more oppressive, probably, in theory and analysis than in any other field of music study; this was apposite not only because the essayist, being one of the most brilliant of younger theorists, is a good witness, but also because so much other quite recent work points to the same conclusion. In addition to the full-scale studies by Narmour, Epstein, and Lerdahl and Jackendoff which we have discussed briefly, many smaller studies can be adduced from the burgeoning theory journals – burgeoning even in Britain, where *Music Analysis* has made a distinctive mark since its foundation in 1982. This is encouraging for the future both of theory and analysis and also of musicology. For it is in an amalgam of analysis and historical studies that I see the main practical catalyst towards a kind of musicology oriented towards criticism.

In musicology itself, much – possibly too much – has been made in the above pages of the surge in activity in nineteenth-century studies. The phenomenon will be more significant, no doubt, as it extends itself chronologically into the twentieth century, and as it bends methodologically towards criticism that is broader and more humane than traditional internalist analysis. And by a willing observer, both of these developments can already be espied. (In this regard, a very valuable feature of *Music Analysis* is that it is allowing younger British musicologists to develop their skills and insights as analysts. They are not bound by the old orthodoxies, any more than younger American musicologists – or analysts – are.) And of course the need to accept a critical orientation in musicology is not limited to work in the nineteenth and twentieth centuries. As Edward Cone briskly remarks in a fine essay on 'The Authority of Music Criticism', it is hard to understand 'how any true historian – as distinguished from an indiscriminate narrator or a compiler of facts – can avoid functioning to some extent as a critic, if only by his choice of subjects and by the relative importance he bestows upon them'.[6] More musicologists of all kinds take this for granted today. Musicology, the stateliest of our means for construing music, is on the move.

Perhaps the very appearance of Cone's essay as a leader in the *Journal of the American Musicological Society* in 1981 also marked a trend. Certainly nothing like it had appeared in an official organ of the society since the days when Charles Seeger was active in it. But in fact Cone's essay leaves the relation of the critic and the historian largely unexplored. What he develops with particular conviction is the parallel between critical interpretation and musical interpretation; and this, by extension, could be highly suggestive for the whole field of historical performance. This field is, just possibly, in the greatest turmoil of all. The interview with Michael Morrow and the essay by Richard Taruskin mentioned in Chapter 6, which questioned the received wisdom in that field, have been followed by a number of others with a similar impetus; they have even been fostered by the new editor of *Early Music*.[7] Historical performers seem to be going through a frenzy of re-examination of their premises, attitudes, and alliances, a process of which the verbal phase, at least, reveals as much destructive as liberating potential. Where all this is going is anyone's guess. The cloudy crystal ball grows opaque. Strike it with a hammer covered by the correctly seasoned layers of special felt: will it ring beautifully again, and newly?

This book has been concerned with ideas and ideologies of music as I have apprehended them, mainly in the United States and Britain, since the Second World War. It would be silly to conclude it on a note of prediction. A coda is no place for presentiments. I draw attention to the above trends as hopes, not as predictions: as hopes for motion.

Notes

1. Introduction

1. See Andrew Porter, *A Musical Season* (New York: Viking, 1974); *Music of Three Seasons: 1974–1977* (New York: Farrar, Straus, Giroux, 1978); *Music of Three More Seasons: 1977–1980* (New York: Knopf, 1981).
2. Charles Hamm, 'Popular Music: North America to 1940', vol. 15 of *The New Grove Dictionary of Music and Musicians* (London: Macmillan, 1980), p. 110.
3. David Fallows, Arnold Whittall, and John Blacking, 'Musicology in Great Britain since 1945', *Acta Musicologica* 52 (January–June 1980), pp. 38–68. Updated in vol. 55 (July–December 1983), pp. 244–53.
4. For example, by J. H. Hexter, in *Doing History* (Bloomington, Ind.: Indiana University Press, 1971), pp. 136–8.
5. In the half-dozen or so years around 1980, there was something like a quantum leap in the number of new English-language scholarly journals, yearbooks, monograph series, and the like in music. The following list makes no claim to completeness: *American Music, California Studies in 19th-Century Music, Composers of the Twentieth Century, Early Music History, Journal of Musicology, Music Analysis, Music Perception, Music Theory Spectrum, Musica Asiatica, 19th-Century Music, Popular Music, Studies in Musical Genesis and Structure, Studies in the History of Music, Studies in Musicology* (dissertations: 83 volumes since 1978, including both English and American series), *Studies in Russian Music, Studies in Theory and Criticism of Music*. This list does not include facsimile series or opera guides.

2. Musicology and Positivism: the Postwar Years

1. Mendel, 'Evidence and Explanation', p. 4.
2. See Joseph Kerman, 'A Few Canonic Variations', *Critical Inquiry*

10 (September 1983), pp. 107–25, reprinted in *Canons*, ed. Robert von Halberg (Chicago: University of Chicago Press, 1984).

3. J. N. Forkel, *On J. S. Bach's Life, Genius, and Works* (1802, trans. 'Mr Stephenson', 1808), in *The Bach Reader: a Life of Johann Sebastian Bach in Letters and Documents*, ed. Hans T. David and Arthur Mendel (New York, revised edition, 1966), p. 353.

4. See Robert Stevenson, 'American Musical Scholarship: Parker to Thayer', *19th-Century Music* 1 (March 1978), pp. 191–210.

5. Harrison, 'American Musicology', pp. 7, 9.

6. Palisca, 'American Scholarship in Western Music', in *Musicology*, p. 210.

7. Robin George Collingwood, *The Idea of History* (Oxford: Clarendon Press, 1946), p. 127.

8. Kenneth Levy, foreword to *Music in the Byzantine World*, by Oliver Strunk (New York: Norton, 1977), p. x.

9. Curt Sachs, 'An Editorial', *Journal of the American Musicological Society* 2 (Spring 1949), p. 6.

10. For a warm tribute to Strunk, see Charles Rosen, 'A Master Musicologist', in *New York Review of Books*, 6 February 1975, pp. 32–4.

11. For a good summary of postwar Bach research see Gerhard Herz, 'Toward a New Image of Bach', *Journal of the Riemenschneider Bach Institute* 1 (October 1970), pp. 9–28; (January 1971), pp. 7–28.

12. See Carl Dahlhaus, *Esthetics of Music*, trans. William W. Austin (London and New York: Cambridge University Press, 1982), pp. 69–71.

13. Walter Emery, 'On Evidence of Derivation', in *Report of the Eighth Congress of the International Musicological Society, New York, 1961* (Cassel, London, and New York: Bärenreiter, 1962), vol. 1, p. 249.

14. Friedrich Blume, 'Outlines of a New Picture of Bach', *Music & Letters* 44 (July 1963), p. 216.

15. Citations in this paragraph: Mendel, 'Evidence and Explanation', pp. 11, 13, 15.

3. Analysis, Theory, and New Music

1. William E. Benjamin, 'Schenker's Theory and the Future of Music', *Journal of Music Theory* 25 (Spring 1981), p. 171.

2. Leonard Meyer, preface to *Beethoven's Compositional Choices*,

by Janet Levy (Philadelphia: University of Philadelphia Press, 1982), p. ix.

3. 'Reflections on Music Theory', ed. Marian Guck and Marianne Kielian-Gilbert, *Perspectives of New Music*, 22 (1983–4).

4. Wallace Berry, 'Dialogue and Monologue in the Professional Community', *College Music Symposium* 21 (Fall 1981), pp. 84–100.

5. E. T. A. Hoffmann's role in the history of criticism has been analysed with great perspicacity by Carl Dahlhaus; for a summary, see his 'Metaphysik der Instrumentalmusik', in *Die Musik des neunzehnten Jahrhunderts*, vol. 6 of *Neues Handbuch der Musikwissenschaft*, ed. Carl Dahlhaus (Wiesbaden: Athenaion, 1980), pp. 73–9.

6. See Ruth A. Solie, 'The Living Work: Organicism and Musical Analysis', *19th-Century Music* 4 (Fall 1980), pp. 147–56.

7. Richmond Browne, Allen Forte, Carlton Gamer, Veron C. Kliewer, Carl E. Schachter, and Peter Westergaard, 'Music Theory: the Art, the Profession, and the Future', *College Music Symposium* 17 (Spring 1977), pp. 135–62.

8. Lewin, 'Behind the Beyond', pp. 62, 63.

9. Cone, 'Mr Cone Replies', p. 72.

10. See Joseph Kerman, 'Tovey's Beethoven', in *Beethoven Studies 2*, ed. Alan Tyson (London and New York: Oxford University Press, 1977), pp. 172–91.

11. Nattiez's main works are *Fondements d'une sémiologie de la musique* (Paris: Union générale d'éditions, 1976) and 'Varese's "Density 21.5": a Study in Semiological Analysis', published in revised form in English translation in *Music Analysis* 1 (October 1982), pp. 243–340. Fundamental objections to Nattiez's whole approach, felt by many, have been expressed by Allan R. Keiler: 'Two Views of Musical Semiotics', in *The Sign in Music and Literature*, ed. Wendy Steiner (Austin, Texas: University of Texas Press, 1981), pp. 138–68. For a more sympathetic view, see Jonathan Dunsby, 'Music and Semiotics: the Nattiez Phase', *Musical Quarterly* 69 (Winter 1983), pp. 27–43, and 'A Hitch Hiker's Guide to Semiotic Music Analysis', *Music Analysis* 1 (October 1982), pp. 235–42.

12. Citations in this paragraph: Hans Keller, 'The Chamber Music', in *The Mozart Companion*, ed. H. C. Robbins Landon and Donald Mitchell (London and New York: Oxford University Press, 1956), pp. 90, 91.

13. Hans Keller, 'FA No. 1: Mozart, K. 421', *The Score* 22 (February

1958), pp. 56–64. While this book was in the press another Keller FA surfaced, at a King's College London Music Analysis Conference in September 1984.

14. Arnold Whittall, 'Musicology in Great Britain since 1945', *Acta Musicologica* 52 (April 1980), pp. 57–62.

15. Theodor Adorno, 'On the Problem of Musical Analysis', trans. Max Paddison, *Music Analysis* 1 (July 1982), pp. 169–88.

16. See Joseph Kerman, 'How We Got into Analysis, and How to Get Out', *Critical Inquiry* 7 (Winter 1980), pp. 311–31.

17. Charles Rosen, 'Art Has its Reasons', *New York Review of Books*, 17 June 1971, p, 38.

18. Lewis Lockwood, 'Eroica Perspectives: Strategy and Design in the First Movement', in *Beethoven Studies 3*, ed. Alan Tyson (London and New York: Cambridge University Press, 1982), p. 93.

19. See Arnold Whittall, review of *Beyond Orpheus*, by David Epstein, *Journal of Music Theory* 25 (Fall 1981), pp. 319–26.

20. Heinrich Schenker, *Harmony*, trans. Elizabeth Mann Borgese, ed. Oswald Jonas (Chicago: University of Chicago Press, 1954), and *Free Composition* (*Der freie Satz*), trans. and ed. Ernst Oster (New York: Longman, 1979); Donald Francis Tovey, *Musical Articles from the Encyclopaedia Britannica* (London: Oxford University Press, 1944); Arnold Schoenberg, *Theory of Harmony*, trans. Roy E. Carter (Berkeley and Los Angeles: University of California Press, 1978).

21. Pierre Boulez, 'Schönberg is Dead' (1952), reprinted in *Notes of an Apprenticeship*, trans. Herbert Weinstock (New York: Knopf, 1968), pp. 268–76.

22. George Perle, 'The Secret Programme of the Lyric Suite', *Musical Times* 118 (August, September, October 1977), pp. 629–32, 709–13, 809–13; Douglas Jarman, 'Alban Berg, Wilhelm Fliess and the Secret Programme of the Violin Concerto', ibid. 124 (April 1983), pp. 218–23.

23. George Perle, 'Babbitt, Lewin, and Schoenberg: a Critique', *Perspectives of New Music* 2 (Fall–Winter 1963), pp. 120–7; Milton Babbitt, 'Mr Babbitt Answers', ibid., pp. 127–32.

24. 'Mr Babbitt Answers', p. 131.

25. Harold S. Powers, 'The Structure of Musical Meaning: a View from Benares', *Perspectives of New Music*, 14–15 (1976), pp. 308–36.

26. Milton Babbitt, review of *Le Système dodécaphonique*, in *Journal of the American Musicological Society* 5 (Fall 1950), p. 266.

27. Boretz and Cone, *Perspectives on Contemporary Music Theory*, p. ix.

28. Stanley Cavell, 'Music Discomposed', in *Must We Mean What We Say?* (London and New York: Cambridge University Press, 1969), p. 186.

29. Milton Babbitt, 'Who Cares if You Listen?' (1958), reprinted widely, e.g. in *The American Composer Speaks: a Historical Anthology, 1770–1965*, ed. Gilbert Chase (Baton Rouge: Louisiana State University Press, 1966), pp. 234–44.

30. John Backus, '*Die Reihe*: a Scientific Evaluation', *Perspectives of New Music* 1 (Fall 1962), pp. 160–7.

31. John Hollander, review of *Silence*, by John Cage, *Perspectives of New Music* 1 (Spring 1963), pp. 137–41.

32. Boretz and Cone, *Perspectives on Contemporary Music Theory*, p. x.

33. Billy Jim Layton, 'The New Liberalism', *Perspectives of New Music* 3 (Spring–Summer 1965), pp. 137–42.

34. Benjamin, 'Schenker's Theory', pp. 169–70.

4. Musicology and Criticism

1. Donald Mitchell, 'Criticism: a State of Emergency', *Tempo* 37 (Autumn 1955), pp. 8–9.

2. Ian D. Bent, 'Thurston Dart', vol. 5 of *The New Grove Dictionary of Music and Musicians* (London: Macmillan, 1980), p. 249.

3. See Davitt Moroney and William Oxenbury, 'Thurston Dart: Bibliography of Publications', in *Source Materials and the Interpretation of Music: a Memorial Volume to Thurston Dart*, ed. Ian Bent (London: Stainer & Bell, 1981), pp. 431–2.

4. Thurston Dart, 'Cavazzoni and Cabezón', *Music & Letters* 36 (January 1955), pp. 2–6; Knud Jeppesen, 'Cavazzoni–Cabezón', *Journal of the American Musicological Society* 7 (Summer 1955), pp. 81–5; reply by Dart, ibid., p. 148.

5. Ian Bent, ed., *Source Materials and the Interpretation of Music: a Memorial Volume to Thurston Dart* (London: Stainer & Bell, 1981).

6. Iain Fenlon, ed., *Early Music History*, vol. 1 (1981), jacket.

7. Philip Brett, 'Facing the Music', *Early Music* 10 (July 1982), pp. 347–50.

8. See David Fallows, review of *Music and Patronage in 16th-Century Mantua*, by Iain Fenlon, and *The Madrigal at Ferrara*, by Anthony Newcomb, in *Early Music* 9 (July 1981), pp. 351–3.

9. Stanley Boorman, 'Petrucci and Fossombrone: Some New Editions and Cancels', in *Source Materials*, pp. 129–54.

10. It would be wrong to leave the impression that no work whatsoever of a critical nature is taking place in 'early music'. Besides studies by Newcomb of instrumental music of the late sixteenth and early seventeenth centuries, papers by Don M. Randel on fifteenth-century song may be cited: 'Dufay the Reader', in *Studies in the History of Music* I (New York: Broude, 1983), pp. 38–78, and 'Music and Poetry, History and Criticism: Reading the 15th-Century Chanson' (unpublished). There is also Richard Crocker's remarkable *The Early Medieval Sequence* (Berkeley and Los Angeles: University of California Press, 1977).

11. James S. Ackerman and Rhys Carpenter, *Art and Archeology* (Humanistic Scholarship in America: the Princeton Studies [Englewood Cliffs, NJ: Prentice-Hall, 1963]), p. 131.

12. Kerman, 'A Profile for American Musicology', pp. 62–3.

13. Edward E. Lowinsky, 'Character and Purposes of American Musicology: a Reply to Joseph Kerman', *Journal of the American Musicological Society* 18 (Summer 1965), pp. 222–34; Joseph Kerman, reply to Lowinsky, ibid. (Fall 1965), pp. 426–7.

14. Curt Sachs, 'An Editorial', *Journal of the American Musicological Society* 2 (Spring 1949), pp. 5–6.

15. Leo Treitler, 'On Historical Criticism', *Musical Quarterly* 53 (April 1967), pp. 188–205.

16. J. H. Hexter, *Doing History* (Bloomington, Ind.: Indiana University Press, 1971), p. 71.

17. Treitler, 'On Historical Criticism', p. 201.

18. Treitler, 'The Present as History', *Perspectives of New Music* 7 (Spring–Summer 1969), p. 50.

19. See note 29, below.

20. Some of the chief Beethoven work issuing from Britain and America has appeared in the serial *Beethoven Studies*,* ed. Alan Tyson, volumes of which appeared in 1973, 1977, and 1982. The *Beethoven Jahrbuch*, issued by the Bonn Beethovenhaus, contains mostly German contributions.

21. Gustav Nottebohm, *Ein Skizzenbuch von Beethoven aus dem Jahre 1803* (Leipzig: Breitkopf & Härtel, 1880); trans. by Jonathan Katz in Gustav Nottebohm, *Two Beethoven Sketchbooks* (London: Gollancz, 1979).

22. See Lewis Lockwood, review of *Beethoven: Ein Skizzenbuch zur Pastoralsymphonie und zu den Trios Op. 70, 1 und 2*, ed. Dagmar Weise, in *Musical Quarterly* 53 (January 1967), pp. 128–35,

and Joseph Kerman, ed., introduction to *Autograph Miscellany from Circa 1786 to 1799: British Museum Additional Manuscript 29801, ff. 39–162 (the 'Kafka' Sketchbook)* (London: British Museum, 1970), vol. 1.

23. Joseph Kerman, 'Beethoven Sketchbooks in the British Museum', *Proceedings of the Royal Musical Association* 93 (1966–7), pp. 77–96.

24. See Joseph Kerman, 'Sketch Studies', in *Musicology in the 1980s*, ed. D. Kern Holoman and Claude V. Palisca (New York: Da Capo, 1982), pp. 53–66; also in *19th-Century Music* 6 (Fall 1982), pp. 174–80.

25. Robert Marshall, *The Compositional Process of J. S. Bach: a Study of the Autograph Scores of the Vocal Works*, 2 vols. (Princeton, NJ: Princeton University Press, 1972).

26. R. Larry Todd, 'Of Seagulls and Counterpoint: the Early Versions of Mendelssohn's *Hebrides* Overture', *19th-Century Music* 2 (March 1979), pp. 197–213; Rufus Hallmark, *The Genesis of Schumann's 'Dichterliebe'* (Ann Arbor: UMI Research Press, 1979), 208pp.; D. Kern Holoman, *The Creative Process in the Autograph Musical Documents of Hector Berlioz, c. 1818–1840* (Ann Arbor: UMI Research Press, 1980), 379pp.; Robert Bailey, 'The Structure of the *Ring* and its Evolution', *19th-Century Music* 1 (July 1977), pp. 48–61; Carolyn Abbate, '*Tristan* in the Composition of *Pelléas*', ibid. 5 (Fall 1981), pp. 117–41.

27. Robert Craft and François Lesure, eds., '*The Rite of Spring*': *Sketches 1911–13. Facsimile Reproductions from the Autographs* (London: Boosey and Hawkes, 1969); Allen Forte, *The Harmonic Organization of 'The Rite of Spring'* (New Haven: Yale University Press, 1978); Richard Taruskin, 'Russian Folk Melodies in *The Rite of Spring*', *Journal of the American Musicological Society* 33 (Fall 1980), pp. 501–43. Another valuable study was made early on by the English composer Roger Smalley: 'The Sketchbook of *The Rite of Spring*', *Tempo* 91 (Winter 1969/70), pp. 2–13.

28. Carl Dahlhaus, *Die Musik des neunzehnten Jahrhunderts*, vol. 6 of *Neues Handbuch der Musikwissenschaft*, ed. Carl Dahlhaus (Wiesbaden: Athenaion, 1980).

29. Carl Dahlhaus, *Richard Wagner's Music Dramas*, trans. Mary Whittall (Cambridge and New York: Cambridge University Press, 1979); *Between Romanticism and Modernism: Four Studies in the Music of the Later Nineteenth Century*, trans. Mary Whittall (Berkeley and Los Angeles: University of California Press, 1980); *Esthetics of Music*, trans. William Austin (London and New York:

Cambridge University Press, 1982); *Analysis and Value Judgement*, trans. Siegmund Levarie (New York: Pendragon Press, 1983); *Foundations of Music History*, trans. J. B. Robinson (London and New York: Cambridge University Press, 1983); with John Deathridge, *The New Grove Wagner* (London: Macmillan, and New York: Norton, 1984); *Realism in Music*, trans. Mary Whittall (Cambridge and New York: Cambridge University Press, 1985).

30. Richard Kramer, 'Ambiguities in *La Malinconia*: What the Sketches Say', in *Beethoven Studies 3*, pp. 29–46; Anthony Newcomb, 'Once More "Between Absolute and Program Music": Schumann's Second Symphony', *19th-Century Music* 7 (Spring 1984), pp. 233–50; 'The Birth of Music Out of the Spirit of Drama: an Essay in Wagnerian Formal Analysis', ibid. 5 (Summer 1981), pp. 38–66; and 'Those Images that Yet Fresh Images Beget', *Journal of Musicology* 2 (Summer 1983), pp. 227–45; Robert Bailey, 'The Structure of the *Ring* and its Evolution', cf. note 26; Walter Frisch, *Brahms and the Principle of Developing Variation* (Berkeley and Los Angeles: University of California Press, 1984); Roger Parker and Matthew Brown, 'Motivic and Tonal Interaction in Verdi's *Un Ballo in Maschera*', *Journal of the American Musicological Society* 36 (Summer 1983), pp. 243–65.

31. D. Kern Holoman and Claude V. Palisca, eds., *Musicology in the 1980s: Methods, Goals, Opportunities* (New York: Da Capo, 1982), 160pp.

32. See p. 200f.

33. Rosen, *The Classical Style*, p. 324.

34. 'Work by "one-off" analysts like Rosen or Kerman [is] frequently held to be suspect in its theoretical focus,' writes Jonathan Dunsby. 'They seem to embed the most penetrating and original insight about specific musical objects in an all-embracing cultural critique that can be ultimately confusing, without the deep-rooted convictions – often hard to live with, but always comprehensible – of the Schoenbergian analytical tradition.' Review of *Beyond Orpheus*, by David Epstein, in *Journal of the Arnold Schoenberg Institute* 3 (October 1979), p. 195.

35. Rosen, *The Classical Style*, p. 35.

36. Peter Westergaard, 'On the Notion of Style', in *Report of the Eleventh Congress of the International Musicological Society, Copenhagen, 1970* (Cassel: Bärenreiter, 1972), p. 71.

37. Rosen, *The Classical Style*, p. 59.

38. See above, pp. 123, 68.

5. Ethnomusicology and 'Cultural Musicology'

1. Charles Seeger, *Reminiscences of an American Musicologist*, interview deposited with the Oral History Program, The University Library, University of California, Los Angeles (recorded in 1966, 1970, and 1971).
2. Charles Seeger, 'Toward a Unitary Field Theory for Musicology', *Selected Reports*, vol. 1, no. 3 (Institute of Ethnomusicology, University of California, Los Angeles, 1970), pp. 171–210, reprinted in *Studies in Musicology, 1935–1975* (Berkeley and Los Angeles: University of California Press, 1977), pp. 102–38.
3. David K. Dunaway, 'Charles Seeger and Carl Sands: the Composers' Collective Years', *Ethnomusicology* 24 (May 1980), p. 168.
4. Alan P. Merriam, 'Ethnomusicology Revisited', *Ethnomusicology* 13 (May 1969), pp. 213–29.
5. Charles Seeger, 'Semantic, Logical, and Political Considerations Bearing Upon Research in Ethnomusicology', *Ethnomusicology* 5 (May 1961), p. 80.
6. Harold S. Powers, review of *The Anthropology of Music*, by Alan P. Merriam, in *Perspectives of New Music* 4 (Spring–Summer 1966), p. 161.
7. George List, 'A Secular Sermon for Those of the Ethnomusicological Faith', *Ethnomusicology* 27 (May 1983), pp. 175–86. This was his address as Distinguished Lecturer at the 1982 annual meeting of the Society for Ethnomusicology.
8. Merriam, *The Anthropology of Music*, p. 6.
9. Mantle Hood, 'Music, the Unknown', in *Musicology*, ed. Harrison, Hood, and Palisca (Englewood Cliffs, NJ: Prentice-Hall, 1963), p. 217.
10. Seeger, 'Semantic, Logical, and Political Considerations', p. 77.
11. Powers, review of *The Anthropology of Music*, p. 163.
12. Alan P. Merriam, 'Ethnomusicology Revisited', cf. note 4 above.
13. John Blacking, *How Musical is Man?* (Seattle: University of Washington Press, 1973).
14. Charles Seeger, 'Preface to a Critique of Music', *First Inter-American Conference on Ethnomusicology*: Cartagena de Indias, Colombia (Washington, DC: Union Pan Americana, 1963); article revised and reprinted as 'Preface to the Critique of Music', *Boletin inter-americano de musica* 49 (September 1965), pp. 2–24.
15. Gilbert Chase, 'Musicology, History, and Anthropology: Current Thoughts', in *Current Thought in Musicology*, ed. J. W. Grubbs

and Leeman Perkins (Austin, Texas: University of Texas Press, 1976), pp. 231–46.

16. Ellen Rosand, 'Music and the Myth of Venice', *Renaissance Quarterly* 30 (Winter 1977), pp. 511–38; Rose Rosengard Subotnik, 'Romantic Music as Post-Kantian Critique: Classicism, Romanticism, and the Concept of a Semiotic Universe', in *On Criticizing Music*, ed. Kingsley Price (Baltimore and London: Johns Hopkins University Press, 1981), pp. 74–98; Iain Fenlon, *Music and Patronage in 16th-Century Mantua* (Cambridge and New York: Cambridge University Press, 1980), 2 vols.

17. Gary Tomlinson, 'The Web of Culture: a Context for Musicology', *19th-Century Music* 7 (Spring 1984), pp. 350–62.

18. See *Report of the Twelfth Congress of the International Musicological Society, Berkeley, 1977*, ed. Daniel Heartz and Bonnie C. Wade (Cassel and London: Bärenreiter; New York: American Musicological Society, 1981).

19. William J. Bouwsma, 'Intellectual History in the 1980s', *Journal of Interdisciplinary History* 12 (Autumn 1981), pp. 279–91.

20. Bouwsma, 'Intellectual History', pp. 287–8.

21. Ibid., pp. 287, 289.

22. See note 10, above.

6. The Historical Performance Movement

1. Denis Stevens, *Musicology: a Practical Guide* (London: Macdonald, 1980, and New York: Schirmer, 1981).

2. For a charming but very rapid survey of developments in Britain and the United States, see Robert Donington, 'Why Early Music?' in the tenth anniversary issue of *Early Music*, vol. 11 (January 1983), pp. 42–5.

3. Theodor Adorno, 'Bach Defended against his Devotees' [1951], in *Prisms* (London: Spearman, 1967; Cambridge, Mass.: MIT Press, 1981), pp. 135–46.

4. Edward T. Cone eloquently develops this view in 'The Authority of Musical Criticism', *Journal of the American Musicological Society* 34 (Spring 1981), pp. 1–18.

5. Laurence Dreyfus, 'Early Music Defended against its Devotees: a Theory of Historical Performance in the Twentieth Century', *Musical Quarterly* 69 (Summer 1983), p. 303.

6. Claudio Monteverdi, *L'Incoronazione di Poppea*: (1) Sylvia Gähweiler, Heidi Juon, Annelies Gamper, Mabella Ott-Penetto,

Friedrich Brückner-Rüggeberg, Rolf Sander; Zürich Tonhalle Orchestra, Walter Goehr, cond.: CHS, 1953. (2) Magda Laszlo, Richard Lewis; Glyndebourne Festival Chorus and Royal Philharmonic Orchestra, Raymond Leppard, harpsichord; John Pritchard, cond.: Angel, 1964. (3) Helen Donath, Elisabeth Söderström, Cathy Berberian, Paul Esswood; Concentus Musicus Wien, Nikolaus von Harnoncourt, cond.: Telefunken, 1974. (4) Carmen Balthrop, Carolyn Watkinson; Il Complesso Barocco, Alan Curtis, cond.: Fonit Cetra, 1981.

7. Edward T. Cone, 'Analysis Today', *Musical Quarterly* 46 (April 1960), p. 174.

8. Heinrich Schenker, quoted in 'Heinrich Schenker as an Interpreter of Beethoven's Piano Sonatas', by William Rothstein, *19th-Century Music* 8 (Summer 1984), p. 10.

9. Charles Rosen, 'Should Music Be Played "Wrong"?', *High Fidelity*, May 1971, p. 54.

10. For a further statement by Taruskin, see his contribution to 'The Limits of Authenticity: a Discussion', *Early Music* 12 (February 1984), pp. 3–12.

11. Marie Leonhardt, '"The Present State of Music in Northern Europe, in Particular the Netherlands"', *Early Music* 4 (January 1976), p. 51.

12. Michael Morrow, 'Musical Performance and Authenticity', *Early Music* 6 (April 1978), p. 233.

13. Greta Moens, 'Baroque Music: New Paths to Old Meanings', *Soundings* 6 (1977), p. 106.

14. Charles Rosen, 'Should Music Be Played "Wrong"?', p. 58.

7. Coda

1. Richard Evidon, 'The Grove of Academe: a Personal View', *19th-Century Music* 5 (Fall 1981), pp. 155–7.

2. See *Music & Letters* 62 (July–October 1981), pp. 249–60; *Times Literary Supplement*, 20 February 1981, p. 139; *Inter-American Music Review* 3 (Spring–Summer 1981), pp. 167–70, 178–94; *Musical Times* 122 (1981), pp. 171–6, 241–2, 304–9, 375–8; also pp. 89–91.

3. The first volumes to appear in Cambridge Readings in the Literature of Music were *Music and Aesthetics in the Eighteenth and Early Nineteenth Centuries*, ed. Peter Le Huray and James Day, and *Greek Musical Writings*, ed. Andrew Barker (London and New York: Cambridge University Press, 1981, 1984).

4. See note 29 to Chapter 4.

5. Blume's articles on 'Renaissance', 'Barock', 'Klassik', and 'Romantik' from *Die Musik in Geschichte und Gegenwart* (1958, 1963) were reprinted as *Renaissance and Baroque Music* and *Classic and Romantic Music*, trans. D. M. Herter Norton (New York: Norton, 1967, 1970). The *New Grove* 'Sources' article is broken down into 'Sources, MS', 'Sources of instrumental ensemble music to 1630', 'Sources of keyboard music to 1660', and 'Sources of lute music'.

6. Edward T. Cone, 'The Authority of Music Criticism', *Journal of the American Musicological Society* 34 (Spring 1981), pp. 1–18.

7. See David Z. Crookes, 'A Turinese Letter: *Semper ego auditor tantum?* A Rant against Present Trends in the Early Music World', *Music Review* 42 (August–November 1981), pp. 169–73; Laurence Dreyfus, 'Early Music Defended against its Devotees: a Theory of Historical Performance in the Twentieth Century', *Musical Quarterly* 69 (Summer 1983), pp. 297–322; and the symposium 'Authenticity' in *Early Music* 12 (February 1984). Since 1983, the editor of *Early Music* has been the critic Nicholas Kenyon.

Main Works Cited

(Marked with an asterisk in the text)

Austin, William. '*Susanna*', '*Jeanie*', *and* '*The Old Folks at Home*': *the Songs of Stephen C. Foster from His Time to Ours*. New York: Macmillan, 1975. 420pp.

Badura-Skoda, Paul and Eva. *Interpreting Mozart on the Keyboard*, trans. Leo Black. London: Barrie and Rockliff, 1962. 319pp.

Bilson, Malcolm. 'The Viennese Fortepiano of the Late 18th Century', *Early Music* 8 (April 1980), pp. 158–62.

Blacking, John. *How Musical is Man?* Seattle: University of Washington Press, 1974. 116pp.

Boretz, Benjamin, and Edward T. Cone, eds. *Perspectives on Contemporary Music Theory*. New York: Norton, 1972. x, 285pp.

Chafe, Eric. 'J. S. Bach's *St Matthew Passion*: Aspects of Planning, Structure, and Chronology', *Journal of the American Musicological Society* 35 (Spring 1982), pp. 49–114.

Chase, Gilbert. 'American Musicology and the Social Sciences', in *Perspectives in Musicology*, ed. Barry S. Brook, Edward D. E. Downes, and Sherman van Solkema. New York: Norton, 1972, pp. 202–26.

Cone, Edward T. 'Analysis Today', *Musical Quarterly* 46 (April 1960), pp. 172–88. Reprinted in *Problems of Modern Music*, ed. Paul Henry Lang. New York: Norton, 1962, pp. 34–50.

Cone, Edward T. 'Music: a View from Delft', *Musical Quarterly* 47 (October 1961), pp. 439–53. Reprinted in *Perspectives on Contemporary Music Theory*, ed. Benjamin Boretz and Edward T. Cone. New York: Norton, 1972, pp. 57–71.

Cone, Edward T. 'Stravinsky: the Progress of a Method', *Perspectives of New Music* 1 (Fall 1962), pp. 18–26. Reprinted in *Perspectives on Schoenberg and Stravinsky*, ed. Benjamin Boretz and Edward T. Cone. New York: Norton, 1972, pp. 155–64.

Cone, Edward T. 'Beyond Analysis', *Perspectives of New Music* 6 (Spring 1967), pp. 33–51. Reprinted in *Perspectives on Contemporary Music Theory*, ed. Benjamin Boretz and Edward T. Cone. New York: Norton, 1972, pp. 72–90.

Cone, Edward T. *Musical Form and Musical Performance*. New York: Norton, 1968. 103pp.

Cone, Edward T. 'Mr Cone Replies [to David Lewin]', *Perspectives of New Music* 7 (Spring–Summer 1969), pp. 70–2.

Dadelsen, Georg von. *Beiträge zur Chronologie der Werke J. S. Bachs*. Diss., University of Tübingen, 1958; Trossingen: Hohner, 1958. 176pp.

Dart, Thurston. *The Interpretation of Music*. London: Hutchinson, 1954; 4th edn., 1967. 192pp.

Dolmetsch, Arnold. *The Interpretation of Music of the 17th and 18th Centuries*. London: Novello, 1915; 2nd edn., 1946. Reprinted Seattle and London: University of Washington Press, 1969. 494pp.

Dürr, Alfred. 'Zur Chronologie der Leipziger Vokalwerke J. S. Bachs', *Bach-Jahrbuch 1957* pp. 5–162. Reprinted Cassel 1976.

Epstein, David. *Beyond Orpheus: Studies in Musical Structure*. Cambridge, Mass., and London: MIT Press, 1979. 244pp.

Fenlon, Iain. *Music and Patronage in 16th-Century Mantua*. London and New York: Cambridge University Press, 1980. 2 vols., 233pp., 151pp.

Forte, Allen. *The Compositional Matrix*. New York: Baldwin, 1961. 95pp.

Forte, Allen. 'Schenker's Conception of Musical Structure', *Journal of Music Theory* 3 (April 1959), pp. 1–30. Reprinted in *Readings in Schenker Analysis*, ed. Maury Yeston. New Haven and London: Yale University Press, 1977, pp. 3–37.

Frisch, Walter. *Brahms and the Principle of Developing Variation*. (Vol. 2 of California Studies in 19th-Century Music.) Berkeley and Los Angeles: University of California Press, 1984. 217pp.

Grove's Dictionary. See Sadie, Stanley, ed.

Harrison, Frank Ll. 'American Musicology and the European Tradition', in *Musicology*, by Harrison, Hood, and Palisca. Englewood Cliffs, NJ: Prentice-Hall, 1963, pp. 1–86.

Harrison, Frank Ll., Mantle Hood, and Claude V. Palisca *Musicology*. (The Princeton Studies: Humanistic Scholarship in America.) Englewood Cliffs, NJ: Prentice-Hall, 1963. 337pp.

Hood, Mantle. *The Ethnomusicologist*. New York, 1971; 2nd edn., Kent, Ohio: Kent State University Press, 1982. 400pp.

Johnson, Douglas. *Beethoven's Early Sketches in the 'Fischhof Miscellany', Berlin Autograph 28*. Ann Arbor: UMI Research Press, 1980. 2 vols., 201pp., 516pp.

Johnson, Douglas. ed., with Alan Tyson and Robert Winter. *The Beethoven Sketchbooks*. (Vol. 4 of California Studies in 19th-Century Music.) Berkeley and Los Angeles: University of California Press, and London: Oxford University Press, 1985.

Keller, Hans. 'K. 503: The Unity of Contrasting Themes and Movements', *Music Review* 17 (1956), pp. 48–58, 120–9. Reprinted in *W. A. Mozart: Piano Concerto in C Major, K. 503*, ed. Joseph Kerman (Norton Critical Scores). New York: Norton, 1970, pp. 176–200.

Kerman, Joseph. *The Elizabethan Madrigal: a Comparative Study.* [PhD diss., Princeton University, 1951.] (American Musicological Society: Studies and Documents, no. 4.) New York: Galaxy Music Corporation, distributor, 1962. 318pp.

Kerman, Joseph. 'Byrd's Motets: Chronology and Canon', *Journal of the American Musicological Society* 14 (Fall 1961), pp. 359–82.

Kerman, Joseph. 'The Elizabethan Motet: a Study of Texts for Music', *Studies in the Renaissance* 9 (1962), pp. 273–305.

Kerman, Joseph. 'On William Byrd's *Emendemus in melius*', *Musical Quarterly* 44 (October 1963), pp. 431–49. Reprinted in *Chormusik und Analyse*, ed. Heinrich Poos (Mainz: Schott, 1983), vol. 1, pp. 155–70; vol. 2, pp. 65–8.

Kerman, Joseph. 'A Profile for American Musicology', *Journal of the American Musicological Society* 18 (Spring 1965), pp. 61–9.

Kerman, Joseph. 'Byrd, Tallis, and the Art of Imitation', *Aspects of Medieval and Renaissance Music: a Birthday Offering to Gustave Reese*. New York: Norton, 1966, pp. 519–37. Reprinted New York: Pendragon Press, 1978.

Kinderman, William. 'The Evolution and Structure of Beethoven's *Diabelli* Variations', *Journal of the American Musicological Society* 35 (Summer 1982), pp. 306–28.

Kresky, Jeffrey. *Tonal Music: Twelve Analytical Studies*. Bloomington, Ind., and London: Indiana University Press, 1977. 167pp.

Lerdahl, Fred, and Jackendoff, Ray. *A Generative Theory of Tonal Music*. Cambridge, Mass.: MIT Press, 1983. 368pp.

Levine, Lawrence. *Black Culture and Black Consciousness: Afro-American Folk Thought from Slavery to Freedom*. London and New York: Oxford University Press, 1977. 522pp.

Lewin, David. 'Behind the Beyond', *Perspectives of New Music* 7 (Spring–Summer 1969), pp. 59–69; Cone, Edward T. 'Mr Cone Replies', ibid., pp. 70–2.

Lockwood, Lewis. 'On Beethoven's Sketches and Autographs: Some Problems of Definition and Interpretation', *Acta Musicologica* 42 (January–June 1970), pp. 32–47.

Lockwood, Lewis. 'The Autograph of the First Movement of Beethoven's Sonata for Violoncello and Piano, Op. 69', in *The Music Forum*, vol. 2, ed. William Mitchell and Felix Salzer. New York and London: Columbia University Press, 1970, pp. 1–109.

Lowinsky, Edward E. 'A Newly Discovered Sixteenth-Century Motet Manuscript at the Biblioteca Vallicelliana in Rome', *Journal of the American Musicological Society* 3 (Fall 1950), pp. 173–232.

Lowinsky, Edward E. Chapter 8, 'Religious Background of the Secret Chromatic Art', and Chapter 9, 'The Meaning of Double Meaning in the Sixteenth Century', in *The Secret Chromatic Art in the Netherlands Motet*. New York: Columbia University Press, 1946, pp. 111–34, 135–75. Reprinted New York: Russell and Russell, 1967.

Marshall, Robert L. 'Bach the Progressive: Observations on his Later Works', *Musical Quarterly* 62 (July 1976), pp. 313–57.

Marshall, Robert L. 'J. S. Bach's Compositions for Solo Flute', *Journal of the American Musicological Society* 32 (Fall 1979), pp. 463–98.

Mendel, Arthur. 'Evidence and Explanation', in *Report of the Eighth Congress of the International Musicological Society, New York, 1961*. Cassel, London, and New York: Bärenreiter, 1962, vol. 2, pp. 2–18.

Merriam, Alan P. *The Anthropology of Music*. Evanston, Ill.: Northwestern University Press, 1964. 358pp.

Meyer, Leonard B. *Emotion and Meaning in Music*. Chicago: University of Chicago Press, 1956. 307pp.

Meyer, Leonard B. *Music, the Arts, and Ideas*. Chicago: University of Chicago Press, 1967. 342pp.

Meyer, Leonard B. *Explaining Music*. Berkeley and Los Angeles: University of California Press, 1973. 284pp.

Narmour, Eugene. *Beyond Schenkerism: the Need for Alternatives in Musical Analysis*. Chicago: University of Chicago Press, 1977. 238pp.

Neighbour, Oliver. *The Consort and Keyboard Music of William Byrd*. The Music of William Byrd, vol. III. London: Faber and Faber; Berkeley and Los Angeles: University of California Press, 1978. 272pp.

Newcomb, Anthony. *The Madrigal at Ferrara, 1579–1597*. Princeton, NJ: Princeton University Press, 1980. 2 vols., 303pp., 220pp.

The New Grove Dictionary of Music and Musicians. See Sadie, Stanley, ed.

Palisca, Claude V. 'American Scholarship in Western Music', in *Musicology*, by Harrison, Hood, and Palisca. Englewood Cliffs, NJ: Prentice-Hall, 1963, pp. 87–214.

Perle, George. *The Operas of Alban Berg*. Vol. 1, *Wozzeck*; vol. 2, *Lulu*. Berkeley and Los Angeles: University of California Press, 1980, 1984. 231pp., 352pp.

Reti, Rudolph. *The Thematic Process in Music*. London: Faber and Faber, 1961. Reprinted Westport, Conn.: Greenwood Press, 1978. 362pp.

Reynolds, Christopher. 'Beethoven's Sketches for the Variations in E Flat, Op. 35', in *Beethoven Studies 3*, ed. Alan Tyson. London and New York: Cambridge University Press, 1982, pp. 47–84.

Rosen, Charles. *The Classical Style: Haydn, Mozart, Beethoven*. New York: Norton, 1971. 467pp.

Sadie, Stanley, ed. *The New Grove Dictionary of Music and Musicians*. London: Macmillan, 1980. 20 vols.

Schenker, Heinrich. See Forte, Allen, 'Schenker's Conception of Musical Structure'.

Schorske, Carl E. *Fin-de-Siècle Vienna: Politics and Culture*. New York: Knopf, 1980. 378pp.

Seeger, Charles. 'The Cultivation of Various European Traditions of Music in the New World', *Report of the Eighth Congress of the International Musicological Society, New York, 1961*. Cassel, London, and New York: Bärenreiter, 1962, pp. 364–75. Reprinted in *Studies in Musicology, 1935–1975*. Berkeley and Los Angeles: University of California Press, 1977, pp. 195–210.

Seeger, Charles. 'Tractatus Esthetico-Semioticus', in *Current Thought in Musicology*, ed. J. W. Grubbs and Leeman Perkins. Austin, Texas: University of Texas Press, 1976, pp. 1–40.

Seeger, Charles. *Studies in Musicology, 1935–1975*. Berkeley and Los Angeles: University of California Press, 1977. 357pp.

Subotnik, Rose Rosengard. 'Musicology and Criticism' [1980], in *Musicology in the 1980s*, ed. D. Kern Holoman and Claude V. Palisca. New York: Da Capo, 1982, pp. 145–60.

Taruskin, Richard. 'The Musicologist and the Performer' [1980], in *Musicology in the 1980s*, ed. D. Kern Holoman and Claude V. Palisca. New York: Da Capo, 1982, pp. 108–18.

Treitler, Leo. 'Music Analysis in a Historical Context', *College Music Symposium* 6 (Fall 1966), pp. 75–88.

Treitler, Leo. 'On Historical Criticism', *Musical Quarterly* 53 (April 1967), pp. 188–205.

Treitler, Leo. 'The Present as History', *Perspectives of New Music* 7 (Spring–Summer 1969), pp. 1–58.

Treitler, Leo. 'Homer and Gregory: the Transmission of Epic Poetry and Plainchant', *Musical Quarterly* 60 (July 1974), pp. 333–72.

Treitler, Leo. 'History, Criticism, and Beethoven's Ninth Symphony', *19th-Century Music* 3 (March 1978), pp. 193–210.

Treitler, Leo. 'To Worship That Celestial Sound', *Journal of Musicology* 1 (April 1982), pp. 153–70.

Treitler, Leo. 'What Kind of Story is History?', *19th-Century Music* 7 (Spring 1984), pp. 363–73.

Tyson, Alan, ed. *Beethoven Studies*. Vol. 1: New York: Norton, 1973; London, 1974. 246pp.; vol. 2: London and New York: Oxford University Press, 1977. 200pp.; vol. 3: London and New York: Cambridge University Press, 1982. 298pp.

Webster, James. 'Schubert's Sonata Form and Brahms's First Maturity', *19th-Century Music* 2 (July 1978), pp. 18–35; 3 (July 1979), pp. 52–71.

Winter, Robert. 'Plans for the Structure of the String Quartet in C Sharp Minor, Op. 131', in *Beethoven Studies* 2, ed. Alan Tyson. London and New York: Oxford University Press, 1977, pp. 106–37. Extracted from PhD dissertation, *The Compositional Origins of Beethoven's Op. 131*. Ann Arbor: UMI Research Press, 1982. 348pp.

Wolff, Christoph. *Der Stile Antico in der Musik J. S. Bachs*. Beihefte zur Archiv für Musikwissenschaft, vol. 6. Wiesbaden: Franz Steiner Verlag, 1968. 219pp.

Index